A FIELD GUIDE
FOR SCIENCE WRITERS

The Official Guide of
the National Association
of Science Writers

• • • • • • • • • • • • • • • •

A Field Guide
for Science Writers

Edited by

DEBORAH BLUM AND
MARY KNUDSON

• •

OXFORD UNIVERSITY PRESS
New York   Oxford

Oxford University Press

Oxford   New York
Athens   Auckland   Bangkok   Bogotá   Buenos Aires   Calcutta
Cape Town   Chennai   Dar es Salaam   Delhi   Florence   Hong Kong
Istanbul   Karachi   Kuala Lumpur   Madrid   Melbourne   Mexico City
Mumbai   Nairobi   Paris   São Paolo   Singapore   Taipei   Tokyo
Toronto   Warsaw

and associated companies in
Berlin   Ibadan

First published by Oxford University Press, Inc., 1997

First issued as an Oxford University Press paperback, 1998

Oxford is a registered trademark of Oxford University Press

Library of Congress Cataloging-in-Publication Data
A field guide for science writers : the official guide of the National
Association of Science Writers / edited by Deborah Blum and Mary Knudson.
p.   cm.   Includes index.
ISBN 0-19-510068-9
ISBN 0-19-512494-4 (pbk.)
1. Technical writing.   2. Communication in science.   I. Blum, Deborah.
II. Knudson, Mary.   III. National Association of Science Writers.
T11.F52   1996
070.4'495—dc20   96-25466

10 9 8 7 6 5 4

Printed in the United States of America

CONTENTS

FOREWORD
Carl Sagan

Cornell University

A general public understanding of science, warts and all, is essential for at least four reasons: a productive technological economy; an understanding of the environmental and other dangers of technologies new and old; a glimpse of the answers to the deepest questions on the origins of the universe and ourselves; and a grasp of the skeptical method of science, which has essential connections with the democratic process. The writers of articles and books on science (and their radio and television counterparts) are the chief means by which adults in our society learn about science. But the coverage of science (especially when distinguished from technology and medicine) in the American media is pitifully sparse. With very few exceptions, every daily newspaper in America has a daily astrology column. How many have even a regular, weekly science column? Yet astrology is bunk, and science is a vital aperture to the future.

Accordingly, it's very much in the public and national interest to have a corps of science writers who understand what they are writing about, have simultaneous appreciation for skepticism and wonder, and who are talented in metaphor and analogy and the ability to make the complex understandable. The National Association of Science Writers is the leading organization of practitioners in this field. In this book these practitioners draw from their experience to advise a new generation of writers. All royalties from the book will go to NASW.

But this book is not just for aspirant science writers. There are wonderful anecdotes, cautionary tales, and revelations of government skulduggery, and the pages are populated by a wide range of scientists with vices and virtues equally on display. The book is illuminating and a pleasure to read.

EDITORS' NOTE

The primary goal of *A Field Guide for Science Writers* is to help train a new generation of science writers who will strive for excellence in writing about science and its many effects on people's lives. This book should also be interesting reading for anyone—writers, scientists, consumers—who would like to better understand how science writers decide what to write about and how to present it.

We have assembled a stellar group of science writers from throughout the United States to talk about how they do their jobs. All our contributors joined in this project in the most generous spirit, giving their time and ideas without hesitation. One of the pleasures in putting the book together was these writers' interest in simply doing something to make science writing better. This is a book chock full of personal experiences and tips on what to do and not do. Yet it is not meant to be an encyclopedia of science writing by any means. Instead, we have chosen to emphasize a mixture of basic skills, key techniques, and fascinating fields to cover—from astronomy to infectious diseases.

Because it is the product of personal experiences, this book necessarily varies in style and content from chapter to chapter. As you will discover, science writers take a variety of approaches to writing about science and its impact on society. But what unites us all is our basic belief that science writing is important and that it needs to be done well.

Preparing this book was an unusual step to take for the National Association of Science Writers, long an organization that existed only for the welfare of its members. It seems to us that NASW and science writing have matured together. The dream started back in 1934 when a dozen science writers, with the goal of strengthening their profession, banded together and somewhat optimistically named their group the National Association of Science Writers. It's taken decades, but now the idea lives up to its name. Over the last 30 or so years, science writing has been transforming itself into something beyond a strange little subculture of journalism. It's become a profession, increasingly respected within both the media and the research realms. As for NASW, it now numbers over 1,800 members in the United States and also has members from 20 countries around the world.

What has driven science writing as a profession? Foremost, science itself: the post–World War II boom in research, the space race of the 1960s, the technologies of today that are opening the subatomic and molecular worlds at a still-dizzying pace, giving rise to a revolution in personal communications and in our knowledge of genetics and biology. Such discoveries have altered the world we all live in, and it has increasingly fallen to the media to explain the new technologies and report on their impact, good and bad.

We used to try to separate science from the rest of society as though they were two different civilizations. Science writers at first acted primarily as scouts, trying to bridge a big divide by bringing back messages from one side to the other. It's to our credit that being good scouts didn't satisfy us for very long. It wasn't enough for science writers to merely translate for scientists, as if that were the whole story. To make science writing work, the understanding had to be real and the questions intelligent and, at times, sharp-edged.

Certainly writing well about science requires bridging the jargon gulf, making technically complicated ideas vivid and alive. You bet, there are times when it's important to share the excitement of science. But excellent science writing doesn't stop there, or science writers would evade their responsibility. You can paint an awesome and adventuresome picture of space exploration with all its glittering planetary rings, but you can also acknowledge its risks and probe its failures. You can point out the medical and agricultural benefits of the new biotechnology or the mapping of the human and other genomes; but you can also question what harm may come of the new knowledge and capabilities, discuss what safeguards will be put in place, and talk about how much big science costs and who pays for it.

The professionalism of science writing has been driven from within as science writers have pushed to refine their craft and become more sophisticated and knowledgeable about what they write. Partly because of their needs, partly because of a similar recognition in the academic community, programs to train science writers have sprung up around the country. And midcareer fellowships for science writers have given many of them the opportunity to return to major universities to gain specialized training.

A Field Guide for Science Writers was written in recognition of the evolution of science writing as a profession and the need to further that evolution.

NASW endorsed this book from the beginning and helped underwrite it. We are especially grateful to those who served as members of the board and officers during 1995–96, when this book became an official project of NASW and was written—particularly Laurie Garrett, president; Richard Harris, vice president/president-elect; and Joseph Palca, treasurer, for their enthusiastic support. We are also grateful to Richard for devoting much time to this project during its last month and, always in good humor, printing the manuscript, putting it in proper electronic form, and helping to organize the back of the book. Thanks to Lori Korleski, who under a tight schedule put half the book on disk. To our colleagues who contributed information about resources for our appendix, we thank you so much—especially Tom Siegfried, who gave freely of his time and was fun to work with. Diane McGurgan, the glue that holds NASW together, has a special place in our hearts for her continuing help and concern for our welfare during heavy work periods.

We are honored that Carl Sagan wrote the foreword for our book because he is uniquely brilliant as both a scientist and as a superb communicator of science. He has achieved the highest distinctions in both fields, including a Pulitzer Prize for *Dragons of Eden*, and Emmy and Peabody awards for the outstanding television series, *Cosmos*. He has a legion of fans, which we are sure will include the next generation of science writers, and we thank him for his cogent opening remarks, for which he generously declined compensation.

We thank Oxford University Press and our editor, Joan Bossert, for believing in our idea and guiding it to publication. Thanks very much to Helen Mules, production editor at Oxford, who spent much time and took great care in overseeing the proofing and production of our book. And much thanks is owed the Alfred P. Sloan Foundation for a grant that helped make the book possible.

Deborah Blum
Mary Knudson

April 1996

A FIELD GUIDE
FOR SCIENCE WRITERS

PART ONE

Getting
Started

• •

1

Introduction

DAVID PERLMAN

David Perlman is the science editor of the *San Francisco Chronicle* and was a reporter, a foreign correspondent, and a political writer for newspapers and magazines before turning to the world of science and technology some 30 years ago.

In addition to his daily reporting in fields as varied as biomedical research, space exploration, and seismology, he writes frequently on major policy issues in medicine and genetics, the environment, nuclear energy, and the technical and political aspects of arms control.

He has lectured on science communication to the public throughout China, and has been a Poynter Fellow at Yale, a Carnegie Corporation Fellow at the Center for International Security and Arms Control at Stanford, a science writer–in–residence at the University of Wisconsin, and a Regents Professor at the University of California at San Francisco.

Perlman has won the AAAS-Westinghouse Award for science writing, the Distinguished Science Journalism award of the National Assocation of Science Writers, and is a recipient of a Fellows' Medal for the California Academy of Sciences.

He is a past president of the National Association of Science Writers (NASW) and of the Council for the Advancement of Science Writing, and is a fellow of the California Academy of Sciences.

Many years ago, when I was laid up from a ski accident after covering politics for my newspaper, a well-intentioned friend brought me an astronomy book.

Immobilized and bored by mindless detective novels, I gave the book a reluctant try, for I had never before paid attention to anything scientific, and in college had been exposed to only one of those "science for poets" sequences that enabled me to acquire enough diversity credits to graduate as an undistinguished humanities major dedicated largely to all-night work on the college daily paper.

The astronomy book, as it happened, was *The Nature of the Universe* by Fred Hoyle, and I had no idea that the steady state theory of cosmology he was propounding would very soon fall into disrepute as the big-bang theory of the origin of the universe swept his model aside.

The book did, however, open my eyes to the possibility that in science there might be excitement, elegance, intrigue, and a way of looking at the world in terms far more filled with wonder than the verbiage expended during the jousting of politicians.

That experience turned me into a science writer, and in conversation with innumerable colleagues since, I have never met one who didn't feel that we chose the best and most rewarding of all journalistic tracks. My newspaper friends may write books on the side, free-lance magazine pieces, write for other media, or even move to radio or television, but they all find the deepest satisfaction in covering the successes, the setbacks, and the personalities—both noble and ignoble—that mark the world of science.

To many of us whose scientific training is as meager as mine, or who may be superbly schooled in a single scientific discipline yet ignorant in all others, reporting on science and writing about it is like attending a never-ending graduate school of unlimited diversity, with a faculty that is most often eager to instruct and patiently explain.

Our sources, of course, are many. Reports in scientific journals and meetings give us fresh results from research that can be intriguing if not vitally important to our readers, whether they describe new progress against disease or the birth of new stars in the galaxy. Universities, research institutions, science-based companies, and government agencies are all eager to let us know the achievements of their scientists and engineers, and reporting them fills our days.

But to accompany a scientist in the laboratory testing a potential vector for gene therapy in a mouse model, to beachcomb with a marine biologist discovering a new species of barnacle, to help a seismologist trenching a fault zone that reveals traces of ancient earthquakes, or to stand by the consoles of mission controllers interrogating an interplanetary spacecraft—these are stories from the field that most enthrall a reporter and best convey to audiences what science is all about.

There are hardships and pitfalls in science writing too, of course. Journals can be filled with deadly jargon. Claims for statistical significance from randomized double-blind clinical trials can be difficult to challenge. Explaining quarks, subatomic particles with their arcane attributes of strangeness and spin and color and charm, may not gladden the hearts of editors or command the column inches that every science writer knows such stories truly demand. And controversy can arise in every field of science to challenge a reporter's confidence in his or her judgment.

What, for example, does one do about evaluating the claims of the disputatious Peter Duesberg on AIDS? How does one profile fairly the brilliantly accomplished but often abrasive Robert Gallo, or describe with equal fairness his long-running controversy with his French rival, Luc Montagnier? What kind of middle course is appropriate when reporting on allegations of misconduct and outright fraud in breast cancer studies of lumpectomy versus mastectomy? How do we cover the issues raised by creation scientists, and their impact on textbooks bought with taxpayers' money and on teachers who must use them? How do we keep our own feelings in check—pro or con—when we write about the deaths of the superconducting supercollider and the near death of SETI, the Search for Extraterrestrial Intelligence?

The science writer is above all a reporter, and as such is not entitled to bias or conflicts of interest. Science writers—if they hope to last in their careers and maintain the confidence of their hard-sought sources—eschew hype (unless they drift to the supermarket tabloids). They obey embargoes set by journals or in press rooms at meetings, and they make scrupulously clear during interviews that both they and their subjects understand what is off the record or not. They are fair, but they must always recognize that merely counting yeahs and nayes in a scientific controversy fails to serve the public and is rarely a real guarantee of fairness.

Just think of the major controversies in science and technology that have recently made headlines and affected society profoundly:

Did the discoveries in recombinant DNA some 20 years ago endanger the world with Andromeda strains, or have the molecular geneticists opened one of the great transforming eras of medical progress, with genetic testing and gene therapy now imminent?

Were the space-based, nuclear-pumped X-ray lasers of Star Wars really feasible, or were they merely a febrile and costly Strangelove dream?

Does the ice-core evidence of long-past carbon dioxide levels, with the current record of fossil fuel emissions, provide a valid signal of dangerous global climate change, or are they the overheated warnings of environmental doomsayers?

What does the future hold if nations ignore increasing signs of depletion in the globe's protective ozone layer?

What should be done with the growing tonnages of spent nuclear fuel from the world's power reactors, or the bomb-grade plutonium from dismantled nuclear weapons, now that the Cold War is over?

I cite these few examples merely to broaden the scope of what science writers can offer to the public for whom we communicate. Yes, reporting on major breakthroughs can be exciting (although my own style book now bans that "B-word"). Yes, following scientists as they work in the field or in their laboratories can yield colorful and fascinating stories. And certainly solid investigative reporting is urgent when the deceits and grant maneuverings and corporate conniving of a few scientists foul the enterprise and cheat the public.

But in the media world where our words and images circulate, the public today is sadly unprepared to cope with the swift pace of scientific discovery and technological change. A distinguished panel of the National Research Council has recently posed national guidelines for science education and national standards for what students should understand of science and the scientific method as they approach adulthood. As science writers, our challenge is not only to describe the discoveries and the changes clearly, but to explain their potential impact and their costs and benefits, even while we present the valid sides of the controversies they generate.

In this part, experienced science writers who have written in every medium of communication, both print and broadcast, describe the special career attractions and differing requirements of each, as well as their difficulties and rewards. Some media are public, as in newspapers, magazines, books, radio, and television; some are more specialized, as in trade or science journals. Some writers prefer the security of a salary, while others find the freedom of free-lance work well worth the insecurity.

To be totally realistic for the moment, I should add a warning: Our editors, no matter what they edit, will always be unrealistic; they will invariably demand that we explain it all, interpret it all, and provide all the sober context in no space at all—less than a column of type, or two minutes of air time at most. So good luck!

2

Covering Science for Newspapers

BOYCE RENSBERGER

Boyce Rensberger has been a science writer or science editor since 1966, when he started as the lone science and medical reporter at the *Detroit Free Press*. All but six of those years were with newspapers. Rensberger, who has a bachelor's degree in journalism and zoology from the University of Miami and a master's degree in mental health information from Syracuse University, worked for five years in Detroit. Then he went to the *New York Times* as one of many science writers for eight years. He quit the *Times* in 1979 to be head writer of *3-2-1-Contact!* a public television show on science for children, and to do free-lance science writing for magazines.

In 1984 he returned to newspaper science writing at the *Washington Post*. He was science editor of the *Post*'s national desk for three years and currently edits "Horizon: The Learning Section," a feature section of the *Post* that runs educational stories in science, technology, and history.

Rensberger has won several journalistic awards, including the AAAS–Westinghouse Award for science journalism twice. He is the author of several books. His latest is *Life Itself: Exploring the Realm of the Living Cell.*

Look in the mailroom of any big newspaper, and you will discover one of the telling realities of writing about science for a daily. The mailboxes of the science and medical reporters will be among the most stuffed. If you cover science for a newspaper, hundreds of universities, corporations, think tanks, government agencies, advocacy groups, independent research institutions, museums, public relations agencies, hospitals, and scientific journals all want a piece of your time and a few hundred of your well-chosen words. Newspaper science writers are what the academics call gate-keepers, people whose jobs allow them to decide what developments in the real world get into the news, and hence reach the public. The public

7

relations types at every scientific or medical organization know that if they can win your attention and interest, they will have scored. And they know that if the newspapers do their story, the other media are likely to follow.

Newspapers, in other words, are the front lines of science communication, the places where most science stories show up first, before they appear in magazines, long before they're in books, usually years before television documentaries discover them. To be sure, television and radio sometimes beat a newspaper to the punch with a brief mention of the latest advance on "fat pills" or "killer viruses" because the embargo system gives them a slight time advantage. But most science stories never make it onto the airwaves at all.

And, of course, no other medium of mass communication covers as many science stories as do newspapers. We cover many advances and issues that never reach the public through any other medium, but that often are more important than the blockbusters.

Something else distinguishes newspaper science writing: It is an educational medium. For the vast majority of Americans, newspapers are the sole source of information and continuing education about science. Most people don't read science books or even popular science magazines, and they certainly don't read research journals. So science stories often must also be short courses in the scientific background needed to understand the news.

The science beat on a newspaper is one of the most varied and rewarding. In most other specialty beats, reporters become familiar with a modest body of knowledge (how a city council functions, for example, or the rules of baseball) and turn to the same few, first-name-basis sources every day. The science reporter seldom enjoys this luxury. Today the story may be a claimed advance in treating cancer, tomorrow it may be explaining atmospheric chemistry and, for the weekend, the latest experiment in fusion power research. Obviously, you must be fast, and incidentally, writer's block is not permitted.

The knowledge and sources you called on today will do you no good tomorrow. To be sure, you'll do another cancer story down the road, and you'll use what you learned today, but with most new stories, you must approach new sources, learn new facts and phenomena, and understand new scientific techniques. The general assignment reporter faces a similar challenge but seldom copes with the most difficult task of the science writer—figuring out how to explain technically sophisticated activities in simple but accurate language to readers who know almost nothing about science.

Yet, amazingly, most of us do a fairly decent job of it.

Moreover, science stories are among the best read in newspapers, according to reader surveys. The readership for medical stories is at least as large as that for sports stories—for a simple reason. Medical stories deal with the human body, which every reader possesses, and with the hopes and fears about the well-being of that body. The readership for nonmedical science stories is not quite as high, but there are signs it is growing.

The stories are fascinating and enlightening for the science writer as well as the reader, which is one reason, I think, that so many science writers are lifers like me. While other reporters typically change beats or bureaus every few years, science writers keep writing science. I think it's because we love knowing what we learn, and we love the process of learning.

As I often tell people, I started out in college wanting to be a scientist but chickened out after discovering that researchers must specialize in some very tiny sliver of a field. I was much too interested in all of science to settle for a small piece of the whole. So I switched majors to journalism to become a science writer. I've never regretted it. For me, science writing is a lifelong, self-directed process of continuing education. I can call up top experts in any field of knowledge that intrigues me and ask for private tutorials. And, I am amazed to find, the scientists almost always oblige. They do so not for my personal amusement, of course, but because, like the others who stuff our mailboxes, they want the public to know, to understand, and to be on their side in a world too often given to ignorance, fear, and superstition.

THE CHIEF RESPONSIBILITIES OF A NEWSPAPER SCIENCE WRITER

The most commonly understood duty of a science reporter is to keep readers abreast of important advances in scientific research. Also part of the mandate is to provide scientific background pieces, or "explainers," prompted by events in the news (earthquakes, heat waves, epidemics, etc.) and issues in the news (claims of advocacy groups dealing with environmental, nutritional, or safety issues; politician's proposals with a technical or scientific basis; etc.). A third responsibility, widely ignored because the stories are hard to make scintillating, is to cover science policy—the health of the scientific establishment and the shaping of government policies affecting science.

And, of course, there is the responsibility to your editors. They want the daily stories but also something special for the slow-news weekend papers and maybe the occasional series that gives a newspaper gravitas and cachet. Balancing these demands requires an ability to think of story ideas that go beyond the news—or deeper into the news—and the people skills to keep your editor satisfied that it really does take a little longer to do a science story than he or she might expect.

Remember the mailbox? In it are scientific journals and tip sheets from scientific journals, some of which arrive by e-mail nowadays. The leading journals compete aggressively to get newspaper science writers to cover their articles. Many send tip sheets a week or more in advance of publication, complete with summaries of the most interesting articles and the phone numbers of the scientists. If you accept this advance information, you accept the embargo, which means your story cannot be published until after the date the journal sets. Once disdained by some science writers, the embargo system is now well established and routinely respected with only rare violations. This is a very good thing because science stories are more complex than ever and it takes time, sometimes several days, to do a good job. The embargo system removes the temptation to beat the competition, giving us more time to do our jobs well and giving the readers better-written stories.

One possible complication for the embargo system has arisen with the Internet. Many scientists are fairly casual about discussing new research in the so-called newsgroups. Data that may be embargoed next month or next year, ironically, can be freely available for anyone to read online. Draft versions of major scientific reports may also circulate online. Does the presence of information online, however tentative, make it fair game for reporters? The question is likely to be debated for some time, but one thing is clear now. If you want the information in your stories to be accurate and scientifically reliable, you'll be very wary of what you find online.

The typical newspaper science writer receives *Science, Nature, the New England Journal of Medicine,* and *the Journal of the American Medical Association* (JAMA). All are well-respected journals in which you can be pretty sure the reports have passed some kind of peer review system attesting that they are good science. Every week American newspapers publish several good science stories based on discoveries and findings that scientists have reported in these journals. This is not, despite what some editors may claim, simply rewriting material from other news agencies. Journals are one of the main ways scientists use to announce their most important advances. Writing a story based on a journal article is the science writing equivalent of a political writer covering a candidate's speech or a courts reporter covering a written decision handed down by a judge. In fact, if a scientific claim is announced and it has not been published or accepted for publication in a major journal, that is reason to be suspicious of its validity.

Of course, it is possible to be consumed by journal-based stories. I like to be fairly selective, using staff writers for only the best journal stories and using wires for the others. That way, you keep time to do enterprise pieces at your own schedule on the topics that interest you most, or that are more closely tailored to your local readership.

And, of course, science reporters share the responsibility of all news-people to be accurate and fair. Sometimes the goal is said to be objectivity, but this is virtually impossible, and I think it best that we not claim objectivity. After all, of the dozens of stories we could do on any given day, we reject most or all possibilities. In this we exercise our opinions as to what is a good story.

WHAT MAKES SCIENCE NEWS?

I think newspaper science writers use five basic criteria. Not every story has to score high on each criterion, but if it does, it's that much better a story.

Fascination Value

This is the special commodity that science stories, more than any other kind, have to offer. People love to be fascinated, to learn something and think, "That's amazing. I didn't know that." I sometimes think people have a natural appetite for fascination. It's very much akin to the sense of curiosity. The best way to explain fascination value is to give some examples and let you judge your own reactions. Which would you rather read about, dinosaurs or extinct species of worms? I thought so. Dinosaurs may be the quintessential fascinating topic for science writers. Close behind are black holes (more fascinating than, to pick another astronomical topic, meteors); human evolution (more engaging than, say, mouse evolution); and animal behavior (the more like a human the animal is said to be behaving, the more fascinating). You get the idea.

Size of the Natural Audience

This is the number of readers who already know that they want to read about the topic. If the story is about a common disease that everyone has had or fears getting, the natural audience will be larger than for a rare disease. Cancer and the common cold score high on this criterion. Kreutz-feld–Jakob disease scores low.

Importance

This is a subjective factor (another reason we're not truly objective). To judge a story idea on this point, you would try to decide whether the event, or finding, or wider knowledge of the event or finding is going to make much of a difference in the real world, especially in that of the average newspaper reader. AIDS is important, bunions are not. Global climate change is more important than regional climate change, unless, of course, the region happens to be your own.

Reliability of the Results

Is it good science? Here the single most useful guideline is science's own peer review system. The system is not perfect, but it's the best that's available, and every science writer must understand how it works and why it is critically important to find out whether a scientific claim or advance has survived the peer review process. It is incredibly easy for scientists (as well as anyone else) to come to believe passionately and honestly that something is true when, in fact, it is false. The peer review system is a time-tested way to minimize the odds that a misunderstanding is promulgated to the world at large. Science writers who ignore the system risk misleading their readers and embarrassing themselves.

Once or twice a week, some scientist or advocacy group tries to get me to write that such-and-such a "fact" is true when it has not passed through even the most rudimentary peer review process. Sometimes it's a perpetual motion machine that can be dismissed instantly (because every science writer should know about the Second Law of Thermodynamics), and sometimes it is a cancer cure, the details of which can't be divulged because the tipster's enemies would steal it (another good clue to quackery). Professional science writers pass up these story ideas routinely.

But not always. One of the most famous instances of non-peer-reviewed science getting into the mainstream press was "cold fusion." Two scientists claimed to have invented a tabletop device that caused nuclear fusion at ordinary temperatures, yielding more energy than was consumed in the process. Ordinarily a scientist would repeat the experiment and, if the results still looked good, submit a paper to a peer reviewed journal. Only after it was accepted or published would the press hear about it.

But not these two scientists. Amazingly, they called a press conference before they had even figured out how to reproduce their own results. Their Utah press conference did not draw the most tough-minded reporters in the business. Their promise of an unlimited source of abundant, cheap energy made the national wires, and a competitive feeding frenzy swept the science writing community.

Because the claims seemed too good to be true (usually a tip-off to something wrong), most good science writers conducted their own peer review process, asking physicists to comment. The dominant response was extreme skepticism. Still, the promise of cheap energy was so tempting that many physicists dropped their own work and tried the experiment, which seemed to be absurdly simple. Most got no sign of fusion and quickly denounced the claims.

Although the press was later criticized as if it had fallen for bad science, the fact is that most science reporters didn't. They simply reported the reaction of the scientific community, which was fascinating in itself. At the time I was in my rotation as the *Post*'s science editor and helped prepare a story with a straight lead followed by "If the claims of the researchers are confirmed and further experiments succeed..." And "Other scientists expressed doubt about the work, however, and one physicist familiar with it said the announcement was 'blown far out of proportion'."

Similar notes of skepticism attended most of the cold fusion coverage, except for that in the *Wall Street Journal*, which, to the astonishment of many science writers, climbed aboard the bandwagon. Although small bands of researchers continue to work on cold fusion, the vast majority of experts long ago dismissed it as a tantalizing illusion.

Timeliness

The final criterion is the old newspaper standard of timeliness. The newer the news, the newsier it is.

EXPLANATORY WRITING

If you've found a story idea that scores high enough on these five criteria, you're ready for the even greater challenge of reporting and writing the story. But first, you've got to sell your editor. If you have an editor who knows some science, this can be easy. If, however, your editor doesn't know his acid from his base, this gives you an advantage. The job of explaining the story idea is likely to show you what you need to explain carefully in your writing. And that can help you in your reporting. If your editor doesn't understand, you can bet your readers won't either.

The place to begin the task of explaining the science is not when you sit down at the computer. It's in your background reading before the interview with your source and in the interview itself. Science Writing Rule No. 1: Never try to explain something that you don't understand. Don't be shy about asking your sources to explain something again, if you don't get it the first time. And don't cop out by quoting the scientist's unhelpful explanation. If your scientist source is not a good explainer, ask him or her to refer you to somebody else, maybe one who teaches the field. Once you think you understand something, check yourself by saying it back to the scientist in your own words.

After you've written a lead to your story, stop, temporarily clear your mind of everything you learned while reporting the story, and even put out of your mind all the science you know. Now pretend you're a reader and you know only what you've read so far in the story. This skill is one of the most important a science writer (or any reporter) can develop, and it takes practice. Be literal-minded. Examine each word, and imagine what alternative (and erroneous) meanings a reader might impute to it.

Here is a lead from a major daily that meets my test:

> Every cell in the human body, according to a new view emerging from one of the hottest fields of cell biology, is poised to commit suicide. In fact, it appears that all cells are already armed with the instruments of their potential destruction and that every hour millions of them in each person's body do kill themselves.

There is not one word that should be unfamiliar to the general reader. The first phrase says the story is about the reader himself. The next says this is a hot field of research. The third delivers what most should find a startling bit of information. You don't need to know anything else to grasp the first sentence. The second sentence picks up from there and delivers more surprising scientific findings.

Once you are satisfied with your lead, write on. But stop every few paragraphs and reenact the naive reader exercise from the top.

If you have a lot to explain in your story, try to get away from the inverted pyramid as quickly as possible. It's a terrible form for explanatory writing. Far easier to report, to write, and to read is a chronological sequence. It's the dominant form for all good story telling, fiction or fact. Once when I had a huge story to write on a public health mystery (a man died of botulism after eating vichysoisse), I shamelessly imitated Berton Rouche, who wrote the wonderful "Annals of Medicine" stories for the *New Yorker*. I reread some of his pieces and imitated the step-by-step style. Twenty-five years later, I still meet people who remember that story. It can work any time you're unraveling a medical or forensic mystery, but it does eat up column inches.

WHEN SCIENCE IS USED TO GRIND AN AXE

One tricky area for science writers is science that comes from advocacy groups. All advocacy groups have axes to grind, no matter how noble or beautiful their causes are. One of their biggest goals is to keep the public aroused over their cause, and good science writing can conflict with that.

I was reminded of the difficulty advocacy groups have with good news when I did a long explainer on ozone depletion and pointed out another bit of good news. Emissions of ozone-depleting substances were dropping so quickly, thanks to an international agreement, that the worst of ozone depletion would arrive around 2000, much sooner than expected and that after that the ozone layer would begin a slow recovery.

Environmentalist groups were outraged. The ozone hole was a big, visible, carefully built issue, and environmentalists said my story would lead to public complacency. They attacked. Some even accused me of reporting that ozone depletion was a hoax. But because the advocates could not challenge my facts, they said my story was wrong in "tone." That puzzled me for a long time until I figured out what they meant. I had taken great care to make the tone of my story as neutral and as strictly factual as possible. And that was the problem. The tradition in environmental writing, unfortunately, is to be rather alarmist in tone. Environmental stories are usually bad news, warnings of impending disaster. My mistake, as the advocates saw it, was in pointing out that corrective measures were working very well and that doom was being averted. A carefully built advocacy issue was undermined by straight reporting.

HOW DO YOU ENSURE ACCURACY?

A generation ago, one newspaper science reporter actually referred to researchers at the National Institutes of Health (NIH) as "those medical wizards with their magic potions." Also in those days, major newspapers wrote major stories about the development of the Salk polio vaccine without referring to viruses, antigens, and antibodies or the immune system and, amazingly, without explaining how vaccines work. Now not only has today's science gotten vastly more complex, the tradition has developed in science writing of explaining things in much more detail. Imagine writing about AIDS without discussing viruses and antibodies. Today's tradition means readers learn more.

But the growing complexity does make it much easier to get a fact wrong in a story—which makes accuracy all the more difficult to achieve. So how do we do it? The main way, of course, is to do careful reporting and, when interviewing scientists, to check your understanding repeatedly with the source. Science Writing Rule No. 2: Never try to explain something that you don't understand. Sound familiar?

Until recently, I believed the traditional dogma in journalism, still held by many science writers, that it is wrong to let anybody outside the newspaper read our copy before publication. Freedom of the press. No prior restraint. No time. And so on. Finally, after spending far too much time with a reference book or on the phone trying to figure out if my simplification of the scientist's explanation was right, I reexamined my religion

and realized that the evil was in letting people change our copy in ways
we don't want it changed. If I've got a fact wrong, I definitely want it
changed. So I started faxing portions of stories and sometimes entire stories to scientists and asking if I had made any errors. I don't do it all the
time, just when I think I'm working at the edge of my understanding.

Amazingly enough, I found most scientists quite happy to respond
quickly without meddling in the story. Now, with e-mail, it's even more
convenient. Most of the changes they suggest are ones I am very thankful
to make before publication.

Although I advise all science writers to do the same, you should know
that a number of outstanding colleagues are opposed. They would never
think of showing anyone, especially a source, their copy. I respect that.
It's a matter of religion.

THE FUTURE OF NEWSPAPER SCIENCE WRITING

When the future of the newspaper industry is being questioned, you may
wonder whether it makes sense to aim for a career in this sector of science
writing. It still does. Newspaper science writing is the core of the field and
will remain so, even as the medium evolves new forms. Just as so many
great writers of literature started as reporters, many of the most accomplished science writers in other media learned their craft at newspapers
and moved on.

What you learn as a newspaper science writer is to be a quick study, to
understand much about how the natural and technological worlds work,
and how to share that information effectively and succinctly with the wid-
est possible readership. That's a service of high calling and a solid preparation for what is increasingly an Information Age.

3

Writing Science for Magazines

JANICE HOPKINS TANNE

Janice Hopkins Tanne began her career as a newspaper reporter and held executive editorial positions in medical publishing and continuing medical education companies before launching a career as a freelance medical writer. She is the author of *New York* magazine's bestselling issue ever: "The 1,085 Best Doctors in New York," part of an award-winning series that includes "The Best Hospitals in New York" and "How to Be a Savvy Medical Consumer." Her articles have also appeared in *Associated Press Newsfeatures, Family Circle, GQ, Mademoiselle, Mirabella, Parade, Reader's Digest, Redbook, The Times* (London), *Vogue,* and many other periodicals. She is a frequent contributor to the *British Medical Journal.*

Janice has won numerous awards for medical writing from organizations that include the American Medical Writers Association, the American Society of Journalists and Authors, the Society of the Silurians (New York journalists), the Newswomen's Club of New York, and the American College of Emergency Physicians.

Currently, Janice is a contributing editor at *American Health* and *New York* magazines. She is a two-term president of the American Society of Journalists and Authors, and is vice president of the Newswomen's Club of New York.

Magazine science stories begin with a query letter, like this one I wrote to *New York* magazine:

"HEPATITIS B: THE MODEL FOR AIDS."
Hepatitis B is spread by sex, including kissing; blood-to-blood transmission by dirty needles and transfusions, and from mother to infant during pregnancy or birth. And, unlike AIDS, it is also spread by casual contact. Much of our knowledge of AIDS is extrapolated from experience with this similar disease. Hepatitis B is much more infectious than AIDS, but more than half the people who get sick with hepatitis B have no identifiable risk factor: They don't know where they got it or how.

17

Researchers think most of them got it from sexual contact with an apparently healthy person who is an unknowing carrier of the disease. . . .

. . . The good news is that hepatitis B, unlike AIDS, is totally preventable by a vaccine. . . .

. . . *New York*'s readers are unaware of this serious, growing, but
preventable threat that affects them intimately through their sex part-
ners, exercise clubs, day-care centers, barber and beauty shops, medical providers, and ordinary work-a-day activities. I want to do this story
for two reasons. It can help save readers' lives and health. And it hasn't
been done. I have never seen an article on this major disease in any
consumer magazine, although I have written a state-of-the-art update
for doctors. . . . Hepatitis B is too important to ignore and *New York*
could be the first to alert readers. The enclosed Xerox shows you the
level of concern at a local medical center.

The proposal was accepted and assigned. The lead of the published
article went like this, because I found a moving story to illustrate my scientific tale:

Four months before she died from hepatitis B, a 23-year-old secretary—we'll call her Kathy—had her ears pierced at a jewelry store near
her midtown office.

"It was the only risk factor we ever identified. She had no sex part-
ners. She never used IV drugs. She was a healthy young woman," says
Dr. Harold Neu, an infectious diseases expert at Columbia–Presbyterian Medical Center and a member of the medical team that fought
to save Kathy's life.

About three and a half months after the ear-piercing, Kathy got
flulike symptoms and stayed home from work. . . . A few days later, she
became so sick that she was hospitalized . . . she slipped into a coma.

"Her liver failed. Her blood wouldn't clot. Despite everything we
did, she died within two weeks," Dr. Neu said.

Hepatitis B, the disease that killed Kathy, is the model for AIDS:
The patterns of infection of the viruses that cause the two illnesses are
very similar. But hepatitis B is at least fifteen times more common than
AIDS, and it is far more infectious.

Unlike AIDS, it is entirely preventable by vaccines. . . .

This story, "The Other Plague," appeared in *New York* on July 11, 1988,
and won a Front Page Award from the Newswomen's Club of New York.

IDEAS

Where did I get the idea? I had been writing about AIDS for years and
had been struck by the fact that AIDS researchers always commented on

hepatitis B as the model for AIDS. I covered an international conference on hepatitis and was amazed to find out that, although a vaccine was available, few people were immunized. I proposed the story to *New York*. And I got myself immunized.

As with the hepatitis B story, many stories grow out of previous ones. Write about AIDS, and you discover hepatitis B. Cover a scientific conference, and you'll see a story for the public.

Sometimes a story that doesn't fly leads to one that does. I had discussions with the Commonwealth Fund about a health story that never worked out, but I learned that the Fund had helped develop the concept of patient-centered care. That story idea proved to be just right for *American Health*, for whom I interviewed doctors and patients at three different patient-centered care facilities.

One of my major sources of story ideas is journal articles. Usually they don't suggest a specific story, but they let me know what topics are currently of scientific interest and who the players are.

Conferences can lead to feature stories as well as news articles. For example, for the *British Medical Journal*, I covered a New York Academy of Sciences conference on the threat that health reform posed to academic medical centers. New York City was especially endangered because its many academic health centers were already tightly regulated by the state and strapped for cash. To *New York* magazine I proposed an article stressing the risk to medical care and to the city's economy, and the story was used with a prominent headline.

A holiday party for science writers in New York gave me another story idea. The speaker was Dr. Patrick Kelly, head of neurosurgery at New York University Medical Center, who described his work in developing computer-aided stereotactic neurosurgery. That became an article for *Parade* that got reader response from around the world.

Half my assignments come from editors who present me with an idea. This is more likely to happen when you've written for a magazine for several years or when you're well known in the field. Often these ideas are "in the air" and editors want them covered fast.

Medical center public relations people sometimes offer me exclusives. For example, Columbia–Presbyterian Medical Center in New York gave me (for *New York*) a print exclusive for a story about the separation of Siamese twins. The medical center trusted me to present a thoughtful, balanced report, and they wanted to avoid a media circus that would upset the parents and foster parents. They did not ask for or get any right of review.

Commercial public relations people, as opposed to public relations people representing medical centers, universities, and professional medical associations, are generally dismal as sources of story ideas. They send a press release announcing the Mark III model of their client's toothbrush and then call to ask if you got the release and plan to use it. Turn the press release over and recycle it as paper for taking notes.

PROPOSALS

Stories begin with a proposal, also called a query letter. The proposal has several parts and aims.

First, it must catch the editor's attention. Writers think, "I'd like to write about genetic testing and counseling." Editors think in headlines: "10 Ways Genetic Testing Can Save Your Life." So give your proposal a headline. It will help you focus your approach (see box).

The proposal must also show the editor how you can write. Many of my successful proposals open with the sentences that become my story's lead, or something close to it. For example, my proposal read:

SEPARATED FOR LIFE

Carmen and Rosa Taveras are healthy, adorable, curly-haired eight-month-old twins, as lively and cute a pair of babies as you'll ever see. They have every prospect of growing up to healthy adulthood. Except that they will never be able to sit, walk, stand, or lead normal lives, because they are Siamese twins joined at the buttocks and sharing parts of the spine and many internal organs.

As printed, the headline and lead were:

FREE AT LAST

When Dr. Peter Altman of Columbia–Presbyterian Medical Center got his first look at Carmen and Rosa Taveras, he saw bright-eyed, wavy-haired 2½ month old twins—as lively and adorable a pair of babies as he'd ever seen. They had every hope of growing up to be healthy adults—except, without a million dollars' worth of risky, sophisticated, delicate medical treatment, they would never sit, stand, walk, or lead normal lives.

They lay on their backs, Carmen's head pointing toward one end of the examining table, Rosa's pointing toward the other end. They were fused together, pelvis to pelvis.

Next, your proposal must tell the editor where your story will go from here and what it will cover. I said I'd be in the operating room, would describe the surgery, and would interview the family members and the surgeons, covering both technology and emotions.

Then your proposal has to tell why you are the right person to do the story and describe your background. This should take no more than two paragraphs. If I hadn't written for a magazine before, I would describe

Ten Tips for Writing a Query Letter

1. Give it a headline.
2. Open with what will probably be your lead.
3. Go on for two or three paragraphs, then describe how you'll cover the rest of the story.
4. Then include one paragraph each on: Why you are the right person to do the story; your background; and why this story is important for their readers.
5. No more than a page and half, single-spaced.
6. You have to do enough research to write a convincing query, but not enough to write the story. You should know whom you want to interview, although you may or may not identify all these people in the proposal.
7. You need an angle: Low-fat diet for the pregnant woman; low-fat diet for the traveling executive.
8. Include three clips.
9. Read three issues of the magazine before you submit a query.
10. Wait three weeks before calling the editor to ask what happened to your query, unless you specify this is a time-sensitive query.

Copyright by Janice Hopkins Tanne.
Reproduced with permission.

my expertise and connections, mentioning prizes or significant stories. I'd enclose three of my best clips, ones appropriate to the magazine's style.

Finally, you must explain why this story is important for their readers. For example: It will improve their health or let them avoid a risk. It will bring them up-to-date on an undiscovered issue of importance.

Before you send a proposal, read a few issues of the magazine and discover whether it accepts free-lance articles. Some magazines are entirely staff-written. If you can't find the magazine on a newsstand or get the information from sources such as *Writer's Market* (published annually by Writer's Digest Books), call the magazine and ask for writer's guidelines and a sample issue.

Submit your proposal. Today this is still done by mail or fax. A few magazines accept queries by modem or e-mail.

Now the bad news. Unless the magazine has asked you to submit a proposal, and even if you have written for them before, your query may well be ignored.

When I became a free-lance writer fifteen years ago, after holding staff positions, most magazines responded to queries even from unknown writers, within three weeks. Today—and I speak as two-term president of the American Society of Journalists and Authors and former chair of its Contracts Committee—your query is likely to meet dead silence at many magazines.

What can you do? Some writers attach postcards to the proposal, asking the editor to check the status (yes, no, we're thinking about it). If you haven't heard within about three weeks, call. The editor may never have seen your proposal and may ask you to resubmit it.

Since the level of rudeness on the editorial side has escalated dramatically, I see no need for writers to be polite. Multiple queries means that you submit your proposal to several magazines at the same time. I would focus the same idea quite differently for different magazines, but many writers send a generic query letter. I wouldn't tell the magazines it's a multiple query. If two of them want it, take the highest bidder.

THE CONTRACT

Write nothing without a contract that specifies what rights the magazine is buying, the amount it will pay and when, and the story length. Copyright and all rights to your story belong to you unless you license the rights or give them away. You do not have to do anything to claim copyright, although (for articles published in the United States) registering your story with the Library of Congress will give you major protection.

In days past, contracts were verbal. Then it was a simple letter: 2,000 words by date ____, ____ pay, and ____ kill fee (fee due to the writer if the story doesn't work out), First North American Serial Rights.

Read your contract carefully and understand what the terms mean. Most magazines have two or more contracts (bad, better, best, and for our special friends).

The most desirable contract calls for First North American (often, today, Print) Serial Rights, which means the magazine has the right to print your article once, on paper, in North America. (In Britain, it's first British serial rights.) Contracts should always say that expenses will be covered, although you may need prior approval for major expenses.

Avoid contracts that describe your article as "work made for hire" (U.S. copyright law says such agreements must be signed before the work is started) or contracts that require you to give up your copyright to the publisher. Writers have made big bucks out of movie, reprint, anthology, and other secondary rights.

The electronic age is a new ball game. When your publisher takes all rights (or electronic rights in addition to print rights) and puts your article on a database, everybody makes money except you. The phone company gets money for telephone access. The publisher receives revenue from the database producer and the access provider, such as CompuServe. You get nothing. The money is significant: *Forbes* magazine estimated the *New York Times* will make $80 million from electronic uses in the next five years.

Major writers' organizations feel that writers should share in this revenue. Your contract should either specify a flat fee for a limited time for use of your work in a specified manner ($____ for 1 year on ____ database). Or it should pay you on a fee-plus-royalty arrangement. The Authors Registry, set up by leading writers' organizations, now represents nearly 50,000 writers and writers represented through 90 literary agencies. It provides a method of contacting writers and paying them for electronic and other uses.

Your contract will specify an approximate article length and a fee. Editors talk fee per word—a dollar a word is the McDonald's of the industry. Writers should think time per project. How much money do you need to make per day or week? How much time will this project take?

Magazine articles have been getting shorter for years, but you have to do the same amount of research to write 1,200 words as to write 3,000. Consider how much time it will take you and price the assignment accordingly.

SOURCES

You've done enough research on the story to write the proposal, but not enough to do the article. Now you need to read review articles, and perhaps textbooks, and interview the experts.

When I'm doing interviews, I try to start with the least important ones, so that I am more knowledgeable with my major interviews.

Ask everybody you interview who else you should talk to. Ask them who disagrees with their point of view and interview them.

Call the major medical centers. Their public affairs people are usually helpful and know who their experts are. Call the disease associations and the professional associations (such as the American College of Obstetricians and Gynecologists).

I read basic journals (*British Medical Journal, JAMA, The Lancet, Morbidity and Mortality Weekly Report, New England Journal of Medicine, Science, Science News, The Sciences*), so I am usually up to date on current science. I use review articles for background; the references are also useful sources for other experts. It helps when you call an expert for an interview to be able to refer to an article he or she wrote. Learn to do electronic searches.

Do your interviews in person if at all possible. You get more out of them, just from facial expressions and the warmth that comes from being in the same room with somebody. If not, do a phone interview.

Don't call to set up an interview unless you're ready to do the interview. It may be your only chance to talk to the expert.

People have different methods of dealing with interview notes. I tape all my interviews, phone and in person, and I always take notes. I almost never transcribe the tapes. I do listen to the key quotes to make sure they're correct.

WRITING AND SUBMISSION

Writing an article is a process of gathering too much information and winnowing it down. Before I start writing, I go through my notes and highlight the key points and good quotes. Then I reread my query. Stories sometimes drift away from what you proposed, but what you proposed is what the editor expects. If you're way off, you should have alerted the editor. If you didn't, do it now.

Ease into writing by doing the source list: the names, correct titles, and phone, fax, and e-mail numbers of the people you interviewed. The fact checkers will need it, and doing it will refresh your memory.

I usually know the way I'll begin my story and the way I'll end it, so I write straight through from beginning to end. Every once in a while I run into a real bastard of a story—I've never known what causes one. When I do run into a bastard, I write the individual parts of the story and string them together, like beads on a necklace.

I started on daily newspapers, where you don't have the luxury of time to write and revise. I learned to do most outlining in my head so that I wrote the story right the first time. Daily newspaper or wire service training is unmatched for teaching you to be a professional.

Sometimes you will write in different styles for different magazines. For *New York*, I write more slangy and hip for savvy New Yorkers, and my readers are evenly divided between men and women. For *American Health*, I write more plain vanilla for a more middle–America audience, more women than men, who are seriously interested in health and nutrition. For the *British Medical Journal*, I'm writing with a more professional tone for doctors, more men than women, who are interested in political issues affecting medicine, but less aware of the nuances in American society. Some magazines treasure writers' different voices; others try to make them all sound the same.

Writers claim they hate to "dumb down" for the women's magazines, but it can be a rewarding experience to have to really understand complex medical ideas and explain them, rather than just repeating the textbooks and standard wisdom.

Your article will be too long. Try not to be over by more than 10 percent; that's comfortable for both you and the editor.

You will have some clever phrases or anecdotes you love. Kill them before they make your editor gag.

The traditional way to submit a story is double-spaced on white paper with generous margins. Today, many magazines request submission on disk or by modem or e-mail, but most also want a hard copy (i.e., paper) as well.

The writer should hear whether a story has been accepted within hours to three weeks, depending on its urgency and the editor's efficiency. If you haven't heard, call after two or three weeks.

Your editor may want revisions, and the contract should have addressed the point. If you turned in a story that fulfills the outline set out in your proposal, you should not have to do more than one revision. Usually, this should be minor or structural. Editors must be specific. You want to avoid endless rewrites while the editor changes focus or decides what he or she likes.

Kill fees range from about 10 to 100 percent. Most are in the range of 25 to 35 percent and come into play when everyone has made their best effort and the story isn't working. A magazine should pay 100 percent when the writer has fulfilled the contract but the magazine has decided not to run the story for its own reasons.

When your article has been accepted and edited, it will probably be fact-checked by a bright young person. Sometimes fact checkers save you from errors. Provide this person with your printed sources, marked to show what supports what statement, much the way a journal article is referenced. Provide a complete list of the names, titles, and phone numbers of the people interviewed. Check the galleys to make sure errors have not been introduced in the editing process.

AFTERPLAY: PROMOTION

Your job isn't done. When your article is published, you need to promote it to make it easier for you to do future articles for this magazine and for others.

Send copies of the article to the people you interviewed and to the people who helped you, such as medical center public relations people. You can give your editor or the editor's assistant stick-on labels, or you can get your editor to send you copies of the magazine and do it yourself. Try to include a brief thank-you letter and your business card.

Tell the magazine you're available to be interviewed on a reasonable number of radio and television programs. Start small, on local stations, and you'll learn how.

Say thank you to your editor if he or she did an excellent job. In special circumstances, send a thank-you letter to the editor's boss, with a copy to the editor. Good editing is extremely rare, and thanks for good editing is rarer yet.

Remember that editors cherish good, reliable writers. Now may be the time to chat about ideas for your next proposal to the magazine.

REWARDS

Your greatest reward will be the sure knowledge that you helped somebody, perhaps saved a life. I know I have, and that knowledge is worth every editorial hassle I've ever been through.

4

Writing for Trade and Science Journals: Trade Journals

JULIE ANN MILLER

I am currently the editor of *Science News* magazine, and was formerly the editor of *BioScience*. Before coming to *BioScience*, I covered biology for *Science News*. I wrote about the potential value of recombinant DNA when scientists were debating whether a gene from one organism could be expressed in another, and I wrote about AIDS before it had a name.

I was recently the science adviser to "Find It! Science" (Computer Access to Children's Literature). I edited the content of descriptions of 3,000 selected children's science books for an innovative CD-ROM that will be used by children, teachers, and librarians.

I have served on the boards of the NASW and the D.C. Science Writers Association. I received my journalism training at the University of Wisconsin at Madison, and also completed a doctorate in neuroscience there.

Think not only about who reads trade journals but also about where they are read. Instead of being skimmed on the subway or browsed at the beach, the trade journal is likely to be studied at the reader's desk or laboratory bench. Envision the reader with pen in hand underlining passages that may be useful in shaping research plans, collaborations, and even financial investments.

I am not saying that trade journals should not be enjoyable, or that other types of publication aren't informative, but trade journals' primary function is to provide specific information about a field to practitioners. And the readers have high expectations of the trade journalists' judgment and accuracy.

Scientific trade journals are targeted to researchers in a particular area, which may be as broad as biology, chemistry, or physics, or as specific as oil chemistry. These publications are often an activity of a professional association of scientists, but some—like the *Journal of NIH Research*—are commercial ventures. These publications may be written entirely by science writers, whether staff or free-lance, or they may contain sections written by scientists.

Trade publications are near one end of the continuum of scientific writing. They are not as detailed and specialized as the journals that carry only articles written by scientists, but they tend to be more so than the publications that cover all the sciences, such as *Science* and *Nature*. The articles written by science writers for trade journals are light, pleasurable reading for the scientists, compared to the technical reports of their peers.

The science writer for a trade journal gets story ideas directly from the same sources the scientists use: meetings, journals, and, of course, other scientists. Press releases tend to be less useful, because the topics are generally chosen to appeal to a broader audience, but occasionally an information-packed press release will point a writer in the direction of an appropriate story.

The trade writer can often be more thorough and persistent in coverage than can writers for more general publications. Having written a major story on brain structure, for example, most other journalists would then have to put that topic aside for a while. At a biology trade journal, the writer can keep tabs on the field and revisit it as often as important discoveries are made.

The trade journal writer can report research in earlier stages of development than can more general publications. Trade journals inform their readers about new approaches to research—some of which reach dead ends or are soon surpassed by other techniques, while others, like the early recombinant DNA work, result in a scientific revolution. Therefore, the trade journal is often a valuable source of ideas and information for other science journalists.

Trade writers must be comfortable in dealing with scientists who are speaking scientific jargon. Whether writers have had academic training in the area or have just picked up the vocabulary on the job, they must be able to identify and comprehend the meaningful information in a meeting, talk, or journal article. They must ask questions of scientists who do not have experience in giving explanations to the general public or in putting their work in context. And they must be firm about requiring the scientist to define terms and explain ideas. A scientist once told me that "all biologists" know the meaning of "conidium." I was biologist enough myself to tell him confidently, "No, they do not." (A conidium is an asexual spore of certain fungi, according to a biology dictionary.)

In a trade journal story, it is critical to make clear the importance of a development within the specialty. I recently began reporting on what seemed like only some interesting observations about species differences. (I had been attracted to the story by a great closeup photo of a moth's face.) Through follow-up questions I learned that the observations upset a longstanding assumption about coevolution. My story was suddenly much stronger.

At a trade journal, the writer is not pressured to link every story to a person's everyday life or a grand philosophical question—each finding does not need to cure AIDS or reveal the origin of the universe. The trade journal writer often has the luxury of going into more depth than most other writers can. He or she can report stories where the beauty is in the details—the shape of a molecule or the way a series of reactions form a feedback loop.

In general, in a trade journal one can assume that the reader knows how scientific research works. Unless the scene is unusual in an interesting way, there is no need to describe the field or laboratory experience.

Accuracy is uniquely important in writing for specialists. First, they are likely to catch you in an error. (Whatever you do, don't refer to a protozoan as a bacterium.) Second, they often forget where they read a report and fail to distinguish between authors who are science writers and authors who are scientists reporting their own work. So there is the risk of readers incorporating misinformation directly into their research plans.

When collecting facts for a story, try to get some written statement from the scientists—an abstract, manuscript, or reprint—in order to check the basics, such as what species were studied and the spelling of the species names. It is well worth repeating to the scientist your understanding of each concept. You should check back to ask further questions as you write and perhaps even fax the scientist portions of your manuscript if you are uncertain of the precise terminology, facts, or implications.

Because you may be explaining difficult concepts, it is extremely important to write in a logical, well-organized manner. In an interview, a scientist may often change topics and then return to add additional comments. Articles written by scientists typically group descriptions of all the methods, then of the results, then of the conclusions, so there is no continuous story line. But the writer must pull out the pieces of the story he or she has chosen to tell and arrange them so they smoothly convey ideas to the reader.

Because trade journals help scientists to communicate with their peers, it is important to include in the story the mundane information needed by readers wanting to contact your sources and find the relevant journals. Otherwise, you may spend your days fielding phone calls from readers trying to track down a researcher or an article. Trade journals are usually more generous than other publications in mentioning the various scientists who have contributed to the research described or who work on similar problems, again in the interest of establishing direct communication, if not collaborations.

As a trade journal writer, you may need to be more adamant than other writers about your autonomy. Your job is to use your judgment about what stories are important and how they should be presented. Especially when a publication is an activity of a professional society, members of that society may assume that they can dictate what scientists and what stories are covered. Although, in fact, your sources are indirectly paying your salary, remember that the publication benefits from its writers independently evaluating the newsworthiness of potential stories. Otherwise, a few well-established researchers and approved topics (the importance of biodiversity; the value of rational drug design) tend to get covered repeatedly. Even the specialists' eyes eventually glaze over at the topics their colleagues insist are good for them.

While insisting on intellectual autonomy, you may also need to be more tactful than other journalists. If the field is specialized, there may be a smaller group of potential sources, so you can't afford to offend them needlessly. Some trade journals have scientists as editors, sometimes as working editors, and sometimes as figureheads. There may be conflicts of interest, especially when these scientists have industry connections.

While trade journals should be intellectually enjoyable, some are more conservative in writing style and appearance than other kinds of publications. A staff writer once had to remove a reference to "a snatch of an old song" in the lead of a story for a chemical trade journal, because the word "snatch," he was told, is inappropriate for family reading.

What does the future hold for trade journals? Their continued existence, in some form, seems assured. Although public interest in science may wax and wane, the scientists will always need impartial information about the progress of their specialties.

However, the distinctions between writing for trade journals and other publications may be fading. Many associations and private publishers, dissatisfied with the revenues generated by their specialty audiences, are attempting to reach a broader audience—teachers, policymakers, scientists in other fields, and even the general public—in the hope of increasing sales. To that end, some have split their publications, separating the technical papers of the scientists from the news and features written by journalists. Some are hiring general newspaper writers instead of journalists who specialize in science. Stories are becoming shorter and less detailed.

Therefore, there appears to be a trend toward the trade journals becoming more like general magazines. If this trend results in livelier presentations of stories, it may be for the good, but it is also likely to decrease the breadth and depth of coverage in these journals. That scenario would make them less useful to other science writers. And the scientists would be left with nothing between the dry articles of their peers and general magazines suitable for reading at the beach.

● ●

Science Journals

RICHARD KERR

Richard Kerr has been a reporter at *Science* since 1977, arriving a week after successfully defending his Ph.D. dissertation on the dissolved humic substances in seawater ("yellowstuff" in oceanographic parlance). His formal training in journalism consists of two night classes—magazine story writing and introduction to news reporting—taken surreptitiously while a graduate student at the University of Rhode Island. On-the-job training from generous colleagues on the research news staff of *Science* was crucial to his more formal preparation.

At *Science,* which publishes scientific papers as well as news for a broad range of scientists, a reporter must deliver facts that are fresh and enticing even to insiders, accurate enough to satisfy world-class experts, and understandable by biologists and physicists alike. Writing for scientists requires an approach to reporting that emphasizes in-depth, long-term coverage of a relatively narrow beat—the Earth and planetary sciences in my case—and the exercise of a sort of critical judgment that is often missing in today's science journalism. Rather than asking "Is this a story or not?" and then filling out the skeleton provided by a press release, a science journal reporter must ask how good the science is, whether the science addresses central questions that researchers care deeply about, and how to balance the inevitable uncertainties with the story's news appeal.

But the rewards can be in proportion to the intensity of the focus and the demands of analytical reporting. If, as veteran *San Francisco Chronicle* science reporter David Perlman once wrote, science writing is a continuing graduate education, then writing for scientists is a Ph.D. in science news reporting.

So if reporters are going to be out there on the scientific frontier, shouldn't they have much the same career preparation as the researchers they cover? When I came to *Science* in 1977, every reporter for the Research News section had to have a Ph.D. The thinking was that Ph.D.-trained reporters will instinctively understand the care and feeding of scientist sources and will more readily gain access to practicing scientists, and, besides, the factual knowledge picked up on the way to a Ph.D. can only help a reporter.

True enough, but there is also some truth in the old adage that a good reporter can cover any beat. Walter Sullivan admirably covered the earth sciences for more than 30 years for the *New York Times*, inventing the beat as he went along, on the strength of some undergraduate science he picked up. A good middle ground might be a combined approach like the science journalism program at the University of California (UC) at Santa Cruz. Applicants are required to have a bachelor's degree in science; a master's would be even better, I suspect, to the extent that it would carry the student away from textbook science toward the real world of research. And every student at UC Santa Cruz does get an internship, providing that essential on-the-job experience.

Of course, no amount of training in science is going to guarantee that you produce technically flawless copy story after story, but scientist readers are the pickiest readers around. One error in a story in their own field—like whether 90 percent of species or genera disappeared in the Permo–Triassic extinction—and they will assume all your stories are similarly flawed. To avoid that, or at least to produce the most accurate copy possible, reporters on the Research News staff of *Science* routinely send their draft stories to a couple of their sources for review. Allen Hammond, the first editor of the Research News section of *Science*, instituted expert review 25 years ago, perhaps because, like the staff that he eventually hired, he had no journalism training or experience. Not being steeped in journalistic lore, he did not feel bound to observe the tradition that showing draft stories to sources is a no-no. With this review process, copy comes out nearly free of those niggling little order-of-magnitude errors or outdated institutional affiliations. Review by sources does require some judgment about who makes a good reviewer—expert in the field, knowledgeable about the specific story, not too opinionated. It can all be a bother on deadline, but after more than 500 stories, sharing copy with sources has never threatened to compromise my journalistic integrity.

Turning out 45 to 50 pages of news stories a year for the 140,000 scientists who receive *Science* takes a degree of concentration unusual in journalism of any brand. But then, for me, having been a scientific dilettante since the fifth grade, teasing out a good story idea by wading through a sea of information is the greatest reward of the job. In an attempt to stay ahead of the ever-increasing flood of press releases in this country, I belong to half a dozen scientific societies so that I get their news publications as well as discounts on their journals. All told, there are about a dozen journals each month, not including *Nature* and *Science,* plus assorted publications such as the Smithsonian's volcano monitoring bulletin or the monthly climate analysis of the National Oceanic and Atmospheric Administration (NOAA). Meetings constitute the other main source of information I use to cultivate stories. Three large, interdisciplinary society meetings form the backbone of a year's itinerary, but two to three other meetings may be drawn from a wide variety of sources. To make good use of a large meeting, you'll have to scan 4,000 or 5,000 abstracts ranging over fields from atmospheric science to volcanology. Close attention to meeting abstracts not only suggests which dozen talks to catch in a day's thousand but also provides lots of material for background and future stories. I was a number of years in the job before I could bring myself to tackle a big meeting; after 18 years on the same beat, it's obvious that experience—the deeper the better—is crucial to the efficiency of the whole process. At the 1981 American Geophysical Union (AGU) meeting, for example, the late Charles Orth, an amateur geologist but expert analytical chemist at Los Alamos National Laboratory, presented pivotal geochemical evidence that the impact theory of the extinction of the dinosaurs was more than just wild imaginings. No news release heralded his talk, his talk was misplaced in an unrelated session, and his abstract title said nothing about dinosaurs, but knowing the field in depth made his abstract stand out.

Broad reading and attending meetings provide stacks of paper (the copier room is a favorite haunt) that go into five file drawers holding maybe 400 subject folders running the gamut from accreted continental terrane through magnetic fields to weather satellites. A mental sifting of this welter of information for gems of news leads to checking with file material and a couple of calls to scientist sources. Then, with luck, a story emerges that tells the reader where a field is going before the first press release is written. All this groundwork might be short-circuited by an unsolicited call from a news-savvy scientist anxious to let you in on a hot development, but don't count on it. Scientists are a wonderfully cooperative lot, always willing if not anxious to explain their work, even if they didn't catch your affiliation. Still, their news sense is usually not that acute. I get precious few unsolicited calls, and they often don't pan out. Cultivate potential sources, but depend on your own digging.

In controversial areas, scientist readers are going to be looking for more than the he-said/she-said treatment they get in a news service story.

The debate over whether an asteroid impact or a huge volcanic eruption did the deed went on for almost a decade after Bruce Bohor of the
U.S. Geological Survey (USGS) published powerful evidence of an impact
imprinted on shattered grains of quartz found round the world, evidence
that was never seriously challenged. But the evidence didn't seem to matter as reporters timidly wrote "fair and balanced" stories year after year
until the same few volcanists who always loomed so large in those stories
of imagined controversy finally retired from the scene. At *Science*, I usually
ignored the volcanists; they had trouble publishing in peer reviewed journals, and even when they did their arguments crumbled in the face of
evidence for an impact. That prompted some heated letters to the editor
about my lack of balance and outright bias, but editors feel, probably
rightly so, that you're not writing enough hard-hitting stories if you don't
offend someone once in a while.

Reporters writing for scientists must break out of the if-this-is-Thursday-
it-must-be-a-*Nature*-story rut of reactive, fair, and balanced journalism.
Mindless objectivity without context and critical analysis ill serves any
reader; the scientist reader will be downright offended. Delivering the
facts—accurately, in context, and realistically balanced—while they are
still news should be the goal of any science reporter. The demands of
writing for a science journal can only hone the necessary skills.

5

Broadcast Science Journalism: Reporting News

DAVID ROPEIK

David Ropeik, a reporter at WCVB-TV in Boston since 1978, created the environmental beat there in 1989. He has twice won the DuPont Columbia Award, one of the most prestigious awards in television journalism—in 1991, for a composite of environmental stories. He serves on the national board of the Society of Environmental Journalists (SEJ), and on the advisory board to the Environmental Reporting Council of the Radio and Television News Directors Foundation. He was a 1994–95 Knight Science Journalism Fellow at M.I.T.

A friend of mine, the environmental reporter for a big city tabloid, once remarked that his job and mine, environmental reporter for a local television news room, were much the same. "It's kind of like being a photographer for the *Wall Street Journal.*"

In one sense, it's an apt analogy. Science stories, and environmental stories that often include science, are a tough sell to television news managers used to more "hard" or "breaking" or, to be honest, more "sensational" stories.

Inadvertently though, my friend's comparison focuses on just what makes television news coverage of science, and the environment, so effective: pictures.

We did an investigative series on serious carbon monoxide and nitrogen dioxide pollution at indoor skating rinks, caused by exhaust from ice resurfacing machines running without pollution control equipment in poorly ventilated buildings. No matter how I wrote that piece, the pictures were what really told the story: fumes from the resurfacing machines operating right in front of skating kids, and pictures of air-testing equipment registering "evacuation" levels as we sat taking the tests among spectators in the stands.

35

Beneath the telling pictures, though, there must of course be sound reporting. And the medium of television news throws up some unique challenges to solid coverage of environmental stories, and the science those stories often include.

Foremost among those challenges is the brevity imposed as the industry standard for a television news story. The average reporter "package" is one minute and 40 seconds long. One hundred seconds! That forces you to keep your writing tight and precise. And it forces you to really focus on the heart of the story, get right to the point, and stick to it.

The restrictive length of most stories limits not only the degree of detail you can include, but also your ability to put things in context. Context is critical to many environmental stories. New developments often find their meaning in what has gone before. In climate change, for example, one warmer-than-normal year means little. One warmer year after 10 preceding warmer-than-normal years might mean something more significant.

In one important way, I find the length restriction helpful. It trains me to focus on the center of the story—as I gather it, as I write it, and as I work with a videotape editor to electronically put all the pieces together. It imposes a certain journalistic discipline. With only six or seven hours to gather the facts, to physically travel around to do on-camera interviews and shoot our video, to talk with my graphics department (usually by phone from out in the field), and to get back and put everything together, there is simply no time to waste chasing parts of the story that won't fit in a minute-forty.

And at some point too much detail can turn viewers off. While people are fascinated by science, I think they are quick to turn away from an explanation that seems too complex. So when I explain a scientific element in a story, I try to keep to the essential facts. On ozone depletion for example, no atmospheric chemistry. Just an explanation about how chlorofluorocarbons (CFCs) rise to the ozone layer and break down the molecules that protect us from ultraviolet rays.

But television's imposed brevity creates a serious journalistic compromise for a television reporter. I don't get to inform people in the depth I'd like to. More than context gets left out. Facts get left out. Big ones, sometimes. I did a piece on climate change recently, based on an international report suggesting that human-caused climate change is underway, no longer just a theory. I cited some of the evidence: sea level rising, unusual regional weather, melting glaciers. But I didn't have time to refer to changes occurring in micro habitats at high mountain elevations, or the unprecedented spread of vector-borne diseases.

Leaving facts out hurts. The trade-off is that there are (unfortunately) millions of people who don't read newspapers or watch network newscasts, who get their news only from local television. That's the niche we occupy in the public-information continuum. There are people who only know what they know of the world by watching us. So my viewers didn't learn that diseases spread by bugs are on the rise, or that ecosystems high up on mountains are changing. They *did* learn that some of the top scientists in the world think that humans are altering the earth's climate. Lots of people got the basic story. That's the payoff that keeps me going as I'm shredding the facts to make them fit in my minute-forty.

And that shredding can get extreme when it comes to stories on the environment, especially when they include science. I recently had to explain the entire issue of endocrine disrupters (sometimes referred to as environmental estrogens) in three and a half minutes. That was twice the normal story length, yes. But it's still an absurdly short amount of time to lay out a complex issue and cite and explain the various scientific findings behind the growing concern that human-made chemicals may be damaging nature and human health and even threatening human fertility.

In circumstances like that, I don't spend time explaining how the research was done or by whom or how the scientists reached their conclusions. But I will spend some of my precious seconds emphasizing a central point, even mentioning it more than once in the story, or revisiting it in the summation.

I dwell on the central facts of a story in part because watching television news has the physiological effect of putting the viewer to sleep. Brain studies suggest that perceiving a "passive" medium, such as television, in which the message requires less deciphering, tends to produce alpha waves, the brain pattern characteristic of sleep and meditation. Perceiving an "active" medium, such as print, in which the brain has to work harder to decode the message, produces more beta or active brain waves.

In addition, the printed word is there to be reread. The ephemeral electrons that carry my message are gone like the flash of a photon. So when I'm reporting a science story, or anything complex, I tend to reiterate the core points to make sure they stick.

I also try to write in a style that is very simple and direct. When I read my script, it should sound as though I'm talking in "regular" language, not "news-ese." Instead of the phrase "climate change" I might say something like "weather patterns around the world." Rather than "non–point source pollution" I might try: "pollution that doesn't come out of one big pipe or smokestack, things like oil and the grit from worn tires washing off roads, or fertilizers washing off lawns."

I try to organize each story, and write it, as though I'm telling something to a friend who doesn't know anything about it. This is especially true of my approach to explaining things scientific. I try to find analogies that help viewers understand the scientific theory in real-world terms. Not everyone has a greenhouse, for example. So instead of calling global warming the greenhouse effect, I used the analogy of what happens in a parked car with the windows rolled up on a sunny day.

Sometimes I'll try things out on colleagues around the news room, reading them a section of my script and asking "Do you get it?" Sometimes I'll try to come up with an explanation that would satisfy my bright 14-year-old daughter. The grade-level checker in my word processor often tells me I'm writing at a 10th-grade level. That's fine. It's especially important to be simple and clear, given the brevity and mind-numbing nature of television news.

I think it's also important to embed a sense of enthusiasm in pieces about science—a sense of "Gee Whiz!" or "Isn't this amazing?" or "Doesn't it seem like this is something interesting and valuable to know?" Sometimes I do this by using words like "fascinating" or "amazing" or "incredible." ("Some scientists believe rain-forest destruction is causing plants or animals to go extinct at the incredible rate of six different forms of life erased from the earth per *hour!*") Sometimes it's just the inflection in my voice that gives it that gee-whiz feeling. The feedback I've gotten in my 18 years as a journalist leads me to believe that news consumers are curious. They *want* to know. They *want* complicated things explained to them. They have a gee-whiz button waiting to be pushed. I look for ways to push it, in how I organize, how I write, and literally in the tone of voice I use as I narrate my stories.

But the surest way to do effective environmental journalism on television is to let the pictures do the talking. Whether it's a nearly empty net dumping a sparse load of trash fish on the deck of a trawler to demonstrate the destruction of the fishing industry off the New England Coast, or a graphic showing how hazardous waste spilled on the ground spreads into a labyrinth of tiny fissures in the bedrock and can't be retrieved before seeping into and contaminating a drinking water aquifer, the power of pictures to tell the story is the television newsperson's greatest tool.

● ●

Magazine Style

IRA FLATOW

Ira Flatow has been affiliated with National Public Radio for over 25 years, covering everything from Legionnaires' disease to Three Mile Island, the space shuttle, AIDS, and the South Pole.

Ira currently hosts and produces NPR's *Talk of the Nation: Science Friday.* For six years he was host and writer for the Emmy Award–winning *Newton's Apple* on PBS; he was science reporter for *CBS*

Magazine Style 39

This Morning and host of the PBS series *Earthkeeping*. Ira has hosted
"Halley's Comet" for Westinghouse and "Neptune All Night" for
PBS. His science reports have appeared on cable's CNBC and his
stories for kids on the Fox network.

His most recent book is *They All Laughed—From Light Bulbs to
Lasers: The Fascinating Stories behind the Great Inventions That Have
Changed Our Lives.*

His company, Samanna Productions, produces educational videos
and multimedia projects. Flatow is a board member of the National
Association of Science Writers and a double winner of the AAAS–
Westinghouse science writing Award, the only person to win for both
radio and television in one year.

The longer length of a magazine piece offers you the luxury you probably
did not have in the short spot news story: the extra time to actually tell a
"story."

If you're focusing on a discovery, you can tell the story of the trials and
tribulations of the researcher behind it. Even if your subject is the budget
debate over a local incinerator, the competing priorities of the people
behind the debate make for compelling storytelling.

RADIO

Concentrate on what radio does best: evoke feelings and pictures in your
mind. Find good storytellers who can describe their feelings about their
work—who can make you, and the listener, understand by their tone of
voice why they feel the way they do. Then interview them in their natural
surroundings and capture the sounds of their workplace.

Radio brings you the best pictures available: those that you make in
your head. The finest radio magazine pieces combine ambient sounds,
music, voices, and facts to create a mental picture and elucidate a feeling
of "being there." Good radio reporters understand this and collect the
sounds around them whenever they can. Once your interview is finished,
point your microphone in all directions and spend a full minute or two
collecting ambient sounds. This sound, recorded in each location, will
help you seamlessly mix different sections of your story together and
make editing easier. But most important, it will evoke the feeling of being there.

For example, I recorded an interview with a scientist while we strolled
around the South Pole. While the listener could hear us panting for air,
due to the extreme altitude, nothing drove the point home more about-

"where we were" than the crystal clear "crunch, crunch" sound emanating from our feet as we packed down the snow on every step.

EQUIPMENT

Nothing but the best. And by that I mean the professional standard. Cheap equipment tends to act cheaply just when you need it the most. More and more reporters are recording digitally, either on tape or on disk. Recording and editing studios are already routinely editing digitally. Don't be surprised to watch as your tape gets "cut" on a Macintosh or PC. If you decide to invest in editing equipment, digital hardware may be the way to go.

Don't skimp on the microphone, either. Good audio mikes wear like iron; they get bumped and dropped a lot, and are worth the extra money.

TELEVISION

"No pictures, no story." This is the philosophy of television. Without pictures—and they usually have to be moving ones, that is, video or film—very few television shows will want to give you air time.

That's one reason chemistry or physics stories rarely get on television: Molecules are invisible, and so are subatomic particles. Computer imaging has allowed viewers to see computer simulations of the unseeable, but they hold viewers' interests just so long. Remember: You're competing for television time with Oprah, Geraldo, football, and *ER*.

One of the most daunting problems you'll face will be in getting your editor to take an interest in your story. You'll have to sell the story not on the merits of the science, but on how much human drama you can milk out of it. Remember the motto of television news: "If it bleeds, it leads." So television producers seek out the human drama of a science story. They will look for the stories of the people behind the event or of people whose lives are tied up in it.

Medical stories are ready-made for such treatment. Everyone (including your editor) is interested in health and medicine, so such stories are covered almost by recipe. First, find a victim of the disease, then interview the family to learn its impact on their lives, talk with the physician about treatment, and uncover any controversy. File your report live on the evening news from a suitable location such as the hospital emergency or waiting room. Lots of times a "stand up" on the lawn will work just fine.

The most challenging stories to produce are the ones in the fields of science that people "think" they don't find interesting like physics and chemistry. Just the mention of the words can send viewers to their remote controls. The trick, then, is to disguise the science in the piece, hide it, and spring it on the viewer suddenly. Do this by treating the topic not as a "science" story but as an Agatha Christie mystery. Your scientists are not white-coated laboratory technicians but science sleuths on the trail of a suspect. Nobody can resist a good whodunit.

I once produced a story about a paleontologist who discovered the tiny fossilized bones of an extinct animal. Dry bones are boring. But the drama behind finding the bones allowed people to see the "human" side of a scientist that belies the usual "egghead" stereotype. The scientist explained how he had crawled on his hands and knees for weeks in the hot desert, nose to the ground, sweeping up tiny bits of dirt with a toothbrush. By recreating the event I could reveal how the personality of the researcher—he was either a genius or a "nut" or both—was as important to the discovery as the science behind it. Here was a real-life Indiana Jones of bones.

The challenge of the long-format science story is in finding or creating these dramatic elements. It may also mean finding scientists who are good storytellers, personable on camera, and willing to submit to the rigors of television. This last point cannot be emphasized enough.

An hour of television takes many months to produce. Let's not even talk about the days you spend in the dark editing rooms. That sacrifice comes with the job of being a television journalist. But scientists who agree to become television "talent" may have no idea of the demands that may be made of their laboratory. Dozens of phone calls interrupt their work. Scripts have to be written and rewritten. Schedules must be arranged. Then comes the invasion. Laboratories are besieged by hoards of camera, lighting, and sound people. All work stops while those "TV people" take over. Unsuspecting scientists may balk at the commotion and decide that this is not what they bargained for.

To avoid such a dilemma I suggest two areas of attack: Use experienced scientists who come highly recommended (but try to avoid those already overexposed) or make sure that the unsuspecting scientist knows what he or she can expect. Public relations people can be very helpful in suggesting scientists who know what to expect when the producers come knocking.

But don't be surprised when the public relations office hands you their latest "video news release" (VNR) complete with B-roll (extra footage to be used as background to a voice-over). Many journalists feel VNRs carry too much political baggage and should be viewed, literally, as nothing more than advertising. I disagree. Except in cases where you know or suspect the video to be doctored, they are a great resource. Few television news stations run them as is. Many judiciously cull from them computer-generated images or footage from microscopes they could neither afford nor have the means of obtaining. At all times VNR footage must carry a video tag crediting its source.

No matter what your feeling about using such handouts, VNRs can be very useful as "audition tapes" for both radio and television. One can get a feel for how the expert looks on the tube or comes across in manner and speech. Does he look convincing? Does she sound like she knows what she's talking about? They also serve to highlight interesting stories you may like to cover with the camera crew of your own choice.

THE FUTURE

"Flux" is a favorite word of journalists when describing a state that defies description. Broadcast journalism is very much in a state of flux.

The information superhighway has changed the definition of what we normally call broadcasting. Anyone sitting at a computer terminal can become a "broadcaster" via the Internet by digitizing and sending radio and television pictures to all parts of the world. What this means for the science journalist is not only new tools but new outlets that bear close attention.

Cable television is fragmenting broadcasting, allowing smaller cable stations to survive in "niche" markets. This can only be good for science reporting. Many times large commercial networks will refuse to air a science magazine news show, fearing its audience will be too small to attract advertisers. But since science news has a large enough following to be considered a niche market, we should expect to see cable channels devoted to science programming. And here may be an opportunity for science television journalists to find work.

Television networks are relying more and more on videotape taken by hand-held 8-millimeter cameras—the same type you might buy for home movies. These cameras require no extra sound or light operators—just the reporter. Radio journalists can now routinely carry these lightweight mini-cams with them on interviews and come away with both a sellable radio story and raw footage for a piece for television. Editing equipment for a mini-cam is a fraction of the cost of a standard commercial setup: And now that computer work stations can process videotape, the costs of producing such pieces has come down to a level many free lances or small shops can afford. Let's hear it for the little guys!

One can hope that as television programming expands worldwide, more opportunities will be available to science journalists to take advantage of the upcoming information superhighway about which they love to write.

Writing Books on Science Topics

JOHN NOBLE WILFORD

John Noble Wilford is a senior science writer at the *New York Times* and the author of several books. He has reported on most of the major space missions, including the *Apollo* landings on the Moon, and currently specializes in coverage of astrophysics, planetary exploration, archeology, and paleontology. He won the 1983 journalism award of the American Association for the Advancement of Science (AAAS). He was awarded the 1984 Pulitzer Prize in national reporting for his stories on space and science, and was a member of the *Times* team that won a Pulitzer Prize in 1987 for reporting on the aftermath of the *Challenger* accident. He has taught science writing at Princeton University and the University of Tennessee and has been a Director's Visitor at the Institute for Advanced Study in Princeton. His books include *We Reach the Moon, The Mapmakers, The Riddle of the Dinosaur, Mars Beckons,* and *The Mysterious History of Columbus.*

Any science journalist with energy, imagination, and ambition has at one time or another thought of writing a book. What a triumph of efficiency it would be to take those notebooks from stories past, add some more research and reporting, and have yourself a book. What a way to secure a wider audience and more permanence for your words. What a stride toward wealth, or at least some extra income. What a way to vault to the big time and show your colleagues, especially those hard-to-please editors, that there are more strings to your guitar than they ever suspected.

As understandable as those motivations may be for embarking on a book project—who has not indulged in such thinking?—they overlook some of the hard realities of book writing. You may have learned from experience that there is more to a magazine article than a lengthy newspaper story. There is a different approach to its organization, the weaving together of many more strands of fact and interpretation, the telling of this in a narrative style. So, too, you must be prepared for the fact that sustaining a story for the length of a book, say about 100,000 words, is a quantum leap beyond the requirements for a 4,000-word magazine piece.

It takes an extraordinary commitment of time and self-discipline. It means weekends consumed and vacations forsaken, agonizing spells of self-doubt. It requires a rigorous honesty in reading a chapter you have just written and accepting that it could be told better with a thorough rewrite. The eventual rewards in self-esteem, satisfied readers, critical acclaim, and book sales may justify all the denial and effort. But to avoid disappointment, or the wasted effort from having to abandon a book in midstream, care should be taken in the beginning that your subject is really worthy of a book.

Ask yourself: Is the subject an important one—dealing with research in one of the currently more active fields of science or technology such as astrophysics, biochemistry and genetics, computer sciences, or particle physics? Does it examine issues at the center of public debate and concern? Is it an interesting subject with a kind of inherent appeal, something about nature and animal behavior? Is the subject ourselves, our emotional strengths and weaknesses, our evolutionary past? Is it about a science of emerging importance, as chaos theory proved to be a few years ago? Are there interesting and articulate people to enliven your subject? Is there something new to be said on your subject? After weighing all these questions and investing in some preliminary research, your must finally ask yourself: Is the subject likely to sustain your interest for the long haul? If not, you will probably fail to keep your readers interested from beginning to end.

The first time I felt sure there was a book in me, ready and waiting to be written, happened to be the wrong time. It was in the early 1960s, and I was a writer at *Time* magazine. For several months I had worked on stories about the promising technology of satellite communications. This was a story of scope and revolutionary import, clearly passing the "important" and public interest tests, and I already had more material about it at my fingertips than could ever be squeezed into short magazine pieces. Why not write a book, my first book?

An editor at a large publishing house whom I contacted asked me to write a proposal, which I did. It ran about a dozen pages and included a list of chapter topics—the usual procedure when submitting an idea to a publisher. As I wrote the proposal, however, the magnitude of the undertaking began to dawn on me. I would need to identify and interview many more people to flesh out the exposition. I would have to develop some kind of narrative thread to hold the story together. In the end, I think, I was relieved that the editor responded with a polite turndown. (If I had been really interested, I should have tried other editors. Never accept one editor's judgment as final, for there is sufficient anecdotal evidence—the best-selling *Day of the Jackal* was rejected by at least two dozen publishers—to show that editors can be wrong.) In writing the proposal I had been forced to judge the merits of my original enthusiasm and realize that this was not a book I was ready to commit two or three years to.

At least I had learned from this experience one of the first lessons in book writing: a proper respect for the difficulty of seeing a book through from beginning to end, and the value of preparing a written proposal, or better yet, a sample chapter. This is the way to sell not only a publisher or an agent on the idea, but yourself as well. It is a test of your understanding of what would be required and how interested you really are in pursuing the idea.

The circumstances were different for me the next time opportunity knocked at my door. A publisher came to me with a proposal, the subject was one of obvious popular interest, and it dovetailed with my everyday work.

By then, in 1967, I was at the *New York Times* and covering the *Apollo* project. A publishing house, in conjunction with the *Times,* wanted to produce a book on *Apollo* to be brought out immediately after the first landing on the moon. It would be one of those "instant" books so popular then. I signed a contract and began preparing the early chapters on the Soviet–American space race, the decision to send men to the moon in the decade, the precursor flights and the technological mobilization. The final chapters, on the *Apollo 11* flights, would be produced from my dispatches during the mission.

Bear in mind, there are advantages and disadvantages to a book tied so closely to events being covered by the author. The greatest advantage was that I could harmonize work on the book with my daily reporting tasks; on assignments for the paper I could also collect added material for the book, and in depth stories could be the framework for entire chapters. (I have made this my practice to some extent on several of my books.) As soon as the research reached a critical mass, I would take a few days off to draft a chapter. I rarely write chapters in the order in which they are to appear in the book, but while particular research is fresh in my mind and my notes are still decipherable. Rewriting and polishing can be done later to insure an even tone and logical connection from one part to the next.

Another advantage is that time is of the essence: The manuscript must be completed for publication soon after the event to which the book is pegged. Such a time constraint concentrates the mind, to borrow from the remark by Samuel Johnson concerning the effect of knowing that one is to be hanged in a fortnight. This may be especially beneficial for a first-time author, for it narrows the focus on the story at hand and permits little time for self-conscious writing.

But some disadvantages are obvious. In haste one is likely to overlook important points, and in being close to the events, one cannot have the perspective and cool objectivity that might come upon reflection. Another risk is that with its short attention span, the public may not be so interested in reading a more full account of an event that was yesterday's news. The book may be destined for a short shelf life.

My book, *We Reach the Moon,* came out in paperback in 1969, a few days after the landing, and an expanded edition, including the mission's scientific results, was published in hardcover later that year. I was pleased with the outcome, financially and critically, and was left with no doubt that I could write books. One must have reserves of self-confidence to write a book. But I was also handed a lesson in humility, even before I had the customary 15 minutes to bask in fame. In Chicago, after my first appearance to promote the book, two women came up with pieces of paper (not even copies of my book) and asked for autographs. "Why, of course," I said, pleased as could be to bestow my first autographs as an author. One of the women studied my signature, looked up at me, and inquired, "Now, just who are you, anyway?"

Be prepared to help promote and market your book. That often means packing your bags and going on the road for a couple of weeks of newspaper, radio, and television interviews in several cities. These are arranged by the publisher's publicity people. But it is up to you to respond with enough enthusiasm and charm that the book tour might just ignite sales. One tip: Prepare and rehearse some succinct lines summing up the main points of your book and two or three anecdotes, and no matter what questions the interview leads off with, give an answer that eventually gets around to your own message about the book. Don't expect that the interviewers will have read your book, don't let naive questions annoy you, and don't try to cram too much information into your allotted minutes.

Please excuse yet another personal experience, but the conception, research, and writing of my next book, *The Mapmakers,* was perhaps more typical and instructive of the practice of book writing.

A flattering invitation came to me to write a science book for Knopf, a publisher with a reputation for fine books. The idea for what the book would be came a little later, the result of reporting on a mapping expedition on the floor of the Grand Canyon. The place was being mapped with aerial photography, helicopters, laser distance-measuring instruments, and other modern technologies. At night I listened to the cartographers tell how the canyon was first mapped by mule and transit, and not all that badly either. Impressed with the hardships and resourcefulness of these early mappers, I began thinking about how the rest of the world had come to be mapped.

Several days of library research established that there were no general-audience books addressing that question and had not been any for several decades. Previous histories of cartography generally dwelled on the maps themselves, not the people behind them, and usually stopped well short of the technologies of the twentieth century. I knew then the subject for my next book.

Without knowing it at the time, I hit on a useful practice. On the basis of that preliminary library research and some follow-up reading, I prepared an outline that went beyond an orderly list of chapter ideas to include thoughts on how each chapter should move the story forward, people through whom to tell the story, and details on sources for subsequent research and reporting. As work on the book progressed, research on one chapter would suggest ideas to be included in others, and so the outline was always being revised in details, though not in any broad sense. I had to resist the temptation to encompass too much.

Even so, the research and writing consumed seven years, in part because I frequently became diverted on some peripheral tack too fascinating to resist. But when decisions on narrative flow and content had to be made, I always fell back on the basic question the book was addressing: How did the world come to be mapped?

Always try to reduce the theme and thrust of your book to a simple proposition. As you go along, you can safely allow yourself to expand and amplify if you keep in mind what it is you are expanding on and amplifying.

Here again, I wrote chapters out of sequence, whenever I felt I had enough research on a particular subject or whenever I tired of research and itched to get on with some writing. Some of the research I also combined with reporting trips for the *Times*. It also helped to alternate the writing of chapters on contemporary history with those on earlier history. The contemporary chapters served to keep reminding me where the book was going.

No two people have the same writing habits. I am sometimes embarrassed by how inefficient mine are some of the time. For what it is worth, I cannot write during the week when I am working at my regular job; I can read and do some library work then, but cannot be productive at writing. Before I start a writing session, I prefer to know that I have two or three days of relatively uninterrupted writing time ahead. I may "waste" a couple of hours because, like a pitcher, I need time to warm up, usually by reading what I wrote the time before and reviewing notes or photocopies from source books. Some writers can dash off a chapter and go back to it later to polish and expand it, but I like to edit and rewrite myself as I go, sometimes paragraph by paragraph.

At the end of a day, I usually make a printout of the chapter as it is up to that point. After a drink and dinner, in a different setting from my office, I can read what I had written with some perspective. Then, I often condense, substitute a more apt verb or adjective, turn a phrase better or sharpen a transition. If I can then anticipate the next day's writing with a few sentences and a list of points to make, I am usually able to enjoy untroubled sleep.

Some days you may despair of ever writing another satisfying paragraph. Often, when feeling stymied, I move to a different chair and read about something unrelated to the book at hand. It may be something I once wrote and am proud of, to remind me that I can write. It may be a few pages or a chapter of an author whose style I especially admire; my staff and my comfort have been Winston Churchill, Alan Moorehead, Loren Eiseley, Timothy Ferris, John McPhee, and several others. Relax, read, and ponder, but do not try to emulate. You may go through many such dry spells in the early stages of a book, but at some point you should gain command over your material—rather than being overwhelmed by it—and be able to ride the momentum to the end.

Books come in many flavors, and it is wise to choose yours at the beginning and stick to it. By this I mean that once you settle on a book subject, you should choose an approach to telling the story. This is more than a matter of organization and style or point of view. Let me illustrate with some choices in flavors.

Some books are meant to survey current knowledge in a particular field of science, usually with an ample review of early research leading up to the present. They tell a story of the trials and triumphs of earlier scientists and of the current struggles to understand. Woven through this narrative are the threads of explanation needed to grasp the fascination such research holds on scientists. This was my approach in *The Riddle of the Dinosaur*. In this way, Timothy Ferris told much of the story of twentieth-century astronomy in *The Red Limit;* Walter Sullivan wrote of the search for extraterrestrial intelligence in *We Are Not Alone;* and Jonathan Weiner reviewed geophysics in *Planet Earth*.

Authors of such books usually maintain a third-person distance, though in recent years more of them make their presence felt and let the reader join them in tagging along with the scientist, asking questions, and reacting to a scene or dispute. One of the most effective examples is Dennis Overbye's *Lonely Hearts of the Cosmos,* an overview of current thinking and controversy in astrophysics reconstructed through interviews with participants, notably Allan Sandage. If well researched and engagingly written, books of this genre—with the author keeping a distance or in the thick of the book—tend to have long shelf lives in stores and libraries.

A variation is the miniaturist approach. Instead of writing a broad survey, the miniaturist focuses on one scientist and team of scientists and through their work illustrates the process and progress in an entire branch of science. This requires extraordinary access to the scientists in the field or laboratory and long hours of interviews. John McPhee was one of the finest practitioners of this approach, traveling with a few geologists and recounting their stories in several books on plate tectonics, notably *Basin and Range.* Jonathan Weiner won a Pulitzer Prize for *The Beak of the Finch,* his case history of a study in evolution conducted by two Princeton biologists on the Galapagos Islands, made famous by Darwin.

Adrian Desmond's *The Hot-Blooded Dinosaurs* and James Gleick's *Chaos* are successful examples of books that bring a new concept in science to public attention. Gleick's approach was to focus on the work of different researchers, chapter by chapter. He had first tested the waters by writing a magazine article centered on one of these scientists—a good way of familiarizing yourself with the language, ideas, and people involved in a particular field. If this makes you feel comfortable with the subject and enthusiastic, then move on to the book. If not, at least you have a magazine article to your credit.

Another genre is the advocacy book. The purpose here is to argue a position or sound an alarm, an approach favored for books on environmental issues, new disease threats, new therapies, public policy regarding science, and also subjects at the fringes of traditional science, like UFOs, paranormal psychology, and the secrets of the pyramids. Read again Rachel Carson's *Silent Spring,* and you will see that this type of book can be both fervent and eloquent.

There seems to be a growing market for books written in collaboration between a scientist and science writers. Literary agents, I am told, are always on the lookout for such matches, seeking to capitalize on a scientist or science that is in the public eye. The scientist alone might not have the time or skill to write a general-audience book; the writer alone might not be granted such access to the scientist, and might not have been able to sell the book on his own. One recent match brought Keay Davidson, a science journalist, together with George Smoot to publish *Wrinkles in Time,* an account of the years of research leading to a crucial discovery supporting the big-bang theory.

No one can instruct you in how to write a book in ten easy lessons. If you are persuaded that you have a book in you, talk to other science writers with book-writing experience. They should have some practical advice. Talk to scientists in the field you intend to write about; make sure you will have their cooperation for interviews and referrals to others. By all means, read other popular books on science, perhaps some I have mentioned, to get ideas and inspiration. Read them closely to appreciate how the authors sustain interest, how they impose order on seemingly disparate facts and events, how they communicate ideas and information without being pedantic, how they inform by telling stories. Good writers are good readers.

If there should be times you wish you had never started the book, be assured of the rewards that will follow. Nothing—no magazine or newspaper article—is as professionally satisfying as a book. You have exercised your talents on a grander scale, stretching them here and there, recognizing some for the first time. You have given people pleasure and information. You may have communicated more to people than you could have imagined as you were toiling from chapter to chapter.

A young Italian journalist introduced himself to me recently at Cape Canaveral. As we shook hands, he told of a book he had been given when he was a little boy. It was the Italian edition of *We Reach the Moon*. Reading the book, in the glow of the *Apollo* triumphs, the boy was inspired to write about space and science when he grew up, and so he has. I could not have been more pleased.

7 •

Journalist and Scientist Co-authors

KEAY DAVIDSON

Keay Davidson has been science writer for the *San Francisco Examiner* since 1986. He has won the AAAS–Westinghouse Award for science writing and the NASW Science-in-Society Award. He is co-author, with astrophysicist George Smoot, of *'Wrinkles in Time'* and author of *Twister*, companion book to the 1996 movie.

Immediately after my first (and, so far, only) collaboration with a scientist on a popular science book, I vowed: "Never again. Next time, I go solo." Yet what have I to complain about? My co-author and I are still on speaking terms; our book was favorably reviewed and reprinted in numerous languages; we both made money. Others have been far, far less fortunate. After lengthy reflection and discussion with other collaborators—some with Kafkaesque tales of woe, others with rosy memories of the happiest collaborations since the Lunts—I have amended my vow: "Next time, I go solo . . . unless the money is right."

In cowriting, the frictionless collaboration is the exception rather than the rule. A few years ago, the science writer Dava Sobel co-authored a book with astronomer Frank Drake, whom she found to be "absolutely wonderful to work with—a wonderful father figure." Even so, after publication she and Drake were "at a symposium, and [science writer] Fred Golden walked up, put an arm around both of us, and joked: 'Co-authors still speaking to each other?' "

"I know some people who make their living doing collaborations," says Joel Shurkin, another science writer and author of numerous books, including two collaborations. "They either 'ghost' books for other people or they [share authorship] with a scientist. And in most cases that I know of, it's a very unpleasant experience because you've got two egos: All writers have egos, and, God knows, scientists have egos."

51

Still, many science writers are intrigued by the prospect of a book collaboration with a scientist. In theory, the ideal collaboration unfolds as follows: The writer buys a tape recorder and interviews the scientist who, with nothing better to do, spends weeks and months recounting wonderful stories about her or his career, discoveries, mistakes, encounters with the great and near-great, insights into the underlying unity of humanity and nature, and so on. The writer gains vast knowledge of a scientific field. They become the best of friends; the writer is invited to all the right parties, where Nobel laureates trade gossip with NSF officials. Finally, the writer rents a house in the Santa Cruz Mountains or the Adirondacks, brews a cup of espresso, sits down at the word processor, and translates the scientist's tale into the vernacular—into the humble prose of the taxpayers who probably funded the research in the first place. The writer mails the manuscript to the scientist, who makes a few minor corrections and mails it back to the writer. Next stage: publication of the book, followed by a national publicity tour and a friendly review in the Sunday *Times*.

That's the dream, anyway.

Science writer Dick Teresi has had many happy collaborations, but he considers himself a lucky exception. "I've heard so many sob stories from other writers. [For most collaborators], you have to accept the fact that the best day of the relationship is the day you sign the contract. And it's going to go downhill from there."

By 1992, I had spent much of 20 years dreaming about writing a book. Thousands of pages had passed through my typewriter (and later, word processor), none of which ended up sandwiched between the covers of a book. Age 40 loomed, and I thought: Oh my God, I'm almost 40, and I still haven't written that book!

My break came that April, when I wrote a newspaper story about a historic discovery in cosmology, the science of the birth and evolution of the universe. Scientists detected "ripples" in the cosmic background radiation (CBR), the faint afterglow of the big bang that spawned our universe more than 10 billion years ago. Those ripples were the "seeds" of galaxies such as the Milky Way, a disk-shaped swarm of billions of stars, including our sun. I proposed a book on the discovery to an agent. He got excited and envisioned a potential international bestseller. But he didn't want me to write the book alone; he thought (correctly) that it would attract a much higher price if coauthored with the scientist who led the discovery team.

I agreed and contacted the scientist George Smoot, a noted astrophysicist at Lawrence Berkeley National Laboratory near San Francisco, who had overseen the development of the key instrument—the differential microwave radiometer—on NASA's cosmic background explorer satellite. George was amiable and agreed to a literary collaboration. We signed a contract with an American publisher, William Morrow, and eventually landed numerous foreign contracts. The Morrow contract required that we complete the book in six months—unusually fast—in order to cash in on the incredible publicity that George's discovery had spawned, as well as to beat any competing books into print.

I had already broken the first rule of a collaboration: Know your collaborator. I hardly knew George, and he hardly knew me. Worse, I had a good grasp of popular astronomy but knew little about CBR research.

I sensed trouble early on, right after we launched our collaboration, and George was still jet-setting around the country, starring at scientific conferences and giving television interviews to Ted Koppel and other talking heads. *People* magazine had named him one of the 25 most interesting people of the year. Interesting, yes—but comprehensible?

People's photographer only had to persuade George to don a pair of Rollerblades and roll around Berkeley. I, in contrast, had to get George to explain how he and his team had mapped the cosmic radiation, and in enough detail—complete with anecdotes, jokes, words of wisdom, and so on—to fill a commercially viable hardback book. This would take time, and time was scarce for George. Everyone wanted to meet him—George Bush invited him to the White House, Bryant Gumbel asked him about science and God on national television, Jamie Lee Curtis introduced herself to him backstage at a talk show.

In all the excitement, George tended to forget the mundane things, such as spending time with his co-author on a book whose deadline was steadily approaching. He neglected to read my chapter drafts, so months would pass before I knew whether my writings were scientific gibberish. I cajoled and pleaded with him to get down to business, to little effect. Worse, George's scientific specialty is extremely complex, and he has trouble explaining it to laypeople. Early in our collaboration, I watched George's appearance on Dennis Miller's late-night talk show. Miller asked George an elementary question, and George cheerfully responded with a short lecture worthy of an advanced astrophysics colloquium. Miller gulped and said: "Dr. Smoot, I haven't any idea what you're talking about." The audience applauded. Fortunately this interview ran at 1 A.M., when most of the book-buying public is asleep.

Even so, knowing one's collaborator doesn't guarantee a smooth collaboration. Not by a long shot. One science writer, who requested anonymity, met a famous scientist and they became "instant friends." The writer profiled the scientist for a magazine. Years passed; they developed a warm relationship.

Finally the writer popped the question: Would the scientist like to collaborate on a book? The scientist made vague but agreeable-sounding noises. The writer commenced his research: "I flew up to [the university] and spent a few weeks up there with him, going through his material, of which there is a lot." They contacted an agent, who asked them to submit a book proposal, which is typically 10 to 25 pages.

All of a sudden the writer's dear friend, the famous scientist, was unavailable for help. "He hadn't a clue of what to do," the writer says. "I literally created an outline all by myself—I gave the chapters titles, invented the book's name. . . . What concerned me even at the outset was how uninvolved and uninterested [the scientist] seemed." The scientist glanced over the finished proposal and said it looked fine; he made no changes, offered no suggestions. Result: a six-figure deal with a major publisher.

For a year the writer struggled, almost alone, to write the book. The scientist virtually ignored the project—he offered few ideas, read few chapters. Eventually the writer generated "thousands of pages of raw material that was like wet clay unsculpted. I'm not exaggerating—thousands of pages, thousands! . . . The book was a disaster."

After a year the publisher called: Where in the hell was the manuscript? By that time the writer was exhausted and disillusioned; he wanted out. He, the scientist, and the agent renegotiated the deal: The writer would continue helping with the book, but his name would be removed from the cover. In addition, the writer would receive a flat payment for services rendered—a few tens of thousands of dollars—and would receive no royalties.

Suddenly their relationship regained its former glow. "The minute I got my name off the book, [the scientist] changed. He started being much more agreeable to work with."

By this time you probably think I'm saying, "All collaborations are awful." Not at all. Teresi loved his coauthorship with Nobel Prize-winning physicist Leon Lederman, a modest, bubbly quipster who has been called "a cross between Einstein and Mel Brooks." And Patrick Huyghe's collaboration with controversial space scientist Lou Frank on their book *The Big Splash* sounds a little like the imaginary ideal collaboration that I lampooned early in this chapter. First Huyghe read Frank's papers. Then Huyghe flew to the University of Iowa to interview Frank. Huyghe flew home, wrote draft chapters, Frank critiqued them, Huyghe made the necessary changes, Frank approved the final version, and Huyghe sent it to the publisher. And that was that. Total time spent writing the book: 10 months. Total shouting matches, nervous breakdowns, and contemplations of suicide: zero.

But for every Lou Frank, there's a scientist like the Nobel Prize-winner with whom Yvonne Baskin wrestled for a year. She's a distinguished science writer and the author of several popular science books, and her story serves as the ultimate cautionary tale for those who enter the uncharted waters of co-authordom. The scientist is now dead but, out of respect for his family, she asked that his name be omitted.

"This was a person who had shunned press interviews for 25 years," Baskin recalled. When she first tried to meet him, in order to interview him for a magazine, "he wouldn't speak to me at first; instead, I had to submit lists of questions and to agree that he would have final approval of the transcript. . . . Then, when I finally met with him, he wouldn't answer the questions on the list; instead he listed 'the questions that I should be asking him.'

"We ended up with this long, hellacious transcript, and I edited it into what I thought was an acceptable 'Q and A' for the magazine, then sent it to him for approval . . . and he completely rewrote all the questions and answers and made a new transcript! It was like there had been no interview!"

That experience should have warned Baskin (by her own admission) that the Nobelist was bad news—definitely unfit for a collaboration. But a year later, she was surprised when this reclusive genius phoned and asked her to help him write his autobiography. Flattered, she agreed. The result was a six-figure contract and what, from any writer's point of view, was a year in hell.

She began in-depth interviews with him and quickly learned that this pivotal figure—a man who had risen to the top of his field, who in fact had revolutionized it, "could not remember any anecdotes. There was no day in his life that stood out clearly, no day about which he could say, 'That was one of the great days, and here's how that experiment went.' All he could say was: 'I don't remember.'

"The hardest thing for me was to admit was: It wasn't me. It was him. That's a frightening thing to realize partly because it means you have to admit it's over." She told the publisher the project was doomed. The contract was dissolved. It took her three years to repay her share of the advance.

Fortunate (Baskin observes) are the science writers allowed to go solo, writers such as Horace Freeland Judson (*The Eighth Day of Creation*) and Richard Rhodes (*The Making of the Atomic Bomb*). Unhampered by a co-author's personal agenda, they felt free to talk to anyone and to portray historic scientific events as they saw them. The result was two classic books.

"It's true that those books are standouts, and most of the time books without a celebrity co-author don't sell as well," Baskin adds. "But if you just want to make a lot of money, why write with a scientist at all? Why not write a book with the guy who got his penis cut off? Why not write with Kato Kaelin?''

But what if it's too late, and you're already mired in a nasty collaboration? You may think the nightmare and the craziness will never end; you may contemplate changing your name, fleeing the country, or even suicide to escape the publishing Hades into which you have descended.

My advice is: Relax.

I shall never forget this moment: It was the last days of my collaboration with George, and I lay on the floor of my apartment, depressed beyond measure, staring out my picture window at a gray, wet January sky. I thought: I'm finished. The collaboration is over. The book stinks, and will probably be canceled. And if it isn't canceled, it will get terrible reviews.

If you are collaborating on a book, then in all likelihood you, too, will experience a similar melodramatic, self-pitying moment. (It's rather relaxing, actually. "The thought of suicide," said Nietzsche, "has gotten one through many a bad night.") When that moment comes, just remember that countless co-authors have traveled the same dark road—and survived it. In all likelihood, your career will not end, the gloom will soon lift, and your book will be published.

True, it may get terrible reviews. But you can't have everything.

Scientists Who Write about Science for the Public

MEREDITH F. SMALL

Meredith F. Small is associate professor of anthropology at Cornell University, where she teaches biological anthropology, primate behavior, and the evolution of human behavior. Her doctoral research focused on the reproductive biology and mating strategies of female macaque monkeys. She began writing for the popular audience in 1988 and has published features in *Discover, Natural History, The Sciences, Wildlife Conservation,* BBC World, *Cornell Magazine, American Health, Pacific Discovery,* and *New Scientist,* among others. Her first trade book was *Female Choices: Sexual Behavior of Female Primates.* Her most recent book is *What's Love Got to Do with It? The Evolution of Human Mating.* She is currently working on a book about the biology and culture of parenting.

"My personal muse is the gas and electric bill." This statement, once made by a journalist friend, sums up the reason I found a second career as a science writer. During the early years of my academic career, I was unable to find a "real" job, but I discovered that I could write about my work in a more popular style and pay the rent. Now, eight years later, with a tenured position at a major university in hand, I am still writing science journalism. This only proves that even the most directed life can take a twist, and sometimes what starts out as necessity can end up a calling.

WHY SCIENTISTS WRITE FOR THE PUBLIC

In my particular scientific discipline, anthropology, there is a long tradition of academics writing for the popular audience. Margaret Meade's books about adolescence in the South Pacific were bestsellers in the 1930s.

Jane Goodall gained international attention with her book about observing chimpanzees, *In The Shadow of Man,* now in its second edition and still used in classrooms over twenty years after it was first written. Paleontologists Richard Leakey and Donald Johanson routinely work with journalists to promote their fossil hunting in Africa. And there are numerous "field" books written by people who went off to faraway places to study monkeys and apes. Anthropologists recognize the inherent popularity of their subjects—humans and other primates—and have never shied away from explaining their work and lives to the public. They might have the ulterior motives of gaining funding or enjoying personal fame, but most of all, I think, most anthropologists have an infectious enthusiasm for their subjects that they like to pass on to others. More important, we do user-friendly science; just about anyone can understand the behavior of chimpanzees or envision an Australopithecine walking across the savanna four million years ago. This kind of science tends to be up close and personal, which makes it fun to read and comparatively easy, as science journalism goes, to write.

Other scientists, especially those in the more "hard" sciences, might have grander motives for writing for the popular audience. Some feel a responsibility to inform the public about science, and others hope to educate America's youth, but I suspect they really do it for the same reason I do—we have found an enjoyable way to combine science and writing. Successful scientists who write books, magazine articles, or columns on a regular basis probably do not do it for the money, the supposed fame, or because of some responsibility to the public—they probably do it because they are compelled to write.

SCIENTIST AS JOURNALIST

Many full-time science journalists, including myself, have little or no professional training in journalism, and in several cases, they have master's or doctoral degrees in some sort of science. They, like me, were pulled in the direction of popular print long after they earned the title "scientist." While the subject matter may be familiar, a move toward popular writing does require an adjustment in both an approach to the material and the writing style.

Clearly, writing for the popular audience is different from writing for academic journals; each has its own particular formula. A scientific journal piece is written after months or years of collecting data; the writing is the frosting on a cake that took forever to bake. The writing is dry and free of analogies, and it concentrates on methodology and results. More important, the subject is narrowly focused, any veering off from it is considered "interpretation" and tolerated only in the last paragraph of the discussion. All statements must be backed up by references from older articles, as if in a court of law, and new information is sectioned off as "results." The language is a specially coded dialect that includes liberal use of words such as "however," "thus," and "therefore." After a few years of this kind of writing, I could do it in my sleep. "However, others have demonstrated . . . Thus these data support the notion that . . . Therefore, we conclude . . ."

Journalism has its own formula, and it, just like academics, takes study. Every magazine has a particular format, and reading several articles from the same magazine in rapid succession makes this clear. After a lead paragraph that the editor thinks catches a reader's eye, there is usually some further explanation in the next few paragraphs to let readers know what they are getting into, and then the piece (unlike academic writing) broadens out. Creative writing, especially analogies that clarify difficult scientific concepts, is encouraged. At the end, the piece is wound together, making a complete circle with the lead. This style and structure I cannot yet do in my sleep.

The difference between academic writing and journalism is not just in the language. It is more in the approach—narrow versus broad, information versus education and entertainment, details versus major points. A scientist aims to tell the already informed audience about a particular point, and how he or she came to that point. They want to convince by using evidence, and it doesn't matter how long it takes or how many charts must be used to make a case. A journalist wants to explain, educate, and basically not bore the pants off the reader.

For me, this difference in approach makes science journalism fun. The challenge here is in the writing and the structure, not in the years or months of data collection that went before. Each piece is a new puzzle: How can I fit all this information, and get it right, into a certain word count, and how can I keep someone's eyes moving down the page?

SCIENTISTS VERSUS JOURNALISTS

I have no idea if my method of science journalism is different from those trained as journalists. We seem to end up with the same kinds of pieces, so I assume the approach is basically the same—find a compelling story, query a magazine, interview, write.

There are, however, several mechanical differences between working journalists and scientists who write about science. Journalists have an advantage, I think, in their training. They learn how to interview and have years of daily newspaper practice before submitting a piece for magazine publication. More reassuring, they can make mistakes in school and not be held publicly accountable for them. The scientist-as-journalist learns all this on the run, and only fast learners, or those with talent, are successful. Scientists, on the other hand, have an advantage in that journalism is not their only means of making a living. I am able to pick and choose my subjects, even to not write for a while if I don't feel like it, simply because my job will provide medical insurance and feed me.

Both kinds of writers have their reputations at stake. For journalists, every piece they write leads to another piece, and access to interesting interviews is gained only if the journalist has a reputation for honesty. The scientist has both a writer's reputation to watch out for and his or her own reputation as a scholar. This point was brought home to me when working on a piece several years ago about bonobo chimpanzees. The editor had cut any mention of one major group of researchers from the piece, and I was extremely upset. Not only did the piece suffer from a lack of credibility, but I was also concerned that my academic colleagues would think I was an idiot for leaving out some of the major players in the field—and some did ask me about this.

This special concern about personal academic reputation has compelled me to do things a journalist might not do. I am often writing about people I know and have worked with, people I will see again as colleagues and friends. I want to get their science correct, and I also want them to remain friends. And so I routinely allow the interviewee to look at what I have written—not just quotes, but the paragraphs surrounding those quotes. In one case, when writing about a dear friend's work on ape vocalizations, I allowed him to see the whole piece. My colleagues understand that I am under no obligation to change anything, but I am interested in what they think about the piece. And this has paid off. In every case, so far, the scientists have only made suggestions that clarify content, and in every case I was glad they did because it made the piece more accurate. No one has yet asked me to change their quotes or my writing. In the end, this flexibility toward the people I write about has, I believe, reinforced my reputation as a member of the press who can be trusted, trusted because I have a scientific reputation at stake as well.

I have also found that my scientific side opens doors, and sometimes makes an interview go more smoothly. While interviewing for an article on cross-cultural infant care for *New Scientist,* several of my interviewees were clearly more comfortable talking with me when I mentioned that I was a biological anthropologist at Cornell. My background and current position, we both knew, put us on a level playing field; they knew I understood human physiology, what it means to look at different cultures, and how an ethnographer works. For some more wary types, the journalist-as-reputable-scientist makes the subject somewhat less leery of being interviewed. They are, perhaps, also correct in assuming we are of the same fellowship. My identity is still, at least for now, primarily as a fellow academic, so they assume I am unlikely to exploit my colleagues for a good story.

HOW TO TRANSFORM A SCIENTIST INTO A SCIENCE JOURNALIST

Every scientist-turned-writer has made the switch by altering focus from participant to observer. Most have needed a change because they were disappointed with academics, and were looking for another way to make a living, and a life. Some attend programs such as the science journalism course at UC Santa Cruz. Many learn by studying the trade. And the best way to do that is to approach the new career with the spirit of an academic changing fields—read, study, gain experience, and associate with those in the know.

Any smart novice seeks out the best, asks questions, and listens. I was lucky enough to meet several science journalists who were willing to read my work and give me advice. The bits of advice most important to me in the early years included: study your target magazine by reading several issues from cover to cover; spend endless hours refining the lead paragraph; make sure an idea is "compelling" (a word I think about often when considering a story); meet the deadline, no matter what. This advice was so different from what any academic or scientist ever said to me that the words had an impact. But no one prepared me for some unexpected events that are commonplace in free-lance science journalism, such as the mountain of rejection, and the fact that query letters often receive no answer at all. More important, no one told me about the constant hustle that it takes to be a successful writer—the queries sent to several magazines, the calls to editors, the constant search for stories, not to mention the money spent on postage and telephone calls. A scientist friend recently asked me how he might sell a book on his subject, one that has a lot of popular appeal. By the time I was through giving him advice about agents, editors, proposals, queries, book signings, and marketing, he was no longer interested in pursuing that direction—academic publishing suddenly started looking much better. An unflagging spirit is, perhaps, the best thing a scientist can bring to a new-found journalistic career.

Experience has taught me a few more things that might be a surprise to the scientifically trained. Most important is the relationship between writers and editors. It's imperative to know that when you sell a piece, you have literally sold your idea and your words, and the magazine has the final say. Unlike science, your work is not sacred, not to anybody. Furthermore, no one thinks about your piece for very long, so don't obsess about it yourself—move on to something else. On the practical side, try not to piss off editors, because they are the decisionmakers; choose your battle and don't hassle the little stuff. Those battles should be waged violently over scientific content and weakly over writing style—be right, not petty. I also learned very quickly that every editor will change the writing, but in a way that is so idiosyncratic to the particular magazine that you won't learn much about improving your writing by following these edits. In the end, stick with editors who are pleasant to work with, if you can afford to, and know that when editors you know well don't call you, they don't hate you, they are just busy. Most of all, remember that this is a business, and the check is not in the mail.

WHAT TO WRITE ABOUT AS A SCIENTIST

The path of scientist-as-journalist can take many routes. Most often, the scientist starts out writing about what he or she knows best. In my case, I first wrote about macaque monkeys, my subjects, for *Natural History Magazine* and other natural history–oriented publications. I also wrote broader theoretical pieces that dealt with female mating and reproduction, my subject area. From there, I branched out to other primates, then to other animals, and then to cultural anthropology. Occasionally I have written about subjects I knew little about, and in doing so I have developed a new area of expertise, as happened with a magazine piece I wrote on the biology of homosexuality. I now write about subjects even further afield when the story looks good or I need the money.

I focus on magazines that fit the subject—general science, natural history, and anthropology. But sometimes there are opportunities in less prominent publications. For example, I wrote a piece about my work on Balinese temple monkeys for *Cornell Magazine,* the alumni magazine of my university. I then sold the piece again to *Natural History,* and, with some rewrite, once again to the magazine of Garuda, the Indonesian national airline. In other words, I approached magazines that had an interest in (1) me, as a faculty member, (2) the natural history of animals, and (3) the locality of the study. In all three cases I was thoroughly familiar with the magazine and knew what they published. Not all my sales paths are so successful, but the point is to think creatively about placement, and approach only those that would clearly have an interest in the piece.

Only recently have I begun to say no to assignments. In the past, I have written for local newspapers, free weekly newspapers, museum magazines, and national magazines. I have been paid anywhere from 10 cents a word to over a dollar a word—one month last year I was simultaneously writing two 3,000-word pieces, receiving $600 for one (a story I didn't care about) and $1,200 for the other (which was the background story for my next book, which I care very much about). Until you can afford it, or until you are so overbooked with work you can't think straight, always say yes to an assignment because experience really is the best teacher.

WHAT BECOMES OF THE SCIENTIST AS WRITER

A few years ago, a colleague in my academic department stopped me in the hall and asked what I was working on. "A piece about sperm for *Discover* magazine," I answered. "Well," she responded, "that's just fluff, isn't it?" Fluff? You mean that marshmallow stuff in a jar? Contrast that comment with a statement made to me about the same time by a fellow primatologist: "It is important that we share our work with the public, and I am glad you are doing it because as a scientist, you will get it right."

Academics have an ambivalent relationship with the press. On one hand, universities are enamored of the publicity—in fact, they seek it—and faculty are encouraged to cooperate with the public affairs office. Presumably, publicity about research and discoveries affects the overall reputation of the university, which in turn probably influences grant funding and donations. Yet scientists have been trained to set themselves apart from the public, and many assume their work is beyond the understanding of mere mortals. I have found there are two camps among academics—those who enjoy it and support science journalism, and those who are suspicious of the press and offended that they might be expected to go public. The latter group also often believes that if their work can be explained by a journalist, it must not be sophisticated or important. More disturbingly, they dismiss colleagues who are friendly with the press and enjoy the publicity.

The press also has an attitude. They often see scientists as secretive and unfriendly or cliquish. Yet they usually admire their experiments and love science. I have listened in awe, or read with admiration, as a journalist tackles some of the most difficult concepts in science; as a nonscientist, you have to be pretty bright to understand and then clearly explain both black holes and sexual selection theory in the same week.

The scientist who takes on the additional hat of a journalist ends up not belonging to either of these camps, and straddling fences is never comfortable. Anthropologist Mary Douglas says humans always call something they cannot fit into one category or another a "taboo," and sometimes I feel like the "unclean" viewed from either side. There are writing fellowships I am not eligible for because I am not a full-time journalist.

But the National Science Foundation, the National Institutes of Health (NIH), and other science funding agencies don't support writers. Scientists wonder why I am doing this when there is so much science to be done. They often suspect money or fame as the motive (although it is neither), and find my sniffing for a story rather suspect.

Journalists, on the other hand, can't understand why I keep teaching and thinking about research projects when I obviously love doing this, and there is so much science to write about. The dance is to keep a foot in both camps, which means keeping up on the literature, both academic and popular, going to conferences, and retaining friendly relationships with both sides. The payoff to this mambo is access to the cutting edge of science, enlightening conversations with scientists who are open to interviews, and the fun of putting together a story that will excite and inform the public.

More important, at those conferences you suddenly have two groups of interesting colleagues to hang out with at the bar.

When Your Office Is In Your Home: Freelance Writing Issues

JANE E. STEVENS

Since 1988, I have been a free-lance writer and editor, and recently become a videojournalist as well. I founded Global Quest Feature Service in 1988, and have provided feature articles on science, medicine, and health to many major metropolitan daily newspapers, including *Asahi Shimbun* (Tokyo), the *Boston Globe*, the *Dallas Morning News*, the *Los Angeles Times*, the *San Francisco Chronicle*, and the *Washington Post*.

I have written articles for magazines, including *Discover, National Geographic, Nature, Science,* and *Technology Review.* From 1991 through 1994 I worked and lived in Kenya and Indonesia, which led to my doing editing projects for the International Centre for Agroforestry and the International Laboratory for Research on Animal Diseases, both in Nairobi, Kenya. I've also done editing projects for the former Office of Technology Assessment of the U.S. Congress.

Recently I began doing science videos for New York Times Video News International.

In the nineties I have received five journalism fellowships, including two NSF fellowships to Antarctica.

I departed from daily journalism in 1988 because I wanted to expand my writing skills beyond those demanded of a newspaper. After 2 years copy editing at the *Boston Globe,* and 10 years at the *San Francisco Examiner,* the last two as reporter for the weekly science section, I was ready to move on. I was already doing some free-lancing for magazines. But I knew that to make a steady living as a free-lance science journalist, I had to find a niche.

I chose to specialize in leading-edge science and technology, the story behind the story, and subjects that seemed new, interesting, or ignored by the rest of the scientific press.

I have written about the use of medical biotechnology in developing countries, the emergence of biological control in farming, computerized highways, the use of virtual reality technology in health, as well as articles that coincide with a special event or holiday, such as a story about the science of chocolate for Valentine's Day.

From the beginning, I treated free-lancing as a business, which I divided into three parts: newspapers, magazines, and special projects, such as writing or editing for designers of exhibits that display information about scientific topics, or nonprofit science organizations.

Successful freelancing also calls for diversifying markets, marketing articles continuously, planning work at least two or three months ahead, and discipline, discipline, discipline.

On the advice of other free-lancers, I devoted a quarter of my time to marketing—finding another newspaper, another magazine, another story to pursue. I learned the hard way to market articles more efficiently. I used to hop from one topic to the next, just as I had in my days as a newspaper writer. I began choosing enthralling subjects—those that were so interesting to me that I never got bored writing about them—and augmented them with some that were merely fascinating. With that approach, I began following the example of the Arabian princess who kept herself alive by a telling a single story that stretched on for one thousand and one nights. I chose issues that were in such a state of rapid development that a year after I wrote the first story, enough new information would emerge to warrant another. I often wrote about one aspect of an issue for a newspaper article, then used the story to query a magazine to write a longer article with a broader perspective.

Here are a couple of examples of how I find, pursue, and market articles. I've always been interested in virtual reality technology. I kept an eye on it, but didn't write about it until 1995, when I saw an announcement for a major conference about the use of virtual reality in health care, and I jumped on a plane to San Diego to cover it. The only other journalists to attend were from the local newspaper and a technical journal.

The conference was a gold mine of information that led me along several paths to develop more articles over the next few months. The story that came directly from the conference—the use of virtual reality in psychotherapy to cure people's fear of heights—was published in the *Boston Globe,* the *Dallas Morning News,* the *Los Angeles Times,* the *Washington Post,* *AERA* (*Asahi Shimbun's* weekly magazine distributed in Japan), and *Longevity* magazine. After the conference, I did interviews for an article about the use of new technologies leading to virtual reality surgery. It was published in the *Washington Post,* the *Los Angeles Times,* the *Dallas Morning News,* and *AERA.* An article about robotics in surgery appeared in the

Boston Globe. BioScience magazine used a story about the use of virtual reality in the biological sciences.

A second example involved my longtime desire to go to Antarctica. When I applied for the NSF's Antarctic journalism fellowship program, the program administrator asked if I had time—42 days—to accompany a scientific research cruise on an icebreaker into the Antarctic winter sea ice. Why not? I thought, and went. I found out that no other journalist had ever accompanied any research icebreaker on an extended scientific cruise into the winter sea ice ecosystem or had written about research being done there.

Before I left, I contacted editors at several newspapers and magazines to inquire about their interest in a story from the cruise. Since I had no idea what the cruise would produce, we left it that they'd be interested in taking a look at whatever I came up with.

A couple of weeks into the cruise, I had a better idea of the range of topics that could come out of the journey. There was the obvious story of the journey itself, with all its eventual adventures. Then there were the various aspects of the science of the Antarctic sea ice, which were being studied by the scientists on board. Dr. Martin Jeffries, the chief scientist who led the expedition, was focusing on the physics of sea ice, while other researchers were interested in ocean-atmosphere interaction, microscopic organisms that survive on sea ice, and the physics of snow falling on the sea ice. Since we had e-mail contact with the outside world, I began sending queries to newspapers and magazines as we traveled through the Antarctic winter pack ice. The *Washington Post* was interested in a 1,200-word article about the general science taking place during the cruise; it was published while we were still in Antarctica. The *Dallas Morning News* was interested in a longer piece about the physics of Antarctic sea ice that would be published after the cruise. *AERA* wanted a 1,000-word story about the effects of sea ice on global climate. *Technology Review* wanted a 1,200-word story about the physics of sea ice and its impact on global climate. *BioScience* contracted for a 2,000-word story on the biology of the winter sea ice as told through the cruise, while *Discover* wanted a similar, but longer and more wide-ranging story, without the cruise. *The Sciences* was interested in a profile of sea ice physicist Martin Jeffries, the chief scientist on the cruise, while *Pacific Discovery* wanted to publish a profile of Matthew Sturm, the snow physicist on board. *International Wildlife* wanted a 2,000-word first-person story about the cruise, with a focus on the animals we encountered. *Sea Frontiers* was interested in an article about krill, shrimplike creatures that most animals in Antarctica rely on as a food source.

During my first three years as a free-lancer, I traveled to Central and

South America on a Kellogg Foundation fellowship, which opened my eyes to the fact that the U.S. media do very little international reporting about science, technology, medicine, and public health, particularly in developing countries. Pursuing my goal of writing articles ignored by the mainstream science media, I moved to Kenya in 1991, and then to Indonesia in 1992 for three years. Traveling throughout Africa and Southeast Asia, I wrote articles about the sunflower oil seed press, a low-tech development that drastically changed people's lives in Tanzania; how Burma's civil war is destroying the country's cultures and environment; and about the lack of AIDS in Indonesia and the public health efforts to keep it that way. I've stalked Komodo dragons on Komodo Island in Indonesia, mountain gorillas in the Bwindi Impenetrable Forest in Uganda, and wild orangutans in Kalimantan, the Indonesian part of Borneo.

My annual income over the last seven years has ranged from $25,000 to $70,000, less than a top salary at a major metropolitan daily newspaper, figuring in retirement, health insurance, and paid vacations. As a freelancer, I have taken no vacations and rarely take whole weekends off.

Newspapers and magazines provide most of my income. Depending on the year, from 10 to 30 percent of it comes from writing and editing for science exhibit designers, nonprofit scientific organizations, and government organizations. I choose projects that are explanatory in nature, not policy oriented. I generally take on work that will educate me about a subject in which I am interested. I would consider it unethical to take what I've written or edited and sell it as a newspaper or magazine article. However, if I happen across an interesting subject as a result of the work, I would not hesitate, after the project is completed, to do research and interviews and write about it. An example is a project for a science exhibit designer who had a contract with the U.S. Forest Service to design an exhibit about the southeast Alaskan rain forests. A biologist who was providing information about rain-forest caves mentioned some other research he was doing on bats that migrated from the interior of Alaska to the coastal caves. That information was not part of the exhibit, and I told him that I might contact him later to do an article.

I pay for most of my expenses to produce an article; sometimes magazines will pay for expenses. If, as in the case of the Antarctica articles, a government organization provides funding so that I can accompany scientists—the NSF paid for my room and board on the icebreaker, but not my travel expenses to and from Chile and New Zealand where the ship embarked and disembarked—then that fact is mentioned either in the body of the story or at the end of the article.

The media environment is beginning to undergo some radical shifts. The distinctions between newspapers, broadcast television, cable television computers, and radio will blur as they merge into one medium used by all information-disseminating organizations. Thus I have a word of advice for people who want to become free-lancers. Broaden your ways of presenting a story. Learn how to do still photos, video, and audio. Pay attention to the use of graphics. Plain old print, as well as plain old television and plain old radio all are merging into multimedia stories delivered through a new medium, known now as the World Wide Web. The days of calling yourself a print journalist or a television journalist are waning. The days of the multimedia storyteller are approaching fast.

I'm putting that advice to work now. As a result of my first trip to Antarctica and the resulting spate of articles, I had the incredible opportunity to venture into the Antarctic sea ice a second time to do a story for National Geographic Magazine. I took along a video camera, courtesy of Video News International, which is owned by the New York Times. With three days of training in my pocket, I managed to produce a short video about the research cruise, which was bought by National Geographic Television. The magazine article was published in the May issue of National Geographic; the 11-minute video aired in December. I'm now working full-time for Video News International as a video journalist, doing six- to 10-minute science videos for a one-hour television program called "Science Times."

* *

Freelance Business Issues

JOEL N. SHURKIN

Joel N. Shurkin graduated from Emory University with a degree in the humanities. He spent two years at Temple University Law School, but, he says, "in an act of social responsibility, flunked out." He was a reporter for the *Newark Star-Ledger;* was reporter, bureau chief, and war correspondent for UPI, was national correspondent for Reuters in New York, and for eleven years served as science writer at the *Philadelphia Inquirer.* He was on the team that won the Pulitzer Prize for covering Three Mile Island and has won several other national journalism awards and a Professional Journalism Fellowship at Stanford University. He stayed on as science writer at the Stanford News Service and ran the Stanford science journalism internship program.

His seven books are about science and science history, except for a science fiction novel, *The Helix,* which he coauthored. A new edition of his *Engines of the Mind: A History of the Computer* was recently published. He currently is working on a biography of William Shockley and *Psychotherapy: How Does It Work and How Do You Know It's Working*.

The great mythology about being a freelance writer invokes the image of the lone artist, sitting perhaps in a cabin in the mountains surrounded by trees, writing his or her little heart out. Dress is informal, say jeans, sandals and a T-shirt. Hours are what you make them, maybe 1,000 words before lunch followed by a rejuvenating nap. The life of independence, challenge, romance.

This kind of life is attainable under any of four conditions:

- You have married well.
- You have inherited money.
- You have a day job.
- You have spent years working hard, developing a solid reputation and contacts, and are prepared to risk everything on an existential leap of faith in yourself.

Actually, I live a life something like that by taking the fourth approach—with a little help from the second—but trust me, it hasn't been easy. I work harder now than when I had a job.

This is not a business for the faint of heart. Indeed, the crucial part is remembering that it is a business and has to be approached that way.

For instance, like every good businessperson, you have to have an accurate picture of your overhead, so you know what you have to shoot at to make a profit. Charles Dickens's overhead consisted of pens, paper, and ink. Yours could include such things as health insurance, phone bills (bet on needing a second line), and equipment such as fax machines and computers, both of which are simply unavoidable these days. You will need to be hooked to the Internet both for e-mail and because it has become a sovereign research tool, so that involves computer access fees and modems. Then there's electricity, mail, photocopying, postage, computer programs and maintenance, courier service, and stationery. All of it is tax-deductible, but all of it requires your laying out the money. My expenses run to almost $600 a month, including unreimbursed travel, meals, and entertainment, but not including health insurance, taxes, or capital expenses such as new computers. That's more than $7,000 a year just to run my office. You need accurate accounts. Any of a number of computer programs such as Quicken are mandatory. So is an accountant.

Then there is the product.

In the writing business, you are selling not just your talent but your time. For that reason, taking a week to complete a story for $300 doesn't make much sense, but a story for the same fee that takes you only a day could be worth the trouble.

A $2,000 fee for a 2,000-word story sounds great, but it's only worth your time (i.e., you make money on it) if it doesn't take too long. If you spend two months on that story, you may be losing money. You have to learn to limit the time you will spend on a story or learn to say no despite temptations and bills.

Maintaining cash flow, however, is an entirely different problem. The goal is to make sure you are not only earning enough money, but that it is coming in at an even enough pace to pay the bills regularly. This is not easy, believe me, and the problem is made worse by the fact that much of it is out of your control.

First is the obvious fact that work doesn't come at your convenience. It often comes in clumps with long, discouraging gaps between the clumps. Working hard to get as many assignments as you can rationally handle or getting some regular gigs are the only ways to mitigate that problem. That's the easy part.

Many, perhaps most, publications pay late. The same company that can pay the boss's American Express card within 10 days, or the phone bills or the rent, needs two or three months to pay its writers. If you ask, they will invariably blame the accounting department. Sure.

Second, many stories go awry. Sometimes the writer blows it—it happens to us all. Sometimes stories just don't pan out—there was less there than initially met the eye. More often, however, the magazine changes its mind.

The bane of all writers is editors who are vague about what they want. "I'd like a story about the geological formation of Asia," the editor might say. What about the geological formation of Asia? If you are left to decide for yourself what the story is, the chances are good the editor won't agree.

Editors change often: Some quit, some are fired. When that happens, the odds are your story will wind up in the hands of someone who has nothing at stake in its success, and you are in trouble. Some publications go out of business, and even if they have accepted your story, you may never see a dime.

It's hard to guess, but as much as one-half the work you are assigned may wind up producing little or none of the money you expect. The first law of living as a free lance is that the money is never in the bank until the money is in the bank.

How do you protect yourself? You negotiate the contract terms before you do the story. With honest, professional editors and publishers—the majority, to be sure—that is less of a problem than you might imagine. What is amazing is the number of people who don't try.

Here are some rules. Disobey them at your peril.

Always have a written contract, even if it is just a memorandum reviewing a telephone call. Get the editor's or publisher's signatures on it. Most publishers wouldn't dream of assigning a writer without a contract, but many do, and those are folks you need to watch out for.

You don't need an agent for magazine work, but if you are writing books, get one! Agents know how to negotiate contracts, and proposals or manuscripts sent "over the transom" (without agents) stand very little chance of being taken seriously. Sometimes finding an agent is more difficult than finding someone to publish your book. The best way is ask a friend who has one. Some publications such as *Writers Handbook* list them. Call them and see if they are taking on new clients. Many are looking for new business. Some agents require a contract and insist on representing you for everything you write; others just work on verbal contracts. Fifteen percent is the normal commission, and the publishers' checks go directly to the agent, who then cuts you a check taking the commission off the top. If an agent demands a fee for reading your manuscript or proposal, walk.

Unless it is a weekly publication, and you are dealing with breaking news, never agree to "payment on publication." It could be as long as a year before the story is published (editors like having stories in reserve), and you won't get paid until then. Sometimes stories are never published for lack of room or a shift of focus at the magazine. That is their problem, not yours. Payment on acceptance is the professional standard, and don't deviate from it.

Always put a limit on their rights to publish your story. You are not selling your story; you are selling the right to publish your work. Tell them if they don't publish it in a reasonable time, say six to nine months, depending on the publication, they lose that right, and you keep the money and can sell the piece elsewhere. Do the same with query letters: Tell them that if you don't hear from them in three months, the offer is revoked. Any publication that takes longer than that probably pays the same way.

Avoid work-for-hire contracts. You are giving away all rights to your story (and potential income), and you shouldn't do it.

Sell them first North American serial rights and negotiate electronic rights separately. Some publications are now demanding all rights to all media that exists now or may ever exist anywhere in the universe (and I'm not making that up). Don't give it to them.

Avoid writing on speculation. Sometimes you have a great story, and that's the only way you can get an editor to see it. But some editors take advantage of writers that way, so don't do it unless you absolutely can't help yourself, and then think hard.

Get clear up front what expenses they will reimburse you for and what they won't, and act accordingly. Most government publications, for example, won't pay for phone calls.

Now the really hard part: Insist on prompt payment by sending an invoice with the story containing the words "payment within 30 days" on the invoice. If you don't get paid in 30 days, send them another with the words "due immediately" on it. If that doesn't work, start calling the accounting department or the publisher. At 45 days, be obnoxious. It is usually not the editor's fault, incidentally, who often is as embarrassed as you by the bad manners, so go to the publisher or accounting department.

By convention, the publication is entitled to one free rewrite to make a story satisfactory, and then some free doodling. If it can't be fixed within those constraints, it's probably a goner anyway. If they won't pay for anything more, don't do it. Don't forget to factor in the time rewrites could take when you are deciding if a story is worth your time.

Insist on a kill fee, something to make up for the time you wasted if the story blows up in your face. Writers hate them—there's no very good reason why, if you are contracted to do a piece and fulfill the contract, you shouldn't get full payment—but that's another argument. One-quarter to one-half the fee is the norm. It should be in the contract.

Read the indemnity or warranty clause carefully. Some publishers want the writers to insure them against the risk of being a publisher. If they don't like the risk, they should not be in the publishing business. You are a writer, not an insurance company. There is the potential here for total financial disaster. The American Society of Journalists and Authors and the Authors Guild have sample clauses that are fair to all sides.

The best publications get good in part because they treat their writers professionally and respectfully, hence they can attract the best writers.

The best writers get that good because they understand this is a business, and that, in the immortal words of Samuel Johnson, "No man but a blockhead ever wrote except for money."

Well, my daughter's rabbits just found a hole in the hutch fence, and I have to take a break now to find them before the coyotes do. Good luck.

PART TWO

Techniques of the Trade

• •

Editor's Note

At the 1996 meeting of the American Association for the Advancement of Science, in a session on science and the media, a Virginia researcher stood up and asked, plaintively, why it is that so much science coverage is either wrong or wrongheaded. A journalist replied that daily reporting—done under deadline pressure, sometimes researched and written within a period of several hours—averages about 95 percent correct, a record many laboratories would be happy to achieve.

That percentage, of course, says nothing about whether the errors are big ("Dr. Quick-Story has discovered that carbon monoxide causes the Earth to warm", when you really meant to say carbon dioxide) or small (you say he discovered it Tuesday morning, when it was actually in the afternoon). Nor does it say how the interview went and whether the journalist in question did any homework or instead asked questions such as "Now, are we talking about a gas here?"

Let's also acknowledge that the journalist can do everything right and Dr. Quick-Story can remain convinced the article is wrong because his favorite theory of global warming did not appear. ("The reporter didn't understand at all," the scientist fumes.) In fact, the scientist may not have stressed the theory strongly enough; or the reporter may have struggled to get it in, only to be overruled by an editor who found it incomprehensible.

At a Sigma Xi meeting in San Francisco in 1993, a physician complained that she had given a speech that contained three points, the last being the most important, and the local paper did not report the final point. Journalists in attendance merely rolled their eyes—every reporter knows that you hit the important point *first*. But all this emphasizes the continuing culture conflict between scientists and journalists, which has intensified as popular reporting on science has become more extensive and more influential.

Every writer in this book will tell you that it's all right to ask a dumb question, that scientists don't expect journalists to know it all and frequently welcome a chance to explain their work. If, for instance, the reporter didn't understand Dr. Quick-Story's theory and didn't ask for a good explanation, or if Dr. Quick-Story was affronted by such a request, that probably doomed its coverage from the beginning.

On the other hand, there's probably no area of reporting that has a higher standard for doing your homework than science writing, or more of an imperative to get it right.

Scientists are not like politicians; they don't rejoice in the mere sound of their name sailing over the airwaves. Many remain wary of the media: they don't want to look like showoffs; they aren't certain the audience will understand; and when the reporter ambles in and asks whether CO_2 floats or swims, they aren't sure the reporter gets it either. The whole experience can simply make a researcher nervous, and the result is a sometimes obsessive focus on perfecting every detail.

Of course, perfection isn't going to happen. And as the relationship evolves, as scientists—we hope—begin to understand the journalistic profession better; they may gain a more realistic expectation of media coverage. That is not to say that we want anyone to be comfortable with errors, big or small. Science writers may, indeed, be held to an unusually high standard of accuracy and understanding. That's also to the good. A lot of credibility rests on getting it right.

This section of the book, then, focuses on some of the picky details, the specifics of reaching for such high standards. Here are guides to evaluating and finding sources, using research journals, in-depth reporting, column writing, and investigative reporting—in other words, doing it well.

After all, the end product primarily serves neither scientists or journalists, but readers, listeners, and viewers. Whatever our differences, we share at least one common goal—to make science vivid, real, compelling, and important. In that context, we won't quibble over 5 percent. We all want to aim as precisely at the target as we can.

10 ● ● ● ● ● ● ● ● ● ● ● ● ● ● ● ● ● ●

Telling a Good Tale

MARY KNUDSON

Early in my career at the *Baltimore Sun,* I was assigned the medical beat and found the subjects I covered so very interesting, I never wanted to write about anything else. I covered medicine, and sometimes science and the environment, for 18 years, before leaving for the adventures of free-lance science writing. I've been the Freedom Forum journalist-in-residence for medical writing at Ithaca College; taught a science writing workshop at Johns Hopkins University; and wrote a series of books on science for students in grades four through six.

During a one-year journalism fellowship at the Harvard School of Public Health, I worked in a laboratory and cloned a gene. I've won the NASW's Science-in-Society Award, am a past president of the D.C. Science Writers Association, have served on NASW's board of directors since 1989, and am NASW secretary 1997–1998.

When I tell a tale, I like to write it as though it were a film, using my computer as a camera, creating closeups, medium shots, and long shots through words, so that readers can visualize the story and feel that they are there, watching.

But you can only write those revealing closeups and backgrounding long shots if you did the reporting that brought you the material to work with. Good writing, with its need for fine detail, eloquent quotes, and vivid imagery, depends on good reporting. There are no shortcuts. Be willing to spend the time it takes to get to know the facts of the story, the characters in the story, and the issues the story raises.

I've told tales from places quite distant from my home base in Maryland. But there are many good tales to be told right in your own city or state. They're in the lives of ordinary people who encounter extraordinary situations.

A child gets a life-threatening disease; a person goes through the stages of Alzheimer's; someone else battles to overcome a phobia, a depression, or an addiction to gambling or alcohol. You can uncover a good tale by chronicling a day in the life of a neurosurgeon or heart surgeon or by spending a weekend at the emergency room of a local hospital. Former *Baltimore Evening Sun* science writer Jon Franklin won one of his two Pulitzer prizes by writing a gripping tale about a brain operation.

Doing the reporting for some tales takes much more time. I spent seven months working in a basic research laboratory and taking notes to prepare a tale told in a series of articles, about how science gets done.

In some tales, an aspect of medicine or science gets intertwined with the legal system, politics, economics, and societal norms as it plays itself out in the lives of ordinary people.

My story, "A Matter of Life and Death," which appeared in the March 8, 1992 *Baltimore Sun,* is one of those. My goal was to try to vividly re-create the true story of what one man, his family, and his fiancée went through when he suddenly was thrown into a coma from which it seemed he would never recover, and he had not left instructions through a living will telling doctors whether, under these circumstances, he would want to be allowed to die. It was a nightmare that could happen to any one of us, one reason it was a compelling story to tell.

There are two ways to do this kind of story. One is to embark on the journey with the family from the beginning, be a close observer, and interview as you go along, following the story to its conclusion. The other way, which is what I had to do since I learned about the situation after it had played itself out, is to re-create the story. Interview, reinterview, reinterview. Try to interview every person who is mentioned in the story. You may interview one or more principal characters a dozen times.

At the first interview it is crucial to gain the trust of the person you are going to write about and secure the story. Don't make the subject of your story come to you—go to him or her. Say why you think it is important to share the story with the public.

The second meeting should be a lengthy, tape-recorded interview in which you try to go from beginning to end, gathering all the facts you can about the story you will tell. Ask permission to tape the interview. Explain that it is very important in this type of story to get down small details that might be missed if you only took notes. Those revealing closeups—you only get them from garnering significant small details. You want to horde those precious details like a squirrel hordes nuts.

Donald Drake of the *Philadelphia Inquirer* is a master at gathering details and deftly weaving them into his long medical tales. This is from a scene that opened part two of a series he and Jim Detjen did on gene therapy:

Dressed in a long white lab coat, the dark-haired woman came out of the research building carrying a Styrofoam box.

Mariann Grossman edged her way into the crowd of students rushing by the lab building on the University of Pennsylvania campus. She was afraid a student whizzing by on a bike would jostle her and dump the container's invaluable contents.

In the box was dry ice surrounding a test tube that contained one trillion viruses.

Grossman crossed Spruce Street, walked into the Penn Medical Center, and took an elevator to a lab on the sixth floor.

She donned a paper gown, bonnet, booties and gloves, and entered the super sterile environment of the human application laboratory—HAL—of the Institute for Human Gene Therapy.

It was there, in a sci-fi world of hooded lab tables, freezers, petri dishes and microscopes, that Grossman would use the viruses to produce what hopefully would be the first gene therapy drug effective against a major genetic disease, cystic fibrosis.

If all went well, the drug would make medical history.

"Detail and anticipation are two of the most important elements in telling a long narrative story," Drake says. "Anticipation is what keeps them reading.

"In this case the reader is first anticipating what is in the Styrofoam box and then whether medical history will be made. Being specific about what is happening in the scene—students buzzing about, riding an elevator to the sixth floor and entering a science fiction world of hooded lab tables, freezers, and petri dishes—enables the reader to see what is unfolding."

In addition to interviewing, a good writer uses these tools to discover telling bits of information:

Observation. Visit important scenes in the story. Describe what you see, and, sometimes, hear or smell—whatever brings the scene to life.

Record-searching. Read hospital and medical records, police records, financial documents, court documents, lawyers' notes, family diaries.

Research. Familiarize yourself with the topic about which you will write—read medical and science journal articles, pertinent laws, court precedents.

When you begin weaving your tale, often it works best to simply start at the beginning and end at the end. As you write, develop a rhythm. Use direct quotes. Convey a sense of intimacy and immediacy. Use short sentences and graphic descriptions. The secret of telling a good tale is to write enough description to let your readers feel they are there, watching, but not so much detail that it bogs the story down, throwing the readers off track.

If a story is worth telling, it has emotions. Let them come through. If you tell the tale well, a reader should react—cry, tense up with anticipation, feel relieved, laugh out loud, call out to a family member, "You've got to read this!" and, maybe, ponder the issues the story raises.

Here is the opening section of "A Matter of Life and Death":

> *Dinner was particularly good that night. David and I had eaten while we watched* Jeopardy *and talked over the day's activities. I remember so well how happy he was. He and Linda had just become engaged two weeks ago and they were both so excited. He planned to meet her at her house around 8:30 that night, but he hesitated in the hallway while we watched something very funny on TV. Then, because he thought he might be late, he phoned Lin and left a really silly message on her machine, said goodbye and left. That was the last time I saw my son as I had known him. [Nicci Bojanowski, David's mother]*

It was a Monday evening, the first day of October, 1990, and just cool enough for a sweater, as David Bojanowski left home in Mount Washington and drove his old white Ford east onto Northern Parkway toward his fiancée's home in Govans. He was 26 years old.

At the same time, Thomas Mitchell "T.J." Jones, 29, of 4018 Garrison Blvd., was approaching from the opposite direction in a 1979 Chevy van. He and another workman had been drinking through the day on a home repair job. Now he was taking the company van back to his boss. And he was late.

Nicci Bojanowski was standing in her back yard not long after, watching the darkness, when the staccato roar of a Shock Trauma helicopter overhead ruptured the silence of the night. She noticed that it was trying to land nearby. Lin Bauer, David's fiancée, outside with her dog, Rip, heard it, too.

The accident, 15 minutes earlier on Northern Parkway, less than a mile from the Bojanowski home, had been a bad one. Baltimore police said that Mr. Jones, traveling "at an apparent high rate of speed," hit a dip in the road and lost control of his van near the intersection with West Rogers Avenue, close to the Jones Falls Expressway.

The work truck became a clumsy missile, jumping the center curb, crossing the grassy median, ramming the boxy Ford Granada on the driver's side. The car was so crumpled by the cab of the van that Baltimore police listed it as a compact on the accident report.

Here's how that part of the story was reported and written: In order to write the first sentence, I had to check a 1990 calendar to verify that the accident happened on a Monday; get a weather forecaster to look up the records for October 1, 1990, to find out the temperature and whether it was windy or raining; and, in my own car, retrace David Bojanowski's route toward his fiancée's home. The casual writing style is a tip-off that this is a narrative. In the next two paragraphs, anticipation builds and the pace of the story is set.

To write the second paragraph, I checked police and court records of the accident, found the name of the drunk driver's former employer, and got her to talk to me.

In the third paragraph, I worried for some time over how to describe the noise a helicopter makes. I listened to helicopters whenever I had the opportunity, and finally decided it was a "staccato roar" that "ruptured the silence of the night."

In interviewing Lin, I mentioned that Mrs. Bojanowski had heard the helicopter coming to pick up David. Lin said she had heard it, too. I asked what she was doing. She said she was outside walking her dog. I asked what her dog's name was. Any more information about the dog—for instance, a golden retriever that had been her pet for five years—would have distracted the reader and slowed the pace of the story. To find out the distance the accident occurred from the Bojanowski home, in the fourth graph, I clocked the mileage when I traced the route in my car.

In the fifth paragraph, I started to get carried away, giving the "clumsy missile" diabolical motives as it searched for a victim. But my great editor, Dudley Clendinen, held me back, saying it's best to stop short of giving inanimate objects human feelings.

I was able to capitalize on an error in the police report of the accident. The police described David's car as a small compact, but his mother had told me it was a large, boxy car called a Ford Granada. I called her back and she was adamant that it was the Ford Granada, a car David used that had been handed down in the family. I trusted her over the police report, knowing, from my earliest reporting experiences covering police, that police reports often contain errors.

Nicci Bojanowski, David's mother, kept a clear and very poignant diary of this tragic family experience. I used bits from her diary to begin the story and in several other places, putting them in bold italics to separate them from my own words. The story continued:

> T.J. Jones, taken to nearby Sinai Hospital with only minor injuries, registered a blood-alcohol level of 0.19, nearly twice the reading necessary to be charged with driving while intoxicated.
>
> David Bojanowski, smashed in his car, was flown to the Shock Trauma Center at University of Maryland Medical Center.
>
> Nicci Bojanowski's phone rang at 11:30 P.M. It was her eldest son, Michael. The state police had found his name in the phone book. When the trooper said David had been pretty banged up, a sharp pain cut down Mike's back. He felt paralyzed. It was at a wedding just two days before that David and his girlfriend Lin Bauer had told Mike and

his wife, Kathy, that they were going to marry. Now Kathy called Lin. They met at Mrs. Bojanowski's, and Mike drove them all to the Shock Trauma Center.

The Maryland Institute for Emergency Medical Services Systems is world famous for pioneering the best in trauma care. Marylanders know it as the Shock Trauma Center. They expect miracles to happen there. Sometimes they do. And sometimes they don't.

The bad news was delivered by two doctors wearing surgical gowns. "Your son is in a deep coma," one of them told Mrs. Bojanowski. "He probably won't live. If he does, he will probably not regain consciousness. . . ."

The doctors took the family to the admitting area. To Mrs. Bojanowski it looked like a huge airplane hangar with her son lying alone and still in the light.

David was propped up on a stretcher in a sitting position with tubes coming out of him from all directions and machines everywhere. His head was bandaged, his face was covered with blood and dressings. His arm and leg were in splints and he was unconscious. As we moved closer to the stretcher, I felt my knees going out from under me.

The first two paragraphs were from hospital, police, and court records, and a check to find what the blood-alcohol level is for driving while intoxicated. The rest of the section was the result of repeated interviewing.

After letting the drama build and unfold at the hospital, it was necessary to pull away and give some background about David—what kind of person he was, what his interests were, his relationship with family members. Readers are not going to follow a story this long (it took up two-thirds of the front page and jumped inside for two full pages) unless they feel that they know the principal characters and care what happens to them.

Then I took the readers back to the hospital in this next section, which came from interviewing the doctor and family members and visiting the waiting room to see what it looked like:

The force of the accident had caused severe bruising to his brain. It was hemorrhaging, and the bruising and hemorrhaging in turn caused the brain to swell.

At the same time, it was starved for nourishment.

David's other injuries—a right forearm fracture and a fracture that laid his right knee open—likely contributed to a drop in blood pressure before he ever got to Shock Trauma, said Dr. Azik Wolf, the senior neurosurgeon who treated him. The low blood pressure increased the pressure inside his brain, which retarded the flow of blood to his head, and kept oxygen from his brain.

David's two sisters, Janina "Nina" Thornton, mother of the twins, and Leslie Collins, joined the others in the soft gray waiting room for family members on the first floor, where the television flickered and paintings of flowers hung on the walls.

This was too much to absorb. On Aug. 29, Mrs. Bojanowski's father had died. Three weeks later her mother died. And that was only two weeks ago.

We huddled in a corner of the waiting room together, trying to comfort each other. There were no words, only solemn silent promises that if David lived, we would help him with every ounce of strength we had.

The doctors' problem was to bring David's brain pressure under control. They drilled a hole in the right side of his skull, inserting a monitor the size of a pencil lead into the brain tissue to check the pressure. It was high, blocking an adequate blood flow to the brain.

I next described what the doctors did to try to lower the pressure in David's brain.

A tale has passages where the story takes a turn. Here is one:

On Dec. 17, David left behind the world of high-tech medicine which had kept him alive. An ambulance carried him 50 miles away to the Rehab Hospital of York, in Pennsylvania, an institute with a different mission. Medicine had kept him from dying. Medicine had restored his body's health. Now the question was whether he had a mind.

And here is another:

Dr. West watched him, and after two months of care, at a cost of about $1,000 a day, he called a meeting with members of David's family. They came, clinging to every hopeful sign they had found in the daily logs, but Dr. West was emphatic:

"If you're waiting for David to come out of the coma, he's out. That's why he has sleep-wake cycles. This is all he can do. He's in a persistent vegetative state. He cannot get any better. This is it." . . .

The doctor discussed the family's choices: they could put David in a nursing home, take him home, or remove his feeding tube and let him die.

Mrs. Bojanowski decided she should let her son die, and had him moved to a Maryland nursing home while she got a required court order to have the feeding tube removed. This notation from her diary served the purpose of explaining her decision to let David die.

It was heartbreaking to see him lying there knowing he had no options. His legs and arms had withered to flesh and bones. His skin had whitened for lack of sunlight and his face was empty. No feelings or thoughts shown in his eyes. There was no response from him at all.

I could still see in my mind the jogger, the football player, the drummer that

> *I knew so well. David loved to cook and would never even eat another meal.*
> *He loved his nieces and nephews so much and would never have any children*
> *of his own. The pain I felt for him was unbearable.*

The next section of the story was a drama that I wanted to re-create so that the readers were in the hospital emergency room, watching, feeling that they knew the people involved.

> Rather suddenly, David developed pneumonia, which for centuries had ended the lives of the old, the bedridden, the chronically ill. At 2:30 A.M. on April 5, he was transferred to the emergency room at the University of Maryland Medical Center. His temperature was 105 degrees. He was having seizures. Mrs. Bojanowski and Lin arrived to find David lying on a stretcher, shaking violently.
>
> "Tell them to let him die," Lin whispered to Mrs. Bojanowski. "Please, you have the authority. He's trying to die. Make them let him die."
>
> "Please," Mrs. Bojanowski screamed to the doctors, "Just let him go! Let him die!"
>
> Dr. Greg Dohmeier, the family medicine resident on call, had worked an eight-hour shift and was asleep in the hospital when his beeper sounded. He took the elevator down six floors to the emergency room and there found Mrs. Bojanowski and Lin. He asked David's mother if she was her son's legal guardian. He asked if David had signed any advance directives—documents that said whether he would want to be kept alive in this condition or not.
>
> Mrs. Bojanowski had to answer no to both questions. . . .
>
> Only 28, the young physician felt torn. Medicine and the law, empathy and a doctor's training were clashing as a 27-year-old man lay convulsing on a stretcher in the hall. . . .

This was a crucial sentence. Here and in quotes that followed, the doctor revealed himself as a human being, for the moment a significant player in this very human drama. The sentence also summarizes the dramatic controversies enveloping the doctor, the patient, and the family. Dr. Dohmeier treated David and returned him to Deaton. The story goes on to tell of the court proceedings, the family lawyer's conscience, the nursing home's fear of liability, and the police interest in charging the drunk driver with manslaughter if David died.

Finally, a year and a day after the accident, with the court's permission, a doctor wrote an order to stop fluids and food so that David could die. The doctor expected death from dehydration would take place in a week or 10 days. But it seemed someone at the hospital was still feeding David through the tube that had been left in place to give him medications. The story picks up here with the death watch:

Finally, Mrs. Bojanowski, her sister Lollie and Lin began to stand a watch in the hospital room. His brother and sisters came as they could. It was a 24-hour guard, to prevent someone from keeping David alive.

The next three paragraphs described family members waiting moment by moment for David's blood pressure to drop—a tip-off that he was about to die. The story picks up here:

> At daybreak Leslie and her husband and baby left. And then David's blood pressure began to drop again.
>
> Mrs. Bojanowski called all the family back.
>
> Nina sat on the edge of a chair with her hand on David's chest so she could feel him breathing. On the other side Leslie held his hand and arm. Michael was behind her. Lin stayed close to David's head. Mrs. Bojanowski and her sister were at the foot of his bed.
>
> Less than an hour after they all rushed back, David took what appeared to be one last breath. They all looked to each other, with the same silent question: "Is that it?" His lungs heaved again. And then he was still. It was very peaceful.
>
> "He's dead," Nina said. Everyone burst into tears.

Finally, after a long buildup, the climax. It is short and simple, and would have been an effective ending, except that true stories don't have tidy endings. This one ended with a bureaucratic foul-up that prevented David from being an organ donor—somebody from the medical examiner's office wouldn't move the body to the operating room until David's family could get him the number on the traffic ticket issued in David's accident more than a year earlier.

I followed the main story with an epilogue that included the drunk driver's sentence of six months on work release and three years' probation. When you have told your story, get out of it as quickly as possible. Often a powerful quote provides a worthy ending to your tale. In David's, the very last paragraph of the epilogue belonged to his fiancée:

> Lin Bauer still works as a hospital critical-care nurse, wears David's engagement ring, and visits his grave two or three times a week. "Everybody was fighting for his life, and he survived. That's the real tragedy. He survived," she said. "Without medical support, he would have died in the first 36 hours."

11

Investigative Science Journalism

DEBORAH BLUM

Deborah Blum, a science writer at the *Sacramento Bee,* won the 1992 Pulitzer Prize in beat reporting for a series of articles on primate research. The series also won the AAAS–Westinghouse Award for science writing and the Clarion Award for national reporting. She has since written a book on the subject, *The Monkey Wars.* She is currently working on a second book about gender biology. Deborah is a graduate of the science writing program at the University of Wisconsin at Madison and was science writer–in–residence there in the spring of 1993. She serves on the advisory board of the Media Resource Service and on the board of the NASW.

I have a theory—unverified, of course—that most science writers spend a large part of their time as investigative reporters. This gets underestimated because we have such a peculiar attitude toward investigative reporting— if it's not trench coats, deep throats, and murky dealings in parking lots, then it's not the real thing.

Having done all of the above (barring trench coats, which I find bulky and unbecoming), I don't believe it. At its most basic, investigative reporting begins with three questions about a given piece of information:

1. What does it mean?
2. Is it the truth or even close?
3. Can it do harm?

You can't do good science writing without asking the first question. And so far, I haven't met a science writer who will accept a researcher's assessment of his work (brilliant! brilliant!) at face value. By necessity, science writers must investigate the claim. Increasingly, too, the last question has become important in science writing. After all, science is an intensely human enterprise. That is, the gifts are mixed. It gives us antibiotics—to which microbes become resistant. It gives us nuclear weapons—which threaten us all. It gives us soaring human space flight—and loss of life and overburdened budgets because people are much costlier to boost into orbit than robots.

I love breathless discovery stories myself, and sometimes I write them. But more and more—to the benefit of public understanding of science— we anchor our stories in reality. This, I think, is the real benefit of the thread of investigation that runs through many science articles.

Having said that, however, I want to go beyond basics. My purpose is to discuss some classic investigative reporting: public document requests, sometimes hundreds of interviews, leaked information, and yes, even the occasional deep throat. For science writing, just like science itself, does not exist on some weird abstract plane. It often requires the fundamental reporting skills of a good police reporter. I started out on that beat. It taught me some essential lessons. I learned quickly—and dramatically— never to rely only on the official source.

When I was a brand-new police reporter, I covered a fatal accident in a small, north Georgia county. According to sheriffs' deputies, a drunken teenager had crashed his car into a ravine and then staggered away with severe head injuries. The valiant officers struggled through underbrush to find him. Duly awed (I was a pretty naive 21-year-old), I wrote up a thrilling story—which turned out to be a lie. The boy's family called the next day. He had indeed crashed the car and staggered away. But it was his father who found him—after the police got tired of looking. And it was his father who held his son by the side of the road, waiting for the ambulance. The boy died before help arrived.

Twenty years later, I still remember. And there's a corollary: The cops really hated me after that story. But when I left for another paper, about nine months later, they sent me off with flowers, trophies, and honorary memberships in police associations. In the interim I'd done a lot of routine beat reporting. I'd also rappelled off cliffs with the deputies, taken shooting lessons with the city police, and eaten quantities of firehouse biscuits and venison. If you want to report with an edge, you have to learn quickly that making people angry is a survivable event. Almost everyone gets over it. As long as you get it right, good sources learn to trust you, even when they don't like everything you write.

And the people you lose probably would never have been great sources anyway. Edward Teller, for instance, hasn't returned one of my phone calls since 1987. Which brings me back to investigative science reporting: Edward Teller is, of course, a brilliant nuclear physicist. He helped drive the development of thermonuclear weapons in this country. But he may be best known today as their most passionate advocate—for his determined refusal to admit that they even have a negative side. For many years now, he has been the statesman of the bomb, holding emeritus positions at Lawrence Livermore National Laboratory and Stanford University.

I met him a few years after becoming a California science writer. As a newcomer to the state, I was startled by the amount of military research. I began playing around with a proposal, something like "tomorrow's wars are being designed in California." I used that approach to convince the *Bee* to let me do a series, which eventually became "California: The Weapons Master."

The 1987 series illustrates another necessity in investigative reporting, that of strategy. For instance, we chose deliberately to schedule the series over a long time period, gambling that along the way we would develop both good sources and good tips. Our theory was that if we could hang out with the nuclear researchers for a while, we (that is, I) would build a relationship of trust. That relationship might eventually lead to insider stories, impossible to gain otherwise.

When I teach journalism classes, I tell the students to think about their approach toward developing relationships with sources, or simply how to coax the most information possible out of an interview. Everyone does this differently. It's worth recognizing your own style, knowing when it works and when it doesn't.

I like an interview to be a good conversation, so my approach tends to be both friendly and relaxed. In a tense, investigative setting, however, sometimes that simply won't work. As soon as I run into a hostile response, I go from chatty to straightforward. I try to get all my points in before the source walks. And I try not to ring alarm bells early on. I save the most difficult questions for last.

If I suspect a person will be hostile before the interview, I will sometimes try to recruit allies. University/laboratory/agency public information officers (PIOs) can be enormously helpful with this. So can other scientists. In Teller's case, Mike Ross, then a PIO at Livermore, advised me to write a very pleasant letter. Teller liked the letter and had his secretary schedule an interview. Depending on how nervous a source is, I will also provide copies of previous stories I've done on a subject and I will offer references.

Let me emphasize that this is an individual approach. I've known reporters who team up in a good cop–bad cop style. I've known reporters who liked "in your face" questions. I once was teamed with a very good environmental reporter, Tom Harris, on an investigation of our local nuclear power plant. We flew to Bethesda to interview top administrators at the Nuclear Regulatory Commission (NRC). Tom told the director that his answers were bullshit. Mentally, at least, my jaw dropped. But we got a very candid answer in response to that.

On the other hand, the man remained forever wary of us. In an investigation, you have to make that call: Whether a person can be cultivated as a source, whether they are most likely good for one confrontational interview. If the latter, do lots of homework well in advance, have your questions in order, and bring a tape recorder.

When I'm doing an investigation, I try not to booby-trap people. Reporters have a sleazy enough reputation as it is without lying to get information. So I'm candid about what I'm doing. I tell people the basic story concept; I tell them who I've been talking to; and I try to make sure they understand that they won't like everything I write.

Finally, I get fanatic about accuracy. If you are writing a story that you know will make people furious, do sweat the small stuff. You can't afford to lose credibility on misspelled names or fractured titles. In my weapons series, I wrote one story suggesting that lab officials had lied about needing constant nuclear tests to check weapons reliability. I took my unpublished copy to two physicists who went over the technical details. You don't want to stumble over a scientific error and damage your story.

The weapons series ran for six months, during which time, I did in fact, develop some very good sources. And, as with many investigations, I established a relationship with some scientists unhappy with what the laboratory was doing. After all, insider tips often begin with someone's exasperation with an employer.

Livermore was, at that time, heavily engaged in trying to develop weapons for Ronald Reagan's beloved Strategic Defense Initiative (Star Wars), which would theoretically use space-based weapons to shield the United States from a nuclear attack. Many scientists outside Livermore felt the approach was being oversold. I was fortunate enough to find scientists inside the lab who also believed that.

They slipped me internal memos and classified documents. Frankly, the documents made me a little neurotic. I kept changing their hiding place—they moved from office, to home, even to the trunk of my car. And yes, to get them I did drive to people's homes at night and met in restaurants and other neutral locations. The resulting stories sparked a General Accounting Office investigation.

The second point about the weapons series deals with how to recognize a subject worth investigating at all. A journalism teacher once said that every good investigative reporter needs a low level of indignation. The "that's outrageous" reaction is actually a good indicator. For me, that began with my newcomer's shock at the dominance of military science in

California. But—and there are investigative reporters who would disagree with me here—you should also be prepared for your instincts to be wrong. Charlie Petit, the science writer at the *San Francisco Chronicle,* sometimes talks jokingly of "stories too good to check." There are many promising beginnings that simply don't hold up. And there's also the possibility that your instincts will push you in the right direction, but that you've grabbed onto the wrong point. That certainly was true for me in these stories. I started out promising a series on designing tomorrow's wars. As I got deeper into the research, I realized I was becoming more and more depressed. I finally stopped, sat down at the computer, and read my collected notes. At that point, they told me I'd actually discovered a different story: None of the weapons worked. I recast the series. I'd actually done my Edward Teller interview before then. After he read the later stories, he refused to talk to me again.

As I said, it's survivable.

In discussing the weapons series, I alluded briefly to the power of documents. Does investigative reporting require massive use of the federal Freedom of Information Act (FOIA) or state public record act laws? Obviously not. You can get better documents, anyway, if someone leaks them to you.

Does investigative reporting require masses of documents at all? Every good investigation is based on good documentation. An investigation of, say, a local chemical plant dumping toxins? You want the state and federal water quality inspections. An investigation of fraudulent science? You want, if you can get them, the internal investigation documents. In the Livermore case, I had memos between scientists detailing misstatements about the research. Looking into a particular drug? You want the documentation of the Food and Drug Administration (FDA) on clinical trials. Exploring a nonprofit research association? You can get IRS forms that detail its expenses, including what officers are paid.

There's simply a fabulous abundance of information that can be accessed through public record acts. The downside is time. Many agencies are overwhelmed with such requests. Many are grudging about responding. It can take weeks—or months—to get your documents. Further, agencies can and will withhold documents in violation of the law, partly because they know that a reporter may simply run out of time. So budget some drag into your record searches and be prepared to appeal.

Just about every federal agency has a Freedom of Information officer. If you want to do an FOIA, contact the agency, find out the name of that person, and talk to him or her to find out specifically how your request needs to be framed. As a general rule, the more details the better: Names of scientists, companies, research topics, days, months, and years will all help move your request more quickly. Also, be sure to ask for documents in every possible medium: microfiche, CD-ROM, computer tapes, tape recordings, printed documents, and so forth.

With states, the laws vary widely. Again, contact the specific agency. Finally, don't be afraid to ask for trivia. I always ask for all correspondence related to the documents. The perspective in those behind-the-scenes letters can be extraordinarily helpful.

The series I did that relied most heavily on public record act requests involved primate research. The eventual product, called "The Monkey Wars," appeared in the *Sacramento Bee* in late 1991. It won a 1992 Pulitzer Prize for beat reporting, so I want to use it here, as a study of integrating public record requests into reporting.

The idea for the series actually came about in a very indirect way, through the now well-publicized outbreak of the *Ebola* virus in monkeys at a research laboratory in Reston, Virginia. As a consequence of that outbreak (which eventually turned out not to be a public health problem), the local primate center conducted *Ebola* tests of its monkeys and handlers. (This center, the California Regional Primate Research Center, affiliated with UC Davis, is about 15 miles from Sacramento.) In the course of writing a news story about those tests, I discovered that the state of California disliked the federal quarantine system; it maintained its own system. It was, in fact, the only state to do so. And because of that quarantine system, it had records on every single monkey imported into the state of California. That list was the only one of its kind in the country.

As soon as I realized how unique that was, I wanted the list. I called the Department of Health Services, talked to the veterinary medicine unit, and was told to file a public record act request. In fact, the department had stored the import records but had never compiled what I requested— five years' worth of monkeys brought into California, how many, and who brought them in.

When I got the list, I realized it wasn't a story. Yet. But it was a road map to primate research in California. At that point, I decided it would be interesting to use that map to explore animal research, taking monkeys as the model. At first, my editors were dubious. From nuclear weapons to monkeys? They weren't impressed. And I wasn't sure either. So I decided to spend some more time collecting documents.

In the wake of the *Ebola* crisis, both state health services and the U.S. Centers for Disease Control and Prevention (CDC) had been inspecting laboratories for proper health standards. In fact, the CDC had temporarily shut down almost all primate quarantine centers. I filed for all those inspection records (and related correspondence). The U.S. Department of Agriculture (USDA) conducts basic animal welfare inspections of laboratories. I filed requests for those for all primate labs in the state. The USDA also requires any scientist conducting an experiment on an animal which involves pain without pain relief to file an extra report. I asked for all pain reports. I asked the FDA for records on certain drugs that had relied heavily on primate research. It took me close to a year to file requests, analyze the documents, realize I needed more, file additional requests. In addition, the CDC withheld a number of documents. The paper's lawyers filed an appeal and won. Essentially, this was a part-time hobby for a year, until I had the paperwork in front of me.

At the end of the year, I had a lot of paper. I also had detailed portraits of primate research facilities, both public and private: how many animals they'd brought in, how many were still surviving, how many citations for bad care they had received, how many painful experiments had been done. Imagine asking a private pharmaceutical company to tell you that. Yet it's there in the public records.

Let me now acknowledge the limits of record use. First, after I accumulated these documents, just about everyone I called refused to speak to me. They hated taking the topic public anyway. And, partly because I had spent all this time gathering documents, they were worried. Many suspected that I was "out to get them." So to make the series work, I had to fall back on those techniques described earlier: providing references, writing samples, describing my intent. At the UC Davis primate center, I went to two meetings with lab officials simply to build a relationship. It took me a good month to convince people to talk to me.

Slowly, as I built a base of interviews, people relaxed. They were reassured by the interviews already done. In the end, I talked to more than 100 people. The series became an inquiry into the very human and ethical dilemmas of using a closely related species for our own medical benefit.

A final point about documents. What you read may not actually provide an accurate picture. In every case where I had an animal welfare violation from the USDA, I called the researcher. Most didn't hold up to my satisfaction. For instance, one inspector had complained about owl monkeys at the California Institute of Technology (Caltech) being low on water during his morning visit. They were. But that's because owl monkeys are nocturnal. The scientists let them sleep in the morning. They replenished their water in the afternoon.

A final point about documents, leaked or otherwise. It is clear that the Internet is complicating, and will continue to complicate, this picture. My experience is that the electronic world is incredibly leaky. Before, if someone wanted to sneak you a document, they had to photocopy it, mail it, fax it, meet you somewhere. Now, they can leak material with a couple of keystrokes. I've already been leaked e-mail copies of confidential memos, supposedly private correspondence between other reporters and their sources, and internal documents. Further, unlike with hard copy, it's not clear with electronic transmissions if the document has been edited. We should all be very careful in how we handle electronic information.

Finally, you will undoubtedly notice that the most essential element is not brilliant deduction or even incredibly good luck with sources. It's time. In-depth investigative reporting takes time, a commitment of resources by both medium and reporter. Is it worth it?

There are people who don't like investigative reporting in science. They argue that it plays to the anti-intellectual part of our society. I've heard scientists also mourn the good old days, when the public believed what scientists said. I believe that blind faith is dangerous. Today's skepticism about science comes, in part, from a sense of betrayal: "We believed you when you said that science would perfect the world. And look at it now." By reporting on science in all its dimensions, we make it real. In doing so, in letting people inside the process, it is true that we may decanonize the scientific society. But we also bring science back into the real world— where it belongs.

12 • • • • • • • • • • • • • • • •

Using Sources

JOEL GREENBERG

Joel Greenberg has been science and medicine editor at the *Los Angeles Times* since 1988. Prior to that he was the editor of *Science News* in Washington, D.C., which won the George Polk Award for science reporting during his tenure. He also served as the magazine's behavioral sciences editor, and has been a science writer at the *Miami Herald* and the *New York Times*. He is part of the *Los Angeles Times* metropolitan staff that won the 1994 Pulitzer Prize for its coverage of the Northridge earthquake. He also received the American Psychological Association's National Psychology Award for Excellence in the Media for "sustained contribution to the public understanding of psychology." In addition, he has been a Professional Journalism Fellow at Stanford University.

In August 1982, Ivars Peterson called me at my office at *Science News* in Washington, D.C. I assumed that Peterson, who covered policy and technology for the magazine, simply was checking in with his editor, telling me what kind of story to expect from the meeting he was covering, the Society of Photo-Optical Instrumentation Engineers in San Diego. It was the type of meeting meant for *Science News:* dull and low-key, but filled with significant new information that someone like Peterson, one of the country's top technology and mathematics writers, could sniff out and transform into a lead story.

Ivars did more than sniff. He inhaled.

Something strange was happening, he told me. Papers long-before approved for presentation at the meeting were being mysteriously withdrawn—not just a few papers, but scores of them, maybe more than 100. Some presenters were gathering in small groups and talking in low tones; others were walking around the hotel simply looking stunned.

It wasn't long before Peterson found out that some 150 nonclassified scientific papers were withdrawn from the meeting, under pressure from the Department of Defense. The DOD apparently felt the papers—which covered holography, fiber optics, lasers, robotics, and other areas of technology—were too sensitive for a meeting whose participants included a group of four scientists from the Soviet Union.

Peterson's diligence led to *Science News* breaking perhaps the most dramatic instance of government censorship of nonclassified scientific research ever seen in the United States. The story resulted from his ability to spontaneously tap sources he had been developing since coming to the magazine.

Our coverage could have ended there, but the question loomed: Was this an anomaly, merely an isolated case of government reaction (or over-reaction?) during a time of heightened nationalism? Or was it a sign of some deeper policy shift?

The answers would depend greatly on the quality and variety of sources we could cultivate over the next few months. In a story as sensitive as this, it was critical to find people who not only could talk about the big picture, but also had firsthand experience with government censorship.

As Peterson returned to cover his normal policy and technology beat, I pursued those questions raised by the San Diego incident. Jump-started by Ivars's initial reporting, I tracked a network of sources—some confidential, some on-the-record—who helped us come up with a number of stunning answers.

Collectively, they painted a picture of pervasive, growing pressure from the U.S. government—primarily the military—to cut back on scientific exchanges with Eastern Bloc countries. Through these sources we were able to report "a confusing, complex struggle between the federal government and scientists in universities and industries. The struggle centers on the freedom of U.S. scientists to report and exchange scientific and technological data with Eastern Bloc nations, primarily the Soviet Union."

Our sources included scientists and government and university officials. Some were obvious choices: Frank Press, president of the National Academy of Sciences (NAS); Stanford president Donald Kennedy; Richard Perle, assistant secretary of defense for international security policy; Admiral Bobby Inman, deputy director of the Central Intelligence Agency. These people provided important, on-the-record grounding for an in-depth look at the situation. The trail also led to less obvious—but in many ways more valuable—sources who were able to give powerful, firsthand details of the government's crackdown on information exchange.

One such person was Richard Wollensak, vice president of the Itek Corporation in Lexington, Massachusetts, and president of the Society of Photo-Optical Instrumentation Engineers. Wollensak's chilling account of his encounter with the DOD would turn out to serve as the story's lead.

He told of an unexpected phone call to his office from the DOD's Lieu-
tenant Colonel Gary Walters. After expressing concern about the number
of "sensitive" papers to be presented at the meeting, Walters asked Wollensak to provide a room at the San Diego meeting where the DOD could
talk with the authors of various papers prior to the meeting.

Through interviews with Wollensak and other participants at the meeting, we were able to relate the Kafkaesque scene in the inquiry room:

> DOD officials asked scientists two questions: "Was your work spon-
> sored by a DOD Agency?" and "Have you secured clearance?" The
> tactic achieved the desired effect. "They never actually asked me to
> withdraw my two presentations," said one engineer from private in-
> dustry. "But I was scared enough to pull both of them."

Confidential sources at the DOD eventually confirmed that the crackdown orders carried the personal approval of Secretary of Defense Caspar
Weinberger.

But perhaps even more telling of the depth and scope of the government's near-secret policy shift were people on the front lines of dealings
with Russian scientists, like Stanford engineering professor Bernard Roth
and Stanford Linear Accelerator director Wolfgang K. H. Panofsky. Roth
spoke of a "subtle" change in his dealings with Eastern European and
Soviet scientists he had known for years: "People don't write as frequently—I got fewer Christmas cards this year than usual. I don't know,
but I just have a sense that there is caution all around."

Much of the confrontation, we found, had centered around Stanford,
which had a history of serving as a center for East–West scientific
exchange. There was the mysterious State Department cancellation of a
Stanford visit by Soviet scientist Nickolay V. Umnov. And later there was
an incident where the the DOD refused the Stanford library computer
access to unclassified material, a case that led the university to sever its
computer link with the DOD.

It is anecdotes like these, obtained only through persistent tracking of
layers upon layers of sources, that add the necessary texture to a story
such as this.

The picture was completed by Soviet scientists themselves, who submitted to interviews via telex (these were the days before the Internet). They
echoed their American counterparts' lamentations over lost cooperation
and contact as a result of the U.S. crackdown. They also denied charges
that much of the scientific flow of information was one-way, from the
United States to the Soviet Union. Their comments—regardless of their
political expediency—were vital to a tenet of journalism in general: Get
all sides of the story.

Whether a science story involves such long-term investigation or quick-turnaround breaking news, it requires well-rounded, balanced reporting that relies on the savvy and expertise of the writer perhaps more than most other beats.

In general, science reporters start with several basic sources for science and medicine stories:

Journals. Probably the closest thing we have to "pack reporting" in science writing. Although we all want to break our own stories first, there is no ignoring scientific journals, routinely monitored by all major media and probably the steadiest sources of science news. The reason? If a researcher is going to drop a bombshell, chances are it will land smack in the pages of *Nature, Science, JAMA* the *New England Journal of Medicine, The Lancet,* or one of scores of other smaller but respected publications. To miss a major research story in a journal—with every wire service and major newspaper on top of it—is an acknowledged sin.

Meetings. If a scientist is going to announce a major find outside of a journal, it will probably be at a scientific meeting. This does not happen as often as it used to, primarily because refereed journals are considered by many a purer forum in which to divulge advances. For this reason, science writers who used to cover meetings like the AAAS for breaking news now attend mainly for "background" and to "cultivate sources." Often, the best meetings are of the smaller, specialized variety that will enable the writer to focus on a specific area of interest.

Breaking news. Like any other journalists, science writers work at the whim of events. In Los Angeles, we're poised to cover an earthquake every day, and to a lesser extent fires and floods. For science writers it is especially important to develop sources expert in such local phenomena that are likely to recur.

Press conferences or press releases. Beware. Institutions and scientists attempting to publicize their research prior to journal publication must be viewed with a wary eye. There are many real-world agendas that sneak into science, like funding, competition, ambition, and glory. The science writer must be on the lookout. This is not to say that press announcements never yield major stories or that public information officers cannot be valuable sources. The best public relations people are those you can trust to call you only when there is a legitimate story involved. And occasionally, such a relationship can lead to an exclusive story. This was the case recently when, through a long, close working relationship with a public relations person at a local hospital, the *Los Angeles Times* was present and broke the story of the first gene therapy procedure on a newborn.

Unsolicited calls. If "scientists" you don't know want to publish their original "research" in your newspaper or magazine, rather than in a journal, run for cover.

Developing your own sources. Perhaps the most important part of covering science (or any other beat for that matter) is building up a cadre of reliable, informed sources that you can call on for reaction and comment—both on and off the record—about any range of stories. This comes primarily through experience and gaining the trust of such people through consistently accurate and well-written stories.

For the novice science writer, groups such as the Media Resource Service (formerly Scientists Institute for Public Information) in New York offer an invaluable service by providing expert sources in all fields of science. Online, there is ProfNet, an electronic information service that connects to hundreds of universities and institutions around the world (profnet@vyne.com); numerous scientific groups have established talk groups on the Internet and other online services; and many universities now have Web sites on the Internet.

In the end, the worth of any science story ultimately rests on the caliber of its sources.

Where one looks for sources depends to a great extent, of course, on the nature of the story. But in general, the primary sources are universities; federal, local, and state agencies; and private companies and research labs.

A rather straightforward example of source selection can be seen in the *Los Angeles Times*'s coverage of the great Northridge earthquake of January 17, 1994. The paper's science writers were involved in dozens of stories over the next several months. A look at one of those stories illustrates that if you have to cover an earthquake, California is the place to be; experts want to be where the action is (after all, Charles F. Richter of Richter-scale fame lived directly above the San Andreas Fault until his death in 1985).

The piece examined the reasons the 6.7-magnitude quake reverberated so unevenly around the Los Angeles Basin, "violently shaking some areas far from its epicenter in the San Fernando Valley, while leaving closer neighborhoods unscathed." In reporting on this complex question, *Times* science writer Robert Lee Hotz utilized four primary sources: Wilfred D. Iwan, a Caltech earthquake specialist who is also chairman of the California Seismic Safety Commission; Jim Mori, head of the Pasadena field office of the USGS; John Boatwright, a geophysicist at USGS in Menlo Park in northern California; and Hiroo Kanamoori, director of the Caltech seismological laboratory. By using these four sources, Hotz was able to sample a cross-section of expertise—from authorities on ground motion in general, to those with specific local knowledge of the Los Angeles Basin, both its underground composition and its above-ground structures.

The result was a story that painted a picture of quake with dynamics unlike those seen anywhere else:

> Geophysicists now believe that shock waves within the San Fernando Valley crisscrossed like ripples in the cauldron created by the high, hard rock of the surrounding mountains. Where the crests of the waves intersected, the power of the ground shocks was intensified. Where the troughs of the waves met crests, their energy was canceled. As the shock waves spread, the Los Angeles Basin also served as a lens to capture and focus the quake's force, extending the duration of the shocks.

Hotz's selection of sources may have seemed obvious, and in some cases it was. After all, Caltech and the local office of the USGS held daily news conferences for many weeks following the main shock and during the thousands of aftershocks. But it was also the result of an experienced reporter wading through the scores of available scientists to find those with expertise specific to his story idea.

"We talked to far more scientists than we wound up quoting," Hotz recalls. "The story grew out of a question we all had: How come the quake seemed to strike some areas far from the epicenter with more force than those close by? Except there are no 'how come' experts."

What he wound up doing was melding the expertise of Boatwright, "a classic academic geologist who knows generally how things work," with that of Kanamoori, who, Hotz says, "nominated himself" as a source by being "extremely knowledgeable about the structure of the L.A. Basin. . . . It's the same with any 'accident.' People who know the specifics (of a region, a building structure, etcetera) aren't necessarily the best at describing why something happened. Like when a highway cracks, a structural engineer who is familiar with the behavior of materials probably will know more about the cause than the guy who knows what bolt went where.

"This kind of story is more challenging because there isn't a specific place to go for sources."

Hotz, who had been at the *Times* less than a year and had little previous experience covering earthquakes, had to scramble to find sources in a hurry for perhaps the biggest local story in decades. But he had also been laying the groundwork for such an occasion since his arrival by studying earthquake clips, introducing himself to the people at Caltech, the USGS, and the Southern California Earthquake Center, and simply dropping by periodically to schmooze.

While the rules for choosing sources on most science stories are clear, certain kinds of stories can render those rules as gooey as volcanic mud-flows.

One painful example is the infamous "cold fusion" experiment of 1989. From the moment that the University of Utah announced a next-day press conference on what it termed a major new energy development, we were faced with an extraordinary decision: to ignore the story or pursue it aggressively. Here was a claim, to be announced at the press conference (and tipped off before that in a wire story from Europe), of an achievement that some of the world's most prestigious scientists had failed to accomplish in at least two decades of trying: room-temperature nuclear fusion.

Moreover, they said they had done this with a simple, cheap, tabletop device. "The breakthrough," said a university press release, "means the world may someday rely on fusion for a clean, virtually inexhaustible source of energy."

It seemed like a textbook case of a story to avoid. The claim, particularly using such a technique, seemed fantastic. The research paper had yet to be published in a refereed journal. And no one at Princeton or anywhere else fusion research had been pursued for many years had come close to such a result. Most science writers knew this was a sensational story that almost certainly would prove to be not true, at least not to the point of the university's claims.

Nevertheless, the results emanated from a respected university and from two scientists, Martin Fleischmann and B. Stanley Pons, who, as far as anyone could tell, were legitimate members of the research community. And finally, whether we covered it or not, it was obvious that this was a story destined to lead the television news and make the covers of *Time* and *Newsweek* (which it did). To ignore it would have been a mistake.

We made our decision quickly. Early the next morning, science writer Thomas H. Maugh II was on a plane to Salt Lake City, while in Los Angeles, other reporters were busy contacting sources for a response. Our top priority in covering this story was to give it a realistic perspective, and the way to do this was with top-flight sources who would provide the proper skepticism and ask the right questions.

For example, high up in our first story on the announcement, science writers Maugh and Lee Dye wrote: "Their work follows a course that is so different from conventional wisdom on fusion research that many of the leaders in the field were not even familiar with it. Others were very skeptical, but several who were aware of the research said it could not be dismissed." This set up a string of sources who helped give the story the balance we were looking for.

They included a nonplused Department of Energy scientist, who said, "It's one of those ideas that hasn't occurred to other people"; Robert

Conn, director of UCLA's Institute of Plasma and Fusion Research: "It would be surprising if the work were confirmed"; UCLA fusion physicist Burton Fried: "Don't put any money on it."

That initial story was the beginning of months of coverage in which numerous attempts to replicate the Pons and Fleischmann work at first saw some preliminary reports of success, then a steady stream of failures. Through it all, we continued to take the pulse of the fusion community—including sending a reporter to Princeton for a story on the major "hot" fusion research. Most sources held as open a mind as possible on cold fusion, until May of that year, when the American Physical Society met.

Some 40 papers were presented evaluating the quality of the Utah research. The papers documented "numerous errors." In perhaps the death knell to the cold fusion experiment, Caltech physicist Steven E. Koonin concluded that Pons and Fleischmann's results were based on "incompetence, and perhaps delusion." Most knew it would end that way. But because it had become such a high-profile issue, the cold fusion story had to be reported full bore, with all the resources the newspaper would have devoted to any other major story. And most important, it had to be kept constantly in the proper perspective. To do anything less would have run the risk of either blowing the claims out of proportion or dismissing them without proper consideration.

The key to such thorough science writing is to balance as many authoritative sources as possible.

13 • • • • • • • • • • • • • • • •

Coping with Statistics

VICTOR COHN

Victor Cohn is a former science writer and editor at the *Washington Post.* He is the author of *News & Numbers: A Guide to Reporting Statistical Claims and Controversies in Health and Other Fields* and has given many lectures and seminars for journalists on how to evaluate statistics. He has twice received the NASW's Science-in-Society Award. He has been a scientific and public affairs fellow with the American Statistical Association.

I have a confession to make. I'm among those who spent much of a lifetime avoiding mathematics whenever possible. Back in high school in Minneapolis, my kind geometry teacher, Mr. Peterson, said he'd give me a D for the last semester if I promised not to take any more math. I promised and also avoided chemistry and physics and their attendant formulas all through high school and college.

With this wonderful preparation, I naturally went into science writing.

I tell you this because my problem over the years, like the problem of all reporters and of the public, was how to cope with the fact that when it comes to any health or risk or environmental issue—the same can apply to statements about crime or welfare or government or virtually any issue—one side tells us the sky is falling, the other says it's not. Or here's the cure, no it's not.

A politician says, "I don't believe in statistics," then maintains that "most" people think such and such. Based on what? A poll says, "Here's what people think," with a "three-point plus or minus margin of error." Believable? A doctor reports a "promising" new treatment. Is the claim justified or based on a biased or unrepresentative sample? An environmentalist says a nuclear plant or waste dump causes cancers. An industrialist indignantly denies it. Who's right?

What can we believe? What's worth reporting? And—the question that must concern us both as reporters and citizens—What's worth doing something about?

I talked to many statisticians and epidemiologists. I was told that a critical examination of claims about almost anything requires not so much an understanding of formulas as an understanding of the nature of rational evidence, the array of facts or probable facts that make us decide something is believable. This means reporters can adapt the methods of science and try to judge claims of fact, whether by scientists or physicians or others, by similar rules of evidence.

An honest investigator may first form a hypothesis or theory, an attempt to describe truth, then try to disprove it by what is called the *null hypothesis:* that there is no such truth. To back the original theory, the study must reject that hypothesis. In much the same way, a jury is told to start with a presumption of innocence and say to the prosecution, "Provide the evidence to disprove innocence." And we reporters may say, to ourselves at least, "Show me!"

We can do this, I found, by beginning with some simple yet revealing questions.

1. How do you know? Are you just telling us something you "know" or have "observed" or "found to be true"? Or have you done or found any studies or experiments?
2. What are your data? Your numbers? How or where did you get them?
3. How sure can you be about them? Are there any possible flaws or problems in your conclusions? Salespeople are sure. Honest investigators admit uncertainties.
4. How valid? In science, this means: are your numbers and conclusion accurate?
5. How reliable? That is, how reproducible are your results? Have they been fairly consistent from study to study?
6. What is your degree of certainty or uncertainty by accepted tests? (See the discussion of probability that follows.)
7. Who disagrees with you? And why?

The very way someone answers, or dodges, such questions can reveal much.

We can then go a long way toward distinguishing the probable facts from the probable trash, a long way toward judging claims and statistics that are thrown at us, by learning just six basic concepts that apply to all science, all studies, and virtually all knowledge of society and the universe. Remembering these can teach us to ask "How do you know?" with a considerable degree of sophistication.

1. Uncertainty. All science is almost always uncertain, or uncertain to a degree. Nature is complex; people are more so; research is difficult; observation is inexact. Almost all studies have flaws, so science is always an evolving story, a journey taken a step at a time. Almost all anyone can say about atoms or cells or human beings or the biosphere is: There is a strong possibility that such and such is true, and we may know more tomorrow.

This tells us why things so often seem settled one way today and another tomorrow, and why so much is debated, whether the effects of global warming, a pesticide, a low-fat diet, or a medical treatment. Why so much uncertainty? Lack of funds to do enough research; the fact that doing valid research is not easy; the ethical obstacles to using human beings as guinea pigs; and more. And when it comes to health and the environment, a main reason is lack of long continuing observations of large populations.

It is important to tell all this to the public—and, often, our editors and news directors—so they will understand why "they" say one thing today and another tomorrow. Yet uncertainty need not impede crucial action, if society understands and uses the rest of these principles.

2. Probability. Scientists live with uncertainty by measuring probability. A commonly accepted numerical expression is the P value, determined by a formula that considers the number of subjects or events being compared to decide if a result could have occurred just by chance, with no actual cause and effect.

A P value of .05 or less—reported as $< .05$—is most often regarded as low or desirable, since it means there are probably only 5 or fewer chances in 100 that this result could have happened by chance. This value is called *statistical significance.*

Do not trust a study that is not statistically significant. On the other hand, statistical significance may or may not mean practical (or, in medicine, clinical) significance. Nor does it alone mean there is cause and effect. Association is not causation without further evidence. Think of the rooster who thought his crowing made the sun rise.

The laws of probability and chance tell us to expect some unusual, even impossible-sounding events. Just as a persistent coin tosser will sometime toss heads or tails several times in a row, nature will randomly produce many alarming clusters of cancers or birth defects that have no cause but nature's coin tossing. These produce striking anecdotes and often striking news stories, but they alone do not prove a cause.

There is something else to remember when someone says, "How do they know this stuff isn't causing harm?" Science cannot prove a negative. No one can prove that little green men from Mars have not visited earth. The burden of proof should be on those who say something is true.

3. Power. Statistically, *power* means the likelihood of finding something if it's there, say, an increase in cancer in workers exposed to some substance. The greater the number of cases or subjects studied, the greater a conclusion's power and probable truth.

Be wary of studies with only a small number of cases. Sometimes large numbers indeed are needed. For example, the likelihood that women 30 to 39 years old will suffer a heart attack while taking an oral contraceptive was once calculated at 1 per 18,000 women per year. To be 95 percent sure of finding at least one such event in a one-year trial, researchers would have to observe 54,000 women. This tells us why we so often learn of a drug's harmful effects only after it is being used by thousands.

This also explains why it is so hard to identify low-level yet possibly important risks, whether of pollution, pesticides, low-level radiation, or some other cause. For lack of power—enough cases—a condition that affects one person in hundreds or thousands may never be associated with a particular cause, and a large yet scattered number of illnesses may remain forever unidentified as environmental because they remain a fraction of the vastly greater normal caseload.

4. Bias. Bias in science means introducing spurious associations and reaching unreliable conclusions by failing to consider other influential factors—called *confounding variables* or *co-factors*—in plain language, other explanations. Among common biases: failing to take account of age, gender, occupation, nationality, race, income, health, or behaviors like smoking. Among women suffering ill effects from birth control pills, older age and smoking were for years the two most ignored co-factors that helped cause or promote these effects. Polls, political and otherwise, as well as medical and environmental studies, are all subject to sampling bias, since every group studied is only a sample of a larger population.

Watch for bias by asking, "Are there any other possible explanations?"

5. Variability. A common pitfall of science is that everything measured or studied varies from measurement to measurement. Every human experiment, repeated, has at least slightly and sometimes markedly different results.

Among the reasons: our constantly fluctuating physiologies; common errors or limits in measurement or observation; biologic variations in the same person, between persons, and between populations. Persons in different parts of the country often react differently to the same conditions thanks to differences between persons or environments—or pure chance.

A related concept: ask too about any association's statistical *strength*—its odds. The greater the odds against an association's being a matter of chance, the greater its strength. If a pollutant seems to be causing a 10 percent increase above background, it may or may not be a meaningful association. If a risk is 10 times greater—something like the relative risk in cigarette smokers versus nonsmokers—the odds are strong that something is happening.

6. There is a *Hierarchy of Studies,* from the least to the generally most believable, starting with simple anecdotes; going on to more systematic observation; then proceeding to true experiments, that is, comparing one population or sample with another, under controlled or known conditions.

Many epidemiologic and medical studies are retrospective, looking back in time at old records or statistics or memories. This method is often necessary. It is often unreliable. Far better is the prospective study that follows a selected population for a long period, sometimes years. The long continuing Framingham, Massachusetts, study of diet and behaviors that may be associated with heart disease began following more than 6,000 persons in 1948 and still yields riches in information.

If we reporters understand these concepts, and some things about their uses and limitations, we can go a long way toward separating the truth from the trash and reporting some solid information.

For this knowledge tells us that one study rarely proves anything—that when someone tells us "I've done a study," we should ask, "What kind? How confident can you be in the results? Were there any possible flaws?"

Then we must seek out the most credible evidence, the most likely probabilities. The most believable studies and observations are those repeated among different populations with much the same result, and supported, if possible, by animal or other biologic evidence. We must look for a consensus among the best studies and the best, most neutral observers.

Reporting today is vastly better than the reporting of my youth, the day still of the fedora-topped newshound with the dangling cigarette. But we still have a long way to go.

Take medical reporting. Some years ago, tongue only partly in cheek, I decided that there are only two kinds of medical (and environmental) stories, New Hope and No Hope. They make page one and the evening news. The stuff in between gets ignored or buried. And *we like* to run for page one or its equivalent.

As a result, we commonly over-praise medical "wonders" by failure to mention some real numbers rather than just the wondrous-seeming cases, or failure to look at what happens to various cohorts—parts of the population. Kidney dialysis is a wonder that keeps many people alive. But a study showed that fewer than a third of dialysis patients older than 55 live as long as five years, this though more than half of all dialysis patients are 55 or older, treated at huge cost.

Another wonder: heart pacemakers. A woman once phoned me to say, "My son had to have his first pacemaker at age 25. Now he's wearing his fourth. The miracles aren't always miracles."

Sometimes we don't get the numbers quite right. A National Public Radio reporter, a very good one, reported that the bulk of evidence is that "you'll live longer" if you eat a prudent diet and exercise. The evidence is only that people live longer on average. "You" only increase your chance of doing so.

Many news stories simply fail to include some numbers that any of us would want for intelligent decisionmaking. Medical journals are not exempt. Researchers wrote in the *New England Journal of Medicine* that "one to three drinks" a day may help protect against heart attacks. They defined a drink as 13.2 grams of alcohol. But with whiskey, wine, and beer all at various proofs (alcohol content) neither the journal's article nor any news reports I read or saw told, in common language, how much daily booze, wine, or beer one should consume to drink no more than the prescribed grams. A free-pouring drinker could swallow far more.

There is frequent failure to add context or other pertinent information. Stories in both the *Washington Post* and *New York Times* once said, in effect, Don't worry about high cholesterol causing heart disease if you're old (though some disagreement was indicated in both stories). Neither said that the real risk—and not just heart risk—is probably from a combination of factors: diet, obesity, lack of exercise.

When the FDA declares a drug "safe,"—though no drug is completely so—maybe we should start to say "this means relatively safe" and try to indicate, in the best numbers and rates we can get, the degree of safety or risk, the rate of risky side effects.

The danger of bias? The *Wilmington (Delaware) Journal* one day splashed this dramatic display atop page one: "Cradle of Sorrow / 19901: Code for 'dangerous to infants.' " The story said this zip code in Dover, the state capital, had the state's highest infant mortality rate, higher than in any of the state's areas of high poverty, high teen-age pregnancy, et cetera. And "Why . . . is not easily explained." The paper explained why the next day in a correction. The Dover hospital where these deaths occurred is the only hospital in something like a 40-mile area. It draws many childbirths from outside Dover, hence the large numbers in one zip code.

And the *Washington Post* often compares the nation's capital with the 50 states—almost always unfavorably—because it is listed that way in many tables. But Washington, D.C., is purely a city and should be compared not with states but with similar cities.

Cities, moreover, are not the same as metropolitan areas. Washington's murder rate, for example, for some years topped the list of the nation's cities, with about 60 deaths per 100,000. But urban populations are spread today over metropolitan areas. Many cities have been able to incorporate neighboring suburbs with a relatively low crime rate, and in others (like Philadelphia and Kansas City) the high murder rate is in a high-poverty area outside the city. Look at metropolitan areas, and in one recent year the highest murder rates (in the low- and mid-20s per 100,000) were in the Miami, New York, and Memphis metropolitan areas, with the Washington, D.C., area as a whole tenth on the list (with 15.3 per 100,000).

Of course, that still doesn't tell us where it's safe or unsafe to walk. For that you have to—another statistical concept—*disaggregate*.

In the reporting of risk, there is wide lack of understanding of the difference between a plain number and a *rate*. A rate has to mean so many per so many per unit of time. A *Washington Post* headline once read, "Airline Accident Rate Is Highest in 13 Years." The story, like many others misusing the word *rate*, reported no rate at all, merely death and crash totals. A correction had to be printed pointing out that the number of accidents per 100,000 departures—the actual rate, the "so many per so many"—had been declining year after year.

Watch risk numbers. To influence us, someone can choose an annual death total or deaths per thousand or million, or per thousand persons exposed, or deaths per ton of some substance, or per ton released in the air, or per facility. There are lots of choices to make something seem better or worse.

During a 1990 debate over the Clean Air Act, one issue was whether or not to require automakers to remove 98 percent of tailpipe emissions, compared with a previous 96 percent. The auto industry called it an expensive and meaningless 2-percent improvement. Environmentalists said it would result in a 50-percent decrease in automobile pollution. The lesson: In any such reporting, seek all the figures, not just the assertions someone tries to spoonfeed us.

Ways to improve our reporting? Here are three:

1. When a "scientist" or an "environmentalist" or a "public advocate" or an "industrialist" makes a statement or describes a study that lacks credibility, I think we journalists are entitled to ask ourselves: Are we obliged to report every piece of junk or report it without criticism? We are not, I believe, if when we examine what we are told by using some of the rules that make a piece of evidence worth reporting, we decide that it is worthless. We can point out that one study seldom

proves anything, that some so-called studies are full of holes, that it takes large numbers and careful studies to learn almost anything, and that even a Dr. Famous can utter nonsense that no one else believes.

2. We can demand that scientists and others who tell us their conclusions tell us how they meet the statistical tests that good scientists and statisticians prescribe. Don't accept the pretense that conclusions are written in stone. The pursuit of knowledge is a continuing struggle.

3. Journalism schools should require a course in statistics for every graduate, but not the same course given prospective scientists or researchers, rather one tailored to journalists' needs and experiences, using the news as a large part of the subject matter and giving students tests of truth they can apply in their daily work. At the least, journalism schools should build some such material into their reporting courses. To who, what, when, where, why, and how, let's add: How true?

For all of us, there is much more to know. For all of us, telling the probable truth from the probable trash is to a large extent a matter of attitude, of healthy skepticism—not cynicism or believing nothing, but an informed kind of "show me!"

I have said there seem to be only two kinds of health or environmental news, at least the kind that get on page one or the evening news—New Hope and No Hope. If we pay attention to the principles of sound evidence—those of good statisticians and scientists—we can go a long way toward writing New Hopes and No Hopes that stand up, and toward making the vast amount of stuff in the middle, including that important and fascinating area called controversy, compelling and valid too.

Adapted from *News & Numbers: A Guide to Reporting Statistical Claims and Controversies in Health and Other Fields,* by Victor Cohn, Iowa State University Press (Copyright 1989, Revised 1994).

14

Writing Articles from Science Journals

PATRICK YOUNG

Patrick Young has served as editor of *Science News*, as national science and medical correspondent for the Newhouse News Service, and on the senior staff of the President's Commission on the Accident at Three Mile Island. He has written for a number of magazines, including *Smithsonian, Popular Science, Good Housekeeping, Parade,* and *Psychology Today.* His books include *Asthma and Allergy: An Optimistic Future* and *Keeping Young Athletes Healthy.* He has received nearly two dozen national awards for his science and medical writings and was a science writer–in–residence at the University of Wisconsin at Madison.

Science writing offers some wonderful adventures at times. In the course of my work, I've visited the South Pole, stared into a steaming volcano, covered the first human landing on the moon, and dived with an under-water archaeology team investigating an old fur trade route known as the Voyageur's Highway. Friends and acquaintances have ventured into the ocean depths aboard the submersible *Alvin,* participated in a scientific search for the Loch Ness monster, and flown into the eye of a hurricane. But for the most part, science writing is an adventure of the mind, and some of my most exciting and memorable experiences have taken place not on some wind-swept mountain or sweltering desert, but in the quiet of a researcher's office or laboratory.

Scientists do get excited about their work, though some hide it well. Tapping into that excitement, sharing the intellectual process, watching theory become reality, and covering cutting-edge advances make science writing a stimulating and satisfying career. Getting started presents some challenges, but challenges well worth meeting.

JOURNAL ARTICLES

You can't live by press releases alone, and so, inevitably, the novice science writer must confront the dreaded scientific journal article. Scientists do research, and they report their results in published papers known collectively, and perhaps ironically, as "the literature." Journal articles are usually information-dense, jargon-packed, high on passive verbs, and lacking in grace and style. Still, that's where the information lies, and if you want to write about science, you have to learn to read the writings of the culture.

You may find yourself perusing journals either in search of a story or to provide additional information on a topic you've already chosen. Either way, you can get bogged down quickly unless you learn to rapidly assess research reports.

When you read a newspaper or magazine article, you start at the beginning and read through to the end, or at least until you lose interest. Do this with journal articles, and you will waste large blocks of time. Indeed, you may feel cheated if you slog through eight or nine pages of small type, only to learn that the study yielded inconclusive results. So in reading a journal article, it's best to read front, back, and only then, in between.

Typically, journal articles consist of seven parts: a title; an abstract that briefly summarizes the study; an introduction that gives an overview of the research area covered in the report (estrogen's role in preventing heart attacks in premenopausal women, for example); the methods or protocol section that describes how the researchers did the study; the results; the conclusion and/or discussion, which offers the authors' interpretation of the findings; and the references, which list articles, books, and other communications relating to previous research cited in the article.

The title may or may not clue you in to the article's topic; journal titles even baffle scientists sometimes. The abstract gives a quick synopsis of the study, its methods, its findings, and sometimes an interpretation of its significance. Often the abstract alone will tell you whether the journal report fits your needs. If not, scanning the conclusion and discussion should. Once you find something you can use, then you can devote time to reading the full article, gleaning whatever you can from it.

Let's look at an actual scientific article as an example of how a writer might approach a journal report and what information he or she might garner from it. The article—"Identifying Adults at Increased Risk of Coronary Disease: How Well Do the Current Cholesterol Guidelines Work?" by Steven A. Grover, Louis Coupal, and Xiao-Ping Hu of the Montreal General Hospital—appeared in the *Journal of the American Medical Association* (JAMA) on September 13, 1995.

Clearly, this title does not leave you with the sense of confronting an enigmatic, ambiguous, and inexplicable mystery. The title may not tell all, but you quickly pick up that the study, in some way, looked at an issue of considerable interest to many readers: how well the cholesterol concentrations in their blood predict their risk of a heart attack. The abstract, in this example, listed five headings: objective, patients, main outcome measures, main results, and conclusion. Reading these reveals that the researchers sought to assess the accuracy of several guidelines used in cholesterol screening to determine a person's risk of dying from coronary heart disease; that they looked at deaths among 3,678 men and women who participated in an earlier medical study; that they found new guidelines used in the United States proved more accurate than those they replaced; and finally, they concluded that future guidelines should include greater emphasis on high-density lipoprotein (the so-called good cholesterol) and greater use of nonlipid risk factors to more accurately determine people at high risk.

At this point, the writer has a general picture of what the researchers wanted to learn and what they did learn. The details are very sketchy, but it is clear that for someone working on an article on cholesterol and heart disease or seeking a story about new, significant medical findings that may affect large numbers of people, this article demands further exploration. The best place to turn now for a greater understanding of the significance of a scientific paper is the end.

The conclusion or discussion or comment section varies in length and format from journal to journal, but whatever form or title it takes, it tells what every science or medical writer or reader wants to know: "So what does it all mean, doctor?" The answer in this article sprawls over parts of three pages. Reading it, you find that previous studies have demonstrated that the ratio of total cholesterol (TC) measured in the blood to the amount of high-density lipoprotein (HDL), one of the forms in which cholesterol is transported, serves as an excellent way to assess a person's increased risk of coronary heart disease. The new study shows that the TC/HDL ratio is as accurate as existing screening guidelines: those originally set by the U.S. National Cholesterol Education Program (NCEP I) and their updated version (NCEP II), and those set north of the border by the Canadian Consensus Conference on Cholesterol.

The paper also concludes that, while the various screening guidelines recognize the importance of total cholesterol and low-density lipoprotein (LDL), they may undervalue the importance of HDL in determining coronary risk. The authors further suggest that, while LDL concentrations may offer a better number to use in deciding whether to institute efforts to lower a person's blood lipids (e.g., diet, exercise, medications), the TC/

HDL ratio provides "the optimal lipid screening measurement because of its relative accuracy, availability, and low cost." They also criticize the Canadian guidelines for failing to explicitly integrate risk factors other than blood fats (i.e., cigarette smoking, lack of exercise) into the process of determining a person's heart risk. And they rate the NCEP II guidelines as clearly superior to the earlier version. Finally, the researchers conclude that all existing guidelines need improvement because they fail to fully incorporate the knowledge gained from the Framingham Heart Study, which for about half a century has studied heart disease among residents of a Massachusetts community and greatly enhanced medicine's knowledge of coronary risk factors.

At this point, the writer can almost certainly decide whether to pursue a story based on the journal article or drop the effort and move on to something else. If it's a go, then the writer can return to the beginning of the article, which will provide more depth and detail about the research and usually help put its findings in a broader context.

What do Grover and his colleagues offer? They note, for example, that total cholesterol and the specific lipoproteins in the blood increasingly serve as the basis for the screening and treatment programs aimed at reducing heart attacks and death. They also offer a brief review of the data that provide the scientific rationale for lipid screening. They then state that little research has been done to determine if the guidelines assessing risk accurately identify people at high risk, especially those who show no symptoms of coronary heart disease.

From there, the paper gives the source of the patients used in the study (they originally participated in something called the LRC Program Prevalence and Follow-up Studies), and describes how the patients were selected, the data analysis system used, the various screening guidelines now used in the United States and Canada, and the use in the study of a model system based on results from the Framingham Heart Study. Finally, they list their results and follow that with their comments on the findings and their implications.

The process of assessing such journal articles goes on daily among science and medical writers, for scientific papers are the lifeblood of our business. One caution, however: All journals are *not* created equal. A hierarchy exists in quality, importance, and usefulness. Science journalists learn this pecking order and what journals best fit their needs with experience, but as a general rule, don't rely on a journal unless it's peer reviewed—which means other scientists check its articles for flaws before publication.

Once you've digested the journal article, you'll have questions, often a great many. Journal articles not only list the names of the authors, they also provide the names and locations of their institutions, so you know where you can begin getting your questions answered. Start by interviewing the author(s) or someone knowledgeable in the institution's information office—in person or via telephone, fax, or e-mail. (You will find that a number of researchers prefer queries via e-mail and, indeed, respond more quickly to them than to messages left on voice mail or faxed.) But don't let your interview become your downfall.

INTERVIEWING

Reading, asking, and watching all play key roles in the interview process (or you can think of them as a single, integrated activity called RAW). You need to inform yourself, and that means reading background material on the subject. Scientists far more than politicians or cops expect people interviewing them to know the basic subject matter. Fail this, and you may get short shrift. That's exactly what happened to a bureau reporter for a prominent weekly news magazine who began his telephone interview with a geneticist by asking: "What's a gene?" In truth, the more you know about a topic—either from experience or doing some background work yourself—the better your interview will be, giving your story more depth and breadth, not to mention reducing your chances of getting the facts wrong.

For all of modern science's sophisticated concepts and technology, journalism's traditional five *W*s and an *H*—who, what, when, where, why, and how—still form the core of science reporting. Don't overlook them, particularly the how. Often the key part of bringing scientific research alive for readers involves explaining how the researchers found their result, whether it's the discovery of an ancient city or the isolation of a new gene. It helps to visit scientists in their laboratories or in the field, watch how they work, and when possible, see their results—for instance, some genetically obese mice slimmed down to house-mouse size.

So don't fly blind into an interview. You don't want to appear a dolt or waste valuable time, the researcher's or yours. Have your questions firmly in mind, and in a logical order. I write my questions out in an order that builds my base of understanding as the interview moves along. That doesn't mean I ask them dauntlessly, one after the other in plodding order, no matter what twists the interview may take. But a list, written or mental, provides a structure for your interview and helps ensure that you cover all the key points you want answered.

Ask for analogies that will help you and the reader better understand the work; some scientists will surprise you with the excellent ones they've thought up. Before you conclude your session, check your list of questions to make certain you've covered everything you need. I've found it worth-while over the years to ask two final questions: Is there anything I've missed? Is there anything you want to add? The first question sometimes yields a key fact or even an anecdote. That latter question has produced some excellent quotes, often of a philosophical nature that help nicely to explain why the article is so important and fascinating that the reader will want to read through to the very finish.

I recommend tape-recording in-person interviews. Tape-recording tele-phone interviews, however, can create legal problems. Laws and regula-tions vary among jurisdictions, and if you plan to tape someone on the phone, make certain you know how to do it within the rules. And whether in person or via telephone, you will win greater trust if you ask permission. Your tape serves as a backup. It lets you check your quotes for accuracy and pick up on facts or nuances you may have missed, and it serves as proof if your interviewee claims you erred in fact or quote. And yes, sci-entists have been known to deny saying something that a reporter has on tape. It's a human frailty not unique to politicians and sports stars.

Researchers generally deserve good marks for objectivity. Yet even top scientists may bring a hidden agenda to an interview. The possibility of profiting from their research or a fear of losing their research funding may skew their comments or color their judgment of their work's potential for benefiting humankind. Or they may be wedded too intensely to some cause, such as saving the environment or preventing child abuse, or even to some scientific theory. Early in my science writing career I attended the conference at which researchers reported the first results from studies of the lunar rocks returned by *Apollos 11* and *12*. Late one afternoon, in response to my question about a particularly puzzling finding, an eminent theoretician offered an absolutely lucid explanation, based on one of his hypotheses, and did so in the most quotable way. Fortunately, I then worked for a weekly national newspaper, so I had time to talk with other researchers. By the end of the evening it became clear that, excellent as the theory sounded, it was a theory believed only by its creator.

That tale illustrates one good reason to get the opinions of others when reporting new scientific findings.

THE VALUE OF COMMENT

Talking with others involved with or affected by some piece of research can add perspective and depth to your article. People may hold quite different views about the importance of a research project, about the ac-curacy of the work, about the future potential of the findings, either to advancing science or in practical applications. Disagreement often does not equate with right or wrong, but simply represents differing interpretations—a point important to understand, or you might make a fool of yourself. Many scientific studies are so complex, so difficult to do, that their findings do, indeed, lend themselves to two or more interpretations. Simply because a research team concludes that their work demonstrates this or that fact does not enshrine their opinion as truth. Others working in the same field may view the results quite differently, and rightly so.

Many things can skew the results of an experiment. There may be a flaw in the design of the study. Or researchers may fail to precisely follow an experiment's protocol, the rules that outline in precise detail how they intend to conduct their study. Competitors and other knowledgeable individuals often can point out such problems, real or potential, and will sometimes do so with great glee. (But remember, those from whom you seek comment may have hidden agendas as well.)

New findings are not always correct findings. Yes, sometimes new research overthrows a body of studies that scientists or physicians have long held dear. Many times, however, reports that purport to do so turn out to be simply wrong. Beware the extraordinary result, for it may well have an ordinary explanation, something as simple as a miscalculated number. Questioning other researchers gives you the opportunity to set the exciting new report—on, say, the origin of the Moon—in a broader context that will illuminate the issues and the new work's importance for your readers, viewers, or listeners. What is the current theory? How radically do the new findings depart from the old? How do others in the field regard the new explanation—as possible, plausible, potentially revolutionary, or pure pap?

I find, and other science writers I've consulted generally agree, that more scientists now seem more willing to make exaggerated claims for the significance or benefits of their findings. In press conferences, in press releases, and in interviews, some researchers will go well beyond anything said, suggested, or supported in their research papers. So, again, seeking comments on a research report helps you provide a more balanced and accurate article.

●●●●●●●●●●●●●●●●

Voicing Opinion on Science: Science Columns

TOM SIEGFRIED

Tom Siegfried is science editor at the *Dallas Morning News*, where he writes a column appearing in the weekly science section, "Discoveries." His column is distributed nationally on the KRTN news wire.

He graduated in 1974 from Texas Christian University in Fort Worth with majors in chemistry, journalism, and history, and has a master's degree from the University of Texas at Austin in journalism with a minor in physics.

In 1993 Tom received the American Chemical Society's James T. Grady–James H. Stack Award for Interpreting Chemistry for the Public. He won the 1989 American Association for the Advancement of Science–Westinghouse Science Journalism Award for Large daily newspapers. He has served on the board of the National Association of Science Writers and on the national advisory board of the Science Journalism Center at the University of Missouri.

Isaac Asimov, the renowned science writer whose voluminous output included a syndicated newspaper science column, had a wonderful attitude about writing. Although he was perhaps the twentieth century's most successful explainer of science, he had no concern with literary pretension. Or literary critics.

In introductory comments to *Nemesis*, one of his last science fiction novels, he wrote:

> I made up my mind long ago to follow one cardinal rule in all my writing—to be clear. I have given up all thought of writing poetically or symbolically or experimentally, or in any of the other modes that might (if I were good enough) get me a Pulitzer prize. I would write merely clearly and in this way establish a warm relationship between myself and my readers, and the professional critics—well, they can do whatever they wish.

To me, the column, which complements regular reporting by providing readers with explanation and insight, is the ideal vehicle for writing in the direct and friendly way that Asimov advised.

While science columns may appear on the editorial or op-ed pages, they more often are found in the science, health, or other feature sections.

Opinion columns on op-ed pages generally advocate positions on science policy issues.

Science columns appearing elsewhere, especially in science sections, often are more explanatory. These columns will describe the science behind the headlines, explore the foundations or philosophy behind aspects of science and the scientific method, and sometimes discuss speculative or offbeat science. Some science columns go beyond explanation and offer commentary or critical observations.

Whatever topic it tackles, a successful column focuses on a single idea—perhaps a new research finding in the news, or an idea emerging from several new papers. A regular newspaper column is generally fixed in length—about 700 to 750 words—so the writer has to choose what to emphasize and what to omit.

Identifying the single idea for a column to focus on is a major part of the column writing task. There are plenty of idea sources available, from news stories to science journal papers that didn't get daily news coverage, electronic archives on the Internet, and scientific meetings and workshops.

After identifying an idea for a column, the writer must then explore that idea, explain the science behind it, and discuss its ramifications and implications in a style that is fun to read.

WRITING

As with all forms of journalistic writing, the most important sentence of any column is the first one. The lead (or *lede* if you were born before 1950) performs several important tasks. It sets the stage and tone, identifies the general nature of the topic, attempts to convey the message that something interesting will follow, and welcomes the reader to read on in a nonthreatening way.

Here are some examples of leads I have used:

"Memories may be beautiful and yet, scientists are simply choosing to forget a lot of what they used to think about memory."

"Is time travel possible? Only time will tell."

"In science, there's a lot of prejudice against pride."

"When astronomers wish upon an exploding star, they wish they knew why it exploded."

"Its name is bond. Hydrogen bond."

"One of these days the Internet pornography police are going to crack down on NASA for its pictures of naked quasars."

After the Lead

The paragraphs immediately following the lead should spell out the idea the column will explore and give a hint about why this topic has come up—an indication of what's new, or perhaps a tie-in to some recent event in the news. Next, it's often wise to say why this topic or idea is important, or to mention its implications for science and its possible applications to ordinary life.

At some point, depending on the topic, it may be necessary to work in some background information, a brief recounting of the history, or scientific principles involved that a reader will need to know to follow the rest of the discussion.

Here are some excerpts from a column to illustrate some of these points.

First, the lead:

"Except for the scarecrow in *The Wizard of Oz*, every body has a brain.

"Actually, the scarecrow got along OK without one. So the question is, could a brain without a body fare so well? Antonio Damasio doesn't think so."

Next, an elaboration on the lead to convey what the column is about:

It's conceivable (in the mind, at least) to imagine a "brain in a vat," bathed in nutrients and connected by nerves to signals from the outside world. But with no body attached, it's doubtful that such a brain's mind would work very well.

"I believe that this brain would not have a normal mind," writes Dr. Damasio, a neurologist at the University of Iowa. Having a mind rather than just a brain, Dr. Damasio argues, depends on the brain's ability to represent conditions of the body to which the brain is attached. A brain without a body is mindless."

The column went on to discuss the neurologist's new book, *Descartes' Error*, which presented his insights into the connections between body, brain, and mind. He argued that mental activity, or mind, requires both brain and body, with elaborate nerve circuitry to provide the proper connections. Discussing this point further in the column required a bit of background:

That is why the brain and body are wired intricately together by a cellular network known as the peripheral nervous system. The brain sends messages via these nerves to control the body's actions. But the body also sends messages back. Every muscle, joint and organ can e-mail the brain directly. And chemicals in the body travel to the brain in the bloodstream, the biological equivalent of snail mail. . . .

In other words, the body contributes part of the content of the mind, and the mind-body division perpetrated by the French philosopher Descartes four centuries ago is fundamentally in error.

At this point, the column turned to addressing the implications of this science for today's society:

Yet in society today, from politics to medicine, the mind and body are treated distinctly.

The artificial division between physical and mental, bodily and spiritual, distorts society's perceptions of a wide range of human problems. Victims of cancer are pitied; sufferers of schizophrenia are scorned. Persevering despite physical pain is lauded; failure to cope with emotional trauma is widely regarded as personal weakness.

Then, I gave some more background on Descartes' mind-body separation:

"This distinction arose four centuries ago, in the philosophy of René Descartes, who had a brilliant mind but made the mistake of thinking it wasn't in his body. It was Descartes' error that established the separation of mind and body in Western philosophical thought. . . ."

And then, more elaboration on the current situation:

In modern times, science has demonstrated that the mind resides within the brain and that the distinction between physical and mental is illusory. But somehow another illusion has survived, the illusion that mind is only a manifestation of states of the brain, and not of the rest of the body. . . .

Dr. Damasio's insights, gleaned from the treatment of hundreds of patients with neurological disorders, have not yet displaced the old ways of thinking, even among doctors, let alone insurance agents.

After the main point is made and supported and the story about it is essentially told, the column requires a finishing touch, the denouement that closes the column out. In some cases, the closing will be a passage that comments on the ramifications of what preceded, or places it in some context, or provides an assessment of what it all means in the grand scheme of things. In that spirit, I ended the mind–body column with this paragraph:

In reality, mind, brain and body are a unified whole, in need of better medical understanding and societal appreciation. Cultural mind-sets still ostracize people whose problems are perceived to be only in the mind. Changing the collective cultural mind on these matters will be difficult. The impetus cannot come from political policy, since politicians have to pander to existing prejudices. It is left to science to illuminate the darkness of ignorance in these areas, and it will be able to do so only to the extent it can disown Descartes' error.

Generally, I think, the effective ending comments but does not advocate.

To accomplish all that a science column should accomplish, I've found it helpful to keep these points in mind:

1. *Eschew the first person.* I prefer the reader to engage the ideas and substance of the column and see no reason for the writer to get in the way.
2. *Provide some substance.* It's easy to skim over the surface of new science and treat it as a gee-whiz discovery, neat but incomprehensible. Good columns do the work of explaining some of the substance of the science.
3. *Provide credible support.* For the sake of conciseness, the general "scientists say" approach to some information in columns is unavoidable. But for key points and in new developments, it's essential to convey credibility by citing current literature or quoting authorities in the field.
4. *Establish recency and relevance.* Citing current literature is a way to convey not only credibility, but a sense that the topic involves active research. A column should reflect the vitality of science as a living, changing enterprise, and show how the science under discussion is relevant to daily life, important policy issues, or human understanding of the nature of life and the universe.

In short, science columns should do what all good science writing does, only better.

● ●

Op-Ed Writing

DAVID JARMUL

David Jarmul is associate director of communications at the Howard Hughes Medical Institute. He writes about biomedical research and science education and coordinates media outreach for the institute's grants program. Previously, he was deputy director of the news office of the National Academy of Sciences, where he was speechwriter for the president and founder of a nationally syndicated op-ed article service.

An honors graduate in history from Brown University and former Peace Corps Volunteer in Nepal, Jarmul also spent more than a decade as a freelance writer for the Voice of America, specializing in science and technology within the developing world.

He is the author of *Plain Talk: Clear Communication for International Development* (VITA) and editor of *Headline News, Science Views* (National Academy Press), two volumes of op-ed articles from prominent scientists and other experts. His own op-ed articles have appeared in the *New York Times* and other publications, and he has written about the op-ed market for *ScienceWriters, Writer's Digest, The Masthead* (National Conference of Editorial Writers), and other publications. He recently served as program director of the D.C. Science Writers Association.

Should we build the space station? Is fetal research ethical? What should happen to the national labs now that the Cold War is over?

Editorial and op-ed pages of newspapers focus most heavily on political events and other news that is generally unrelated to science. But a study that Leah Fine and I carried out found that roughly one in eight or nine of the editorials in the leading newspapers in 1991 dealt at least indirectly with scientific issues. Science writers can bring special expertise to these kinds of issues—and more science writers should consider the op-ed page as an outlet for their skills.

Larger newspapers typically have editorial boards with one or two members who specialize in such topics. Indeed, some science writers, such as Philip Boffey of the *New York Times* and Loretta McLaughlin of the *Boston Globe*, have gone on to leadership positions on editorial boards.

You don't have to be a staff writer, however, to publish opinion articles.

Most newspapers regularly publish op-ed articles by outsiders who help readers make sense of—and care about—current issues.

It's a great opportunity for science writers. The trick is to recognize that these are opinion pages, where expectations are different from the news section. The following suggestions are based on my experience helping hundreds of scientists and others to place op-ed articles in daily newspapers.

Be opinionated. It should be obvious, but for scientists and journalists trained in other writing styles, it often is not: The first rule of opinion writing is to have an opinion. You can't just describe what's happening to the ozone hole; you need to suggest what to do about it, and not just call for more research. Op-ed page editors want fire and passion on their pages—and so do readers.

Follow the news. Timing is everything. When the O. J. Simpson trial is focusing on DNA evidence, that's when you should prepare an opinion article on the social challenges posed by new genetic testing methods. If you think the media feeding frenzy over an *Ebola* outbreak is distracting us from problems like malaria, then say so while the hot zone is still hot. I once helped an authority on earthquakes to prepare an article calling for tougher building codes. We held the article until an earthquake occurred somewhere. Sure enough, disaster struck in Mexico City, and his article appeared in dozens of newspapers.

Paradoxically, opinion editors also like articles on oddball topics like whether to let young students use calculators in math class. If you can't hit the day's major topic, in other words, shoot in the opposite direction rather than belaboring a story that languished on page A23.

Limit the article to 750 words. The limit for most newspaper op-ed sections is about three double-spaced pages. Some papers have Sunday editions that run longer articles, and magazines publish stories of several thousand words.

Make a single point—persuasively. With such limited space, you're not going to teach readers the intricacies of nuclear fusion or protein folding. But you can change their minds about your main point. If you can't explain it in a sentence or two, you're trying to cover too much. Should we go to Mars or not?

Who cares? Many readers have only a passing interest in issues involving science. But they do care about their health care, the environment, their children's education, and the like. Address these concerns directly. Don't dwell on the biological wonder of oncogenes and tumor suppressor cells. Instead, explain how your proposal will speed new treatments for cancer.

Show, don't tell. As with news and feature articles, provide lots of examples to help readers understand and care about your argument. If you're arguing for "hands on" science education, for instance, describe how a single teacher used fast-growing plants to get students excited about botany. It's easier for readers to make an emotional link with the teacher than with faceless curriculum planners. They also are more likely to remember a colorful account of $125 being squandered than the details of a billion-dollar budget. This is why politicians and advertisers fill their messages with examples. You should, too.

Be a real person. You learned in journalism class to be objective and keep yourself out of the story. Science class taught you to write in an impersonal, passive voice. Now, forget those rules, or at least reexamine them. In many situations, the best way to convince a reader is with your own experiences, feelings, and views. If you are a physician who believes in euthanasia, describe your patients who suffered needlessly. Connect with readers' hearts, not just with their heads.

Other familiar journalistic rules apply to opinion writing. Use short sentences and paragraphs. Avoid jargon. Use the active voice. And, except for the policy forums in *Science* and similar settings, skip the footnotes and citations.

A handful of national newspapers accept op-ed articles only on an exclusive basis. These include the *New York Times,* the *Washington Post,* the *Wall Street Journal,* the *Los Angeles Times,* and *USA Today.* Most other papers require exclusivity only within their city or region. A growing number of newspapers have begun restricting their op-ed sections to syndicated columnists and local authors, and some have cut back the number of pages for budget reasons. So competition can be intense, especially with universities, think tanks, and others churning out op-eds on a regular basis. But a well-written, persuasively argued article on an interesting topic always stands a good chance of being accepted. You just have to apply the science of being opinionated.

PART THREE

Covering the Stories in Science

● ●

16 • • • • • • • • • • • • • • • • •

Introduction

MIKE TONER

Mike Toner is the science writer for the *Atlanta Journal and Constitution,* and the winner of the 1993 Pulitzer Prize for explanatory journalism, awarded for his series of articles, "When Bugs Fight Back," which examined the dangers of antibiotic-resistant microorganisms and pesticide-resistant insects.

A native Iowan, Toner has a bachelor's degree from the University of Iowa and a master of science degree from Northwestern University. He has worked as a reporter, editor, and photographer for United Press International (UPI) and for the *Miami Herald.* As a science writer, he has written extensively about archaeology, agriculture, environmental affairs, the geosciences, public health, the space program, and information technology.

In the chapters that follow, you will meet a handful of journalists who have, for more than a generation, shaped the style and substance of science writing in America. Whether their individual expertise encompasses the distant reaches of the universe or the inner recesses of the brain, the collective efforts of these writers and editors have helped make the frontiers of science, and the people who explore those frontiers, more accessible and more meaningful to millions of people. Many of the writers and editors you are about to meet work for major daily newspapers. Some represent news magazines, specialty publications, and broadcast media. With such a diversity of outlets, and such a diversity of interests, it should be no surprise that each of these journalists has developed a unique approach to science journalism, in part out of necessity, in part by personal choice. In some cases, individual writing styles are so distinctive that I can frequently tell, without looking at the byline on an article, who wrote it. Some individuals' interests are so characteristic that, when in the course of my own reporting, I encounter a source who says, "You know, I was just talking to another reporter from . . . ," I can often guess who got there first.

Each of the journalists you will meet in the coming chapters shares a commitment to lucid, insightful reporting. But while styles and insights reflect each person's unique lifetime of individual experiences, their work shares a common attribute—the energetic application of the one tool that no journalist should ever leave home without. "What's that?" you ask. Ah, good question. We all start life with more of it than we know what to do with. It's called curiosity.

Author Robert Fulghum could not have realized he had coined a metaphor for the ages when he wrote *All I Really Need to Know I Learned in Kindergarten*. In the years since, the book became a bestseller. The notion that we learn important social skills and values at an early age has become a cultural icon, so widely recognized that one need only invoke the partial title "All I Really Need to Know . . ." to be instantly understood. Icons notwithstanding, we never know all we really need to know, and there are some things we probably shouldn't have learned in kindergarten. Almost from the moment of birth, infants are imbued with a boundless, natural curiosity about the world around them. As they grow, their inquisitiveness quickly progresses from *whos* and *whats* to the good stuff: Why is the sky blue? Why is the grass green? Why is Mommy sad?

Like a weed, curiosity has a habit of popping up in the wrong place. It can be unruly and hard to control. It is robust and tenacious. And where one question sprouts, many more are bound to follow. The similarities to weeds may explain why society sometimes seems so determined to root out curiosity. Don't ask so many questions, inquiring young minds are told. Look what curiosity did to the cat. By kindergarten, it's: Not now, Suzy, it's nap time. Teacher doesn't have time to answer questions now, Johnny. As the years pass, there never seems to be time. By the teenage years, everyone knows better than to ask "stupid questions." Youthful energies are spent trying to prove we already know it all.

Over the years, it's been my good fortune to have known a number of teachers, mentors, colleagues, and friends who helped me learn the fundamentals of journalism. As much as I appreciate those who helped me appreciate the finer points of syntax and the elements of style, I am more deeply indebted to the few—a high school history teacher, a grizzled wire service veteran, and a few good editors—who sharpened my gnawing, some might say annoying, sense of curiosity.

All journalists have stories behind their stories—the exotic dateline, the scoop that everyone else missed, the story dictated from notes the day the computer crashed. You will read some of them in the following chapters, but the stories I remember most fondly are those that began, sometimes almost unconsciously, as a trickle of nagging little questions that, like a low-grade fever, would not be ignored.

It was nagging little questions that once sent me rummaging through the records of the Environmental Protection Agency (EPA) seeking an explanation for the continued accumulation of DDT byproducts in the environment more than a decade after the substance had been banned. Many questions later, it was clear that the byproducts were widely being used—registered by the EPA itself as "inert ingredients" in a host of pesticides.

Sometimes, curiosity has provided the nudge a busy reporter needs to put aside the press of daily business and go looking for the story behind the story. During the space shuttle's formative years, nagging little questions about the shuttle's eggshell-like tiles drew me to the oversized Vehicle Assembly Building for a firsthand look at the assembly process. The nightmare I witnessed on the assembly floor—which during some weeks saw work crews removing more tiles than they installed—made it clear that the space shuttle was never going to be the robust, quick-turnaround vehicle it was intended to be.

I often wonder, in the wake of the *Challenger* disaster, what might have happened if any of us who covered the shuttle program had been equally curious about the seemingly minor problem of faulty O-rings on the solid rocket boosters.

Sometimes, questions—once planted—can lie dormant for a long time. At one meeting of the AAAS, the annual smorgasbord of ideas for science journalists, I sat and listened with interest to University of Illinois entomologist Robert Metcalf explain the growing problem of resistance among insect pests and bacteria. The brief story I wrote at the time was published somewhere deep inside the newspaper, but Metcalf had piqued my interest in an issue that lingered for years. It would be several years before the rise of drug-resistant tuberculosis prompted me to take a deeper look at resistant organisms, from the farm to the hospital. The investigation took a while. And it took some space to publish the results. Although some editors feared that a lengthy look at such an esoteric subject might be "more than people wanted to read," the paper eventually published a total of 20 articles. My greatest satisfaction, other than seeing it in print, was the response of our readers. The hundreds of calls I received made it clear that many had read the entire series. Even better, most of them wanted to know more. The seeds of curiosity that Robert Metcalf had planted five years ago were doing quite nicely, thank you.

It is, in fact, the contagious aspect of curiosity that makes it such a powerful tool for science journalists. Readers, listeners, and viewers may appreciate our wit, our incisive grasp of complex issues, and the clarity of our delivery, but by planting the seeds of curiosity, we make our audience accomplices in the pursuit of knowledge.

At first glance, the information revolution sweeping the world might appear to be the perfect antidote for a society with a flagging sense of curiosity. Never before have so many had such speedy access to so much information. But information these days is too often designed to satiate our curiosity, not stimulate it. Whether it arrives at the front door every morning in a plastic bag, or is downloaded from the World Wide Web, the events that affect our lives are being reduced to sound bites and news briefs. Editors insist—and many believe—that busy readers have no time for "the rest of the story." The five Ws that journalists once revered are often reduced to four. Yes, we can fit the who, what, where, and when into the little space on the front page. But skip the why. That fifth W, after all, may only raise more questions than it answers.

Exactly.

One of the most satisfying aspects of science journalism is not just the opportunity to exercise one's own curiosity. It's the chance to give everyone else's curiosity a workout too. And whether their curiosity is the kind that smolders, unnoticed and unrecognized, for years, or whether it is the kind that bubbles over with instant energy, it provides the common thread that binds the journalists that you will meet in the following chapters—as well as the generation of journalists that will follow them.

17

Critical Coverage of Public Health and Government

ABIGAIL TRAFFORD

Abigail Trafford is health editor of the *Washington Post* and a syndicated columnist. Since 1986, she has been in charge of the *Post*'s weekly health section, which covers medicine, health care, biological research, lifestyle issues, and social trends. Her column, "Second Opinion," is syndicated by Universal Press Syndicate. Before coming to the *Post*, she worked for *U.S. News & World Report* from 1975 to 1986 as writer, senior editor, and assistant managing editor. From 1969 to 1974, Trafford covered the *Apollo* space program in Houston as a special correspondent for *Time* magazine and the *Washington Post*. From 1964 to 1967, she worked as a researcher for the *National Geographic*. In 1967, she went to Australia and taught at a Lutheran Mission for Aborigines in the Northern Territory.

Trafford is the author of *Crazy Time: Surviving Divorce,* and a revised edition, *Crazy Time: Surviving Divorce and Building a New Life.*

Trafford graduated cum laude from Bryn Mawr College in 1962. She received a journalism fellowship at the Harvard School of Public Health in 1980.

"No one knows exactly how serious this threat could be. Nevertheless, we cannot afford to take a chance with the nation's health."

With these words on March 24, 1976, President Gerald Ford launched one of the greatest debacles in public health history—the campaign to vaccinate every American against swine flu, the same virus that had swept the world in the great flu pandemic of 1918.

But this time, the disease was a phantom, and the program did more harm than good.

I had been a health reporter at *U.S. News & World Report* for less than a year. The story splashed over the front page and dominated the nightly news on television. It transcended traditional beats—as all big public health stories do—and involved politics and economics as well as science and medicine. Being a generalist and fairly new to the beat turned out to be an advantage, because the swine flu story broke all the rules of conventional medical reporting and would forever change the way public health is covered.

In the beginning, the story was wrapped in fanfare—the staged hoopla events that must be covered and thus build momentum for the government's program. President Ford's announcement was the starting gun. Congress quickly passed special legislation to spend $135 million to inoculate 215 million people by fall, when the epidemic was supposed to hit the United States. The signing ceremony at the White House was duly recorded by an enthusiastic press corps. A supposedly impeccable Harvard study predicted 50,000 flu deaths and costs of $6 billion if the population were not immunized. When President Ford and his family rolled up their sleeves to be vaccinated, it was an irresistible photo opportunity. Meanwhile, editors called for predictable historical pieces showing the death and mayhem caused by the 1918 flu pandemic that took 500,000 American lives. Who could be against a program aimed at saving lives?

The government's launching of the Swine Flu Program was like sending the nation to war, only this time, the enemy was a disease. In the media excitement, it seemed almost unpatriotic to raise questions.

But that, of course, is our job as chroniclers of history in real-time. Covering public health is no different from covering war. Both stories share common elements: lofty national goals and dramatic action, bureaucratic bungling and misdeeds by the "government-industrial complex," political titans and ordinary heroes.

Most important, both stories turn on one essential question: Do the benefits of waging war justify the risks and costs?

And just as important, what is the risk, the cost-benefit ratio of not mounting a campaign against a perceived threat to the nation's health?

Lesson 1. The swine flu story taught me skepticism. I was helped early on by a high-level scientist at the National Institutes of Health (NIH) who pointed out that European countries were far less concerned with the supposed return of the dreaded swine flu virus. He was not involved in the government's immunization program, but in retrospect, his perspective of doubt during those early giddy days of the program helped me shape how I was going to cover the story.

For starters, I turned to the magazine's foreign bureaus to get the official reaction of other countries to the threat of swine flu. About six weeks after President Ford's announcement, the magazine published a roundup from a dozen countries, including France, Great Britain, Germany, Canada, Australia, Japan, and the Soviet Union. The responses were devastating. Not only was the United States alone in its campaign, but officials in other countries universally questioned the threat posed by swine flu. Officials at the World Health Organization (WHO) in Geneva saw "little danger of an epidemic." Asian scientists suspected "Americans of panicking about the flu danger."

This sent me off to question a wide range of experts in medicine, virology, and public health to assess the threat of an epidemic. I found people in local health departments, in drug companies, in universities and medical centers. I also talked to experts in other countries. By June, the early warning network of flu spotters could find no cases of swine flu. Yet by October the dread disease was supposed to strike the United States. Could this whole program be much ado about nothing?

Behind the veil of federal government scientists and health officials was a growing debate over the risk of a swine flu pandemic and the need for a mass vaccination program.

That focused our coverage. While the story shifted to problems in vaccine production and liability questions, we kept returning to this fundamental point. As the magazine reported in July, "For the public, the prospect of increased costs, the malpractice question and delays in some aspects of the plan have raised doubts about the wisdom of the program. Against this background of uncertainty, a basic question remains: Just how great is the risk of a worldwide epidemic of swine flu next winter?"

It took until December for the swine flu story to play itself out. For the most part the press simply followed along. As late as November, the government organized a media blitz to boost vaccination rates. By that time, only one case had surfaced, in a telephone lineman in Concordia, Missouri, who might have contracted the disease from pigs.

The final blow came a few weeks later when government officials announced that 51 people inoculated against swine flu had developed the rare paralytic disease of Guillain-Barre syndrome. At least six people died. On December 31, the swine flu program officially ended.

Lesson 2. The swine flu story taught me to think big. First of all, the failure of the Swine Flu program was stunning. The government didn't just make a few mistakes in carrying out a high-minded goal. It was completely and catastrophically wrong.

As a story, the flawed campaign wasn't just about statistics, a little viral biology, and a band of well-meaning medical bureaucrats. It involved high stakes: the potential for great harm to the public, the spending of significant economic resources, and the fallout of a highly visible political gamble.

Lesson 3. The swine flu story also taught me compassion. Not only do bad things happen to good people, but good people can do things that turn out to be bad.

In part, this is the lesson of hubris. Once a massive government program gets started, it's hard to pull back. The fallacy of the Swine Flu Program was not in launching it. After all, President Ford had been cautious in his announcement: "No one knows exactly how serious this threat could be." The fallacy was that once the evidence had piled up, over succeeding months, that the threat was not as serious as previously feared, the government didn't change course and stop the vaccination campaign. Instead, the government apparatus tried all the harder to convince the public of the threat.

With the swine flu story, public health issues became recognized as having Big Story potential. Covering government programs and policies emerged as a separate hybrid beat combining medicine and science with politics and economics.

As the swine flu campaign demonstrated, public health stories unfold against a background of scientific uncertainty and misinformation, public confusion, and political spin. To cover public health today means making those elements of uncertainty, confusion, and spin an integral part of your coverage.

Most unsettling is the tendency sometimes for the public to get more confused as the story goes on. Superficial and incremental coverage that jerks readers back and forth over complicated issues of epidemiology, risk analysis, and medical science ultimately makes them feel whiplashed. If the public becomes too confused, it will ultimately get bored and turn off.

This is what happened in the great health care reform debate of 1994, when President Clinton tried to pass a national health care plan. In part, the confusion was fueled by opponents of comprehensive legislation. Polls showed that fewer Americans understood the Clinton plan at the end of the debate than when he announced it nearly a year earlier.

As journalists, we can't do anything about elusive facts—except to assess the current state of knowledge and put it into the context of uncertainty. We can't do anything about the high political and economic stakes—except make them a major element in our coverage. But we can do a lot about public confusion. If people don't understand the complex issues of a public health story, and they get bored, it means we haven't done our job right.

At the *Washington Post,* covering public health is broadly defined. Anything that affects the health status of Americans and involves the government—

federal and local levels—is a public health story. This gives you enormous latitude in coverage. You can unveil a particular health hazard—an outbreak of food-borne illness, for example. Or you can focus on a government program.

In recent years there's been a gold rush of stories. Some are new twists on old stories: updates on childhood immunization campaigns and tuberculosis control programs. Some are futuristic—triggered by new technology. Scientists, for example, have found a genetic defect that increases the risk of breast and ovarian cancer in Jewish women. Should the government someday launch a screening program to look for this culprit gene? What about the potential for discrimination on the job and in health insurance from genetic screening tests?

Other stories expand the public health model beyond diseases to social and legal problems such as violence and drugs. "Guns at Home: Doctors Target Growing Epidemic of Violence" ran the headline in the health section. Former surgeon general C. Everett Koop had labeled the bullet a pathogen and the American Medical Association (AMA) had called on physicians and public health officials to focus on the pathology of violence.

In 1988, the health section produced a special issue on "The Medical Side of the War on Drugs." Until then, most coverage of the war on drugs had focused on the legal system and the criminal aspects of using and dealing illegal drugs. We wanted to look at the public health response to escalating rates of illegal drug use. The peg for our 24-page section was the Omnibus Drug Act of 1988, which called for a major expansion of treatment and education programs across the country.

Nowhere was the drug war more savage than in the nation's capital, so we had our human laboratory in which to investigate the public health efforts at curbing drug use. First, we assessed the "crisis." Washington was in the early phase of the crack epidemic. We surveyed the drugs being used and analyzed the trends in usage among adults and teenagers.

The main articles focused on what the community offered—and lacked—in treatment and rehabilitation. In this way we showed how the network of centers and clinics was overwhelmed and unprepared to meet the needs anticipated with the new funding. In addition, we updated readers on the latest biomedical research on addiction. Most important, we personalized the drug war with photos and personal stories of addicts and counselors.

The product of our investigation was a comprehensive, compassionate—but skeptical—report on the public health and medical strategy to combat drug use.

In its most narrow definition, public health is about government health policies and programs such as Medicare and Medicaid. Sometimes the stories are framed as public debates such as the 1994 health care reform debate or ongoing Congressional proposals to change Medicare and Medicaid. Other times, coverage focuses on how a particular program is working. What about the potential for fraud in Medicare's expanded home-health program? Which public program looks after the homeless mentally ill in your community? Does your state have a waiver from the federal government to design its own Medicaid program?

A critical task when you cover public health is to evaluate your sources. You usually have to start with government officials. In many ways, they are like real estate agents: they are often friendly, knowledgeable, and sophisticated. They show you a lot of properties. They want you to be happy and they answer a lot of your questions. But remember, they are always working for the seller—namely, the government, and in some cases, the president, or the governor or mayor who gave them their job.

At the highest levels, public health officials are usually political appointees. They come and go with whatever administration is in power through a revolving door that links the government with academia and private think tanks. Below the political appointees are the career public health servants, who tend to stay in the government agencies.

Circling the government are several rings of sources. The first ring is made up of high-powered institutions, including schools of public health, hospital systems, medical schools, and research and policy centers. The second ring consists of advocacy and lobby groups. These include disease organizations and grass roots citizens groups, as well as promotional foundations and trade associations for hospitals and drug companies. In the third ring are the bystanders—those individuals who are most affected by a public health problem and the government's plan to deal with it. The fourth ring is the general public.

It's important to have sources in all four rings in addition to the government.

High-level officials are usually accessible (because it's part of their job). They can give you very good information along with political spin, which is part of your story. Mid-level bureaucrats and front-line public health workers are often your best bread-and-butter sources. Over the years, you can develop a relationship and mutual trust. They are essential when a story breaks for both context and information. What do the scientists in the lab who are analyzing the parasite in the water system say about the danger to the community?

To evaluate what the government is doing and saying, your first step is to go to experts in the first ring—many of whom have worked in the government in previous careers. Sources in the second ring of advocacy groups vary tremendously. Some become trusted sources of long standing. They are important not just for information but for the passion they bring to issues.

Getting to people in the third and fourth rings is also essential. Sometimes it's through serendipity: A teacher in your child's school has a cousin who lives next to the landfill.

One trap in writing about public health is to quote everyone you talk to on an equal basis in the name of "balance." But what you're really striving for is fairness and accuracy. Not every source is equal, nor should points of view be equally reported. The reader expects you to make the first cut in evaluating the major points in a story.

In most news rooms there is general agreement that public health stories are important. The problem is that they may be boring. They are known as DBS stories—dull but significant. Studded with numbers from a government tome, public health stories are too often written for constituencies such as specific disease groups or government health officials, instead of the general public.

My colleague, health section senior editor Bob Price, calls these stories "four bowlers." It means when the family gathers at the breakfast table and reads the newspaper, the story is so boring that mom, dad, and the two kids go to sleep, all four faces falling into their cereal bowls.

The challenge is to turn epidemiological trends and motherhood rhetoric into compelling stories on how the government is affecting the nation's health.

Over the years, the health section has developed what's loosely called the PPPM standard, which stands for people, power, passion, and money. The goal is to get at least three of these four ingredients into every story.

PEOPLE STANDARD

Public health is foremost about people, but officials deal in statistics. How many white males, ages 25 to 44, will die if . . . ? Fill in the blanks. The Department of Health and Human Services and state health departments crank out volumes of numbers. So do universities and private research institutes. One of my favorite tip sheets is the weekly Morbidity and Mortality Report from the Centers for Disease Control and Prevention. But phrases like "a two-fold increased risk" and "rate per 100,000" are bloodless. A story that just repeats statistics from a government report is bound to be a four bowler.

That's why it's so important to find the faces of ordinary people to illustrate the drama buried in the gray numbers of a report or the cautious (and sometimes misleading) statements from government health officials.

In the Swine Flu Program, the casualties had faces. There were reports of cases such as June Roberts, 39, of McLean, Virginia, for example, who was so paralyzed after having a swine flu shot that for a while she had trouble speaking. Personal stories like hers illustrate the catastrophic consequences of the mass vaccination program much better than any official announcement on the number of cases and deaths.

Caution: The personal story can become the whole article and not relate to the larger public health issue. As a result the anecdote just hangs out there, another hard-luck victim or gee-whiz survivor story.

That is what ultimately happened in the 1994 health care reform debate. At the eleventh hour, President Clinton brought forward two cases: Daniel Lumley, of Washington state, who was disabled in a motorcycle accident, and John Cox, of Texas, who had temporarily lacked health insurance when his wife was diagnosed with cancer. The problem was that these personal tales were not tied to any specific legislation to show how their plights might have been fixed. By this time, the public was tired of yet another health care sob story.

Tip: Get the face behind the statistic, but make sure the personal story has relevance.

POWER STANDARD

Public health stories are about the exercise of power and political leadership. Sometimes the stories shake the presidency. Certainly President Ford was tainted by the problem-ridden Swine Flu Program. President Clinton was badly damaged by the demise of his health care reform initiative—and so was his wife, who had been in charge of the effort. The Reagan administration has been faulted, most recently in an Institute of Medicine report, for its lack of leadership in protecting the blood supply in the early years of the AIDS epidemic.

Also on the political stage are the leaders in the health community—the generals in the federal government, and their troops in state and local health departments across the country, who plan and implement strategies to protect the nation's health.

When a story breaks, the initial assessment of the severity of a potential public health crisis usually comes from the leadership in the health community. The tendency for government officials is that once they have made a decision to mount a public health campaign such as the Swine Flu Program—or not mount a campaign, as was the case in deciding against stricter blood screening and testing in the early years of the AIDS epidemic—they then characterize the problem in a way that justifies their policies.

The same is true of officials in the private sector who have a stake in what the government is doing—vaccine manufacturers, for example, in the Swine Flu Program, or representatives of the AMA seeking to protect their turf in Medicare and Medicaid programs.

All this translates into political spin. It complicates your job of assessing the severity of the public health problem. This is true whether it's contamination of city water supplies or the plight of Americans who don't have health insurance. That's why you need to find sources who are knowledgeable but not directly involved in the government's program, such as the scientist who helped guide me in the swine flu story. Fortunately, they can easily be found in other government branches, or in academia or private think tanks.

Caution: The power part of the public health story can take over and dominate the coverage. The 1994 health care reform debate quickly became a political story, bogged in legislative maneuverings and covered as a battle between Republicans and Democrats.

Tip: Hang on to the story, because the more political it becomes, the more important it is for you to look beyond the partisan skirmishing to assess the severity of the "crisis" and the health impact of the program.

PASSION STANDARD

Stories have to elicit an emotional response from the reader or viewer. The public has to know why it should care that the suicide rate has tripled among 14-year-olds, or that the government may encourage the elderly to join health maintenance organizations.

A first step toward meeting the passion standard is to write about ordinary people. But the drama of the personal story has to match the drama of the larger story. *Washington Post* health writer Don Colburn described the medical saga of a homeless indigent man who was shot in front of the White House and rushed to a hospital emergency room nearby. The man ultimately died after repeated surgeries to save his life. The individual story, which included doctors and nurses as well as the victim, reflected the larger public health issue: the burden on city hospitals of treating uninsured patients who are injured by gunshot. What is the local and federal government doing, or not doing, to address this problem?

Passion comes in the writing of the story, the description of the people, and the flow of the narrative. As novelist Vladimir Nabokov put it, "Caress the detail, the divine detail."

Public health stories also have plots: Will the heroic health official vanquish the threat to the community? Will the hazard break through the country's defenses and take away the lives and dreams of those stricken in its path? Who wins? Who loses? Who pays?

Caution: One temptation is to overwrite public health stories as a soap opera or to hype the "crisis."

Tip: Assess the severity of the problem and let the substance of the story drive the drama.

MONEY STANDARD

Every year, $1 trillion changes hands in health care. As the Watergate dictum goes, "Follow the money."

Since 1960, spending on health care has ballooned, going from 5.3 percent of the gross national product to more than 12 percent in 1990, and heading for more than 16 percent by the turn of the century. The government is a dominant force, not only as a payer and provider of medical services but also as a regulator and policymaker. The government affects the fortunes of companies and individuals through the tax code and insurance regulations as well as by awarding contracts and research grants. This has given rise to a vast medical-industrial complex and a legion of special-interest groups.

Public health initiatives often translate into bonanzas for certain industries. The Swine Flu Program, for example, poured money into drug companies to manufacture the vaccine. One company produced a batch of the wrong vaccine. For weeks afterward, coverage centered on production and cost problems.

Most stories involve significant sums of money, whether they're about immunization campaigns against measles, regulations on air pollution, or legislative proposals to cut the growth of federal spending on Medicare and Medicaid. Figuring out who stands to benefit financially, and who stands to lose out, is an important part of public health coverage.

Caution: Money isn't everything. Limiting stories to dollars, without people and passion, can be just as boring as limiting stories to statistics.

Tip: Integrate economics into your broader coverage as you constantly ask yourself: Do the benefits to the general public of a government health program or policy justify the costs and the risks?

Every time the government announces a new program, a new study, a new policy, I think of the Swine Flu Program. A call for a national health plan? Free immunizations for all children? Vouchers for the elderly to purchase health insurance? Tobacco regulations? Cutbacks in the Public Health Service? I apply the swine flu lessons of skepticism, big-picture vision, and compassion. There's no special training for this beat. As Annie Dillard wrote in *Pilgrim at Tinker Creek,* "I'm no scientist. I explore the neighborhood."

It's the same with covering public health. You explore the neighborhood and take its pulse.

18 ● ● ● ● ● ● ● ● ● ● ● ● ● ● ● ● ● ● ●

Reporting on Biology of Behavior

RONALD KOTULAK

A *Chicago Tribune* science writer since 1963, Kotulak has covered many of the most important scientific advances of the last three decades, ranging from space travel to the AIDS epidemic, and from molecular biology to the genetics revolution.

He received the 1994 Pulitzer Prize for explanatory journalism for two related series on brain research: "Unraveling the Mysteries of the Brain" and "The Roots of Violence."

A graduate of the University of Michigan, Kotulak is a past president of the National Association of Science Writers. He has won a number of national writing honors, including awards from the American Psychiatric Association, the American Chemical Society, the American Medical Association, the National Society for Medical Research, the American Heart Association, and the National Mental Health Association.

In 1995, Kotulak received the American Diabetes Association's C. Everett Koop Medal for Health Promotion and Awareness.

Concerned about the growing rate of violence among young people, in 1992 the editor of the *Tribune* began planning a year-long project to bring this problem into public consciousness.

The project, called "Killing Our Children," documented the lives and deaths of all of the children aged 14 and younger who were killed in the Chicago area during 1993. By the end of the year, there were 61 such violent deaths. One of the most dramatic revelations that came out of the project was the sameness of the victims' lives. Usually, they were born to teenage mothers, had no father at home, were abused and impoverished, and lived in violent neighborhoods.

Meeting me in the hall one day, the editor wanted to know if there was something more to this tragic tale. Was anything going on in brain research that might begin to provide some answers to the underlying causes of violence? To a science writer, that's like being given the keys to the candy store. I spent the next two years writing three series—on how the brain gets built; the biological roots of violence; and how the brain heals itself.

Jack Fuller, the *Tribune* editor at the time, had the right instinct about violence. Essentially, he was looking for the "motive." The motive is 1 of 10 general journalistic techniques I use to develop the whole story. The other nine are: dumb questions, red flags, echo interviews, good writing, research, the nut graph, self-censorship, synthesis, and synergy.

THE MOTIVE

People are innately curious. They have an insatiable appetite to know why things happen, probably because it is our nature to be problem solvers. People don't want just the facts, they want an explanation of what the facts mean. Looking for the motive is becoming easier, because science is explaining more and more things.

The new tools of molecular biology are revolutionizing brain research. Scientists have learned more about the brain in the last 5 years than in the last 100. The explosion of new knowledge has led scientists to a greater understanding of the brain's biology and to the discovery of the possible causes of violence. What we thought we knew about the connection between a deprived or bad upbringing and the increased risk of criminal behavior is now being traced to the brain's chemistry. It is the biological smoking gun of violence. We are now finding molecular answers about things that happen in the brain that we could only grope for with older tools such as psychology, psychiatry, and sociology.

The new knowledge is putting to rest the old, contrived argument about which is more important, nature or nurture, genes or environment. Do we come into the world fully programmed to act the way we do, or are we blank slates waiting to be written on? The answer is that genes and environment are probably equally important. The environment affects how genes work, and genes determine how the environment is interpreted.

Here's how the motive was set up in "The Roots of Violence":

> In a startling series of recent breakthroughs, researchers probing the biology of violence have pinpointed how aggression is triggered in the brain—and how it might be prevented.
>
> Underlying the scientific quest, which has revealed genetic and environmental links to abnormal brain chemistry, is the growing suspi-

cion that society may unwittingly be feeding the nation's growing epidemic of murder, rape and other criminal acts by making childhood more dangerous than ever.

The most profound discovery, so new that parts of it have yet to be formally published in scientific literature [although by then it had been accepted for publication in a peer reviewed journal], is that genetic defects produce abnormal levels of serotonin and noradrenaline, two potent brain chemicals that researchers have successfully manipulated to make animals more violent or less violent.

Several studies also suggest that threatening environments can trigger serotonin and noradrenaline imbalances in genetically susceptible people, laying the biochemical foundation for a lifetime of violent behavior.

Such ominous trends as the collapse of the family structure, the surge in single parenting, persistent poverty and chronic drug abuse can actually tip brain chemistry into an aggressive mode—an effect that was once thought impossible.

DUMB QUESTIONS

No question is dumb if the answer is necessary to help you understand something. There's a difference between not being prepared for an interview and feeling embarrassed about asking a question that you think may sound stupid or silly. Don't pretend to know more than you do in hopes of impressing a source. You need to know the information in order to write an accurate story.

The most important tool a journalist has is the ability to ask questions. Answers always raise more questions, and you should keep asking them until you understand the subject.

My first dumb question in the brain series was; "Is there anything fundamentally new in brain research that could help explain behavior?" The purpose of such an elementary question was, first of all, to force myself to take a fresh approach to the subject, and, second, to look for new information that was quickly changing our understanding of how the brain works. The dragnet I threw out to a lot of sources paid off. One of the most profound answers I received from my first dumb question came from the University of Chicago's Peter Huttenlocher. Without any fanfare, Huttenlocher was opening the door to knowledge of the amazing changes that go on in the brain. He was, for the first time, counting synapses, the telephone lines that enable brain cells to communicate. They are so small and so numerous that they had previously defied a scientific census.

From autopsies of fetuses to oldsters, he took samples of brain cells about the size of the head of a pin. Each sample contained about 70,000 neurons. He found that synaptic connections grow at an enormous rate in the fetus and the newborn infant.

When synaptic construction is finished, the entire brain has about 1,000 trillion connections. But after that they begin a gradual decline. By about age 10 or so, half the connections have died off, leaving about 500 trillion that last through most of life.

"I stumbled on the whole thing," said Huttenlocher, who launched the census about a decade ago. "It was something that nobody expected. It took quite a long time until people began to accept that this really happens."

Huttenlocher's answer gave rise to a second dumb question. If synapses go through such astonishing changes, what happens to brain cells? Interviews with other scientists turned up a similar explosion in numbers, but for brain cells it occurs during fetal development. From conception to about halfway through fetal life, brain cells grow from 1 billion to about 200 billion. Then they begin to die, leveling off at about 100 billion at birth, the number that remains throughout life.

Another dumb question: What is the purpose of this tremendous growth and decline in brain cells and their connections? Both phenomena are examples of genetic frugality. Humans do not have anywhere near enough genes to make a fully operational brain at birth. So an overabundance of brain cells and synapses are produced, and the brain then has to learn how to make itself work.

A surplus of brain cells ensures that there are enough available for the awakening body—heart, muscles, lungs, eyes, and so on—to plug into. Brain cells compete for the jobs. It's as if they all come out of the same mold but have to learn different jobs, depending on where they find themselves. Those that don't connect die off. There is some thought that the extra cells also give the brain the ability to evolve new capacities, such as language and abstract thinking.

The more dumb questions I asked, the clearer became the picture of how the brain gets built. Connections between brain cells undergo a fate similar to the cells, but it occurs after birth. Twice as many are made to guarantee that a newborn will be able to receive input from any environment it is born into—whether Borneo or Boston—and to adapt to the food, language, and culture.

After enough questions came the enlightenment: The outside world shapes the brain's architecture. The connections that do not become part of the structure perish. The outside world comes in through the senses—vision, hearing, smell, touch, and taste—teaching the brain what to become.

RED FLAGS

Red flags can pop up in your mind when you have doubts about the trustworthiness of a scientific claim, or when a claim is denounced because it goes against accepted dogma. The history of science and medicine is replete with dogmas and procedures that were once accepted but later abandoned because they turned out to be false. Likewise, new findings that were at first discredited later turned out to be true.

Science is not carved in stone. It is a process of discovery and continual change. Mistakes are made, and occasionally there is even scientific fraud. Ultimately, however, if a finding cannot be reproduced, it is not believed.

The initial report linking brain chemistry to violence was viewed as heretical. Here's how that story unfolded in "The Roots of Violence":

> The first clue that human aggression and violence were influenced by brain chemistry occurred in 1976 when Marie Asberg, chief of neuroscience at the Karolinska Hospital in Stockholm, documented a link between low serotonin and violent suicides.
>
> These involved people who killed themselves with guns, knives, ropes or by jumping from high places. Asberg found that they have a tenfold greater risk of violent death as other equally depressed people who have higher serotonin levels.
>
> Her findings were met with disbelief and hostility. Few people thought that there could exist any correlation between a brain chemical and something as personal as suicide, Asberg recalled.
>
> "For most people, ending your days is more of a philosophical question and a personal question; not a biological question," she said.

One safety net that helps ensure the accuracy of new findings is peer review. Peer review means that an article submitted to a scientific journal is published only after it has been judged by experts to be valid.

But when you're chasing cutting-edge research, sometimes you find yourself ahead of peer review journals. Then you can do one of two things to make sure the information is scientifically sound. The first is to wait for an article to be accepted for publication in a peer reviewed journal. The second is to conduct your own peer review. I chose the first option in dealing with the sensitive subject of genes and aggression.

After years of controversy and difficulty getting people to accept a link between genes and violent behavior, in 1994 a paper was accepted in a peer reviewed journal reporting a groundbreaking link between a relatively common gene mutation and aggression. Here's how I reported it in "The Roots of Violence":

But scientists at the National Institute of Alcohol Abuse and Alcoholism have made an even more far-reaching discovery—a mutant gene that appears to be widespread in the populations so far studied that lowers serotonin levels and increases aggression. The NIAAA scientists, headed by Markku Linnoila, are expected to report their findings in a scientific journal early next year.

I was able to incorporate their findings into "The Roots of Violence" because their report had been peer reviewed and accepted for publication in the *Archives of General Psychiatry*.

You can conduct your own peer review by calling experts and asking them to assess the material either on or off the record. If you're interviewing scientists on a controversial topic, ask them who their worst enemies are, and then call them. It is important to keep an open mind about research results and to view them with a bit of healthy skepticism.

ECHO INTERVIEWS

The better you understand something yourself, the better able you will be to write your story. One of the techniques I find most effective to help me understand new information I call the echo interview. This technique is nothing more than basic feedback. By repeating in your own words key points that a scientist has made and asking him or her if your interpretation is correct, you get an immediate check on how well you are grasping the material. If your paraphrase is incorrect, ask him or her to explain the point in simpler terms.

In one interview, I was trying to find a simple way to describe the relationship between two important brain messengers and violence. I asked: "If serotonin is the brake for aggressive impulses, is noradrenaline the accelerator that can drive them out of control?" "That's right," the scientist said. This is how the interview was reflected in the series:

> "If people are leaving you alone and your brakes are lousy—your serotonin is low—it's okay. You're not going to get into trouble because your car is moving very slow," said Dr. Emil F. Coccaro of the Medical College of Pennsylvania. "But if people are starting to agitate you and your accelerator starts to rev, and your brakes are bad, you can't stop yourself. You lash out."

GOOD WRITING

Good writing is the key to making science understandable. Analogies, anecdotes, examples, and metaphors are very effective in helping people understand new ideas and concepts. They allow you to translate complex information into examples that people experience in their everyday lives.

Example:

> Normal aggression has a set point, like body temperature, which is regulated by brain chemicals. Most people are born with a balance of these chemicals that enables them to react to events in reasonable ways. But changing that set point can either increase aggression or lower it.

RESEARCH

My research involves reading about a specific topic as much as possible in journals, press releases, Medline, and other sources. The next step is tracking down leads and interviewing as many scientists as necessary to enable me to fit all the pieces of the puzzle together. I interviewed about 80 scientists for each of the three brain series.

I tape-record all my interviews and transcribe them. Although transcribing can be tedious, I find it extremely valuable. Listening to a tape, typing the words, and reading them on the screen provide a triple dose of reinforcement for learning new information. I not only get great quotes from the transcripts, I invariably learn things I missed during the interview. I also find transcripts useful when my research changes the direction of the story. Information that I may not have written down in my notes, because I didn't think it was important at the time, is there in the transcript. One of the biggest advantages of this kind of research is that it enables me to become familiar enough with a subject to write about it in my own words.

Example:

> In probing the biology of violence, scientists have found it useful to take an age-old question—Why do some kids turn out bad?—and pose it like this:
>
> What happens inside a developing brain to turn a child into a killer?
>
> Their discoveries are shedding new light on the epidemic of violence that is being inflicted on children and that they are inflicting on others.
>
> Consider the infant brain: its main job is to figure out the kind of world it will have to live in and what it will have to do to survive.
>
> For millions of American children, the world they encounter is relentlessly menacing and hostile. So, with astounding speed and efficiency, their brains adapt and prepare for battle. Cells form trillions of new connections that create the chemical pathways of aggression; some chemicals are produced in overabundance, some are repressed.

THE NUT GRAPH

Because science articles tend to be complex, anecdotal leads and other writing devices are useful for attracting the reader's interest. But somewhere close to the top of the story, the "nut graph" a summation paragraph, should give the reader a basic idea of what the story is about and why he or she should continue reading it.

Here's the nut graph I used in the series about how the brain gets built: "At the core of the revolution in brain research is the 'plasticity factor,' a term that scientists use to describe the brain's amazing ability to constantly change its structure and function in response to experiences coming in from the outside."

SELF-CENSORSHIP

Self-censorship usually occurs when writers or editors base their evaluation of a story more on emotion or preconceived notions than on facts or reason.

When federally sponsored meetings to discuss the "Genetics of Crime" are canceled because of opposition to such research, how do you handle this hot topic? Most people are delighted with the new knowledge about the brain. But some people don't believe it, and others are afraid of it, convinced that such research is a plot to discriminate against some groups or gain mind control over others. They are fearful of genetic screening tests that may unfairly stigmatize people.

Part of the answer to handling controversial topics is fairness. Violence, after all, affects all socioeconomic, racial, and ethnic groups, so everyone stands to benefit from the new findings. The research should be done openly. But it is important to point out possible dangers from new research as well as potential benefits.

Here's one example of how I put the role of biology in violence into perspective:

> The link between brain chemistry and violence "is extremely interesting and fascinating," said Marie Asberg, chief of neuroscience at the Karolinska Hospital in Stockholm. "But it's also a bit dangerous.
> "It's the power in it. If we know the biology of how aggression works, we might also be able to manipulate it in ways that we don't like. We don't want to stigmatize people as aggressive . . . because of their brain chemistry. But we do want to use it to help them."

At the *Tribune,* there were no questions about the scientific accuracy of the information, but there was a sensitivity among editors about making sure the information was presented fairly. After the violence series ran, only three readers called or wrote to complain that they thought the articles portrayed African Americans in a poor light. Scores of other readers said the new information gave them a better understanding of the environmental and genetic factors involved in aggression.

SYNTHESIS

Because related research is done at many institutions and by many different investigators, science writers are increasingly called on to be synthesizers. They have to make sense out of information that is frequently complex, controversial, and contradictory. Individual reports are often confusing. Are electromagnetic waves dangerous or harmful? Is coffee good or bad? Do silicone breast implants cause autoimmune disorders or are they safe? Science writers have to be creative, putting together individual reports in fresh new ways to give readers a better understanding of a topic.

It's like putting together the pieces of a puzzle. Researchers themselves, because they are so busy and narrowly focused, often see only their own piece of the puzzle. The job of the science writer is to find and put together as many of the pieces as possible to provide readers with a perspective of the whole picture.

Here's an example of how I summed up a number of different research findings:

> The first three years of a child's life are critically important to brain development. Unfortunately, for a growing number of children, the period from birth to age three has become a mental wasteland. Society needs to focus on this period if it is to do something about the increasing rates of crime.

Such a synthesis was only possible after conducting dozens of interviews, reading tons of journal articles, and realizing that children growing up in bad environments usually are ignored by society until they enter school. Then it is often too late.

SYNERGY

Synergy means putting something together to make the whole greater than the sum of its parts. It goes a step beyond synthesis. Piecing together the results of related research enables me to develop new insights into a subject. When I do this I usually check my interpretation with experts in the field to see if they agree.

Here is an example from "The Roots of Violence" of how I developed new concepts from my research and explained their implications:

> New insights about the causes of violent behavior are also challenging the notion that violence is something a person always does on purpose and should be punished for.
>
> Now it appears that many types of violence, especially impulsive violence, may be just like other mental disorders—a dysfunction of the brain—that can be treated and prevented.

I checked my interpretation with a researcher. He agreed with it and gave me the following good quote:

> "We view people who are violent in the same way we used to view people who were mentally ill. In the old days, schizophrenics, manic-depressives and others were thought to be bad people who had to be punished," said Dr. Stuart Yudofsky of the Baylor College of Medicine in Houston.
>
> "The brain is left out of the whole paradigm in the criminal justice system," he said. "We got nowhere punishing mentally ill people, and we're getting nowhere with our population of criminals. We're just building more prisons."

Bringing new concepts like this to light is vital to our understanding of complex issues, and is for me one of science writing's greatest rewards.

19

Covering Infectious Diseases

LAURIE GARRETT

I never studied journalism or writing in college; those are crafts I
continue to learn every day. I majored in biochemistry, at UC
Berkeley, and did graduate studies in cellular immunogenetics
there.

While still in graduate school I started working as a science
reporter for KPFA-FM in Berkeley. What began as a hobby became
an obsession, prompting diversion to journalism. Over the last 15
years I have covered science, medicine, and other news for Pacifica
Radio, various non–American broadcast outlets, and National Public
Radio. I am currently a medical writer for *Newsday*. I've written
articles for many magazines and have co-authored several books. In
1994–95, I wrote a bestselling *The Coming Plague: Newly Emerging
Diseases in a World out of Balance.*

Some of my awards include the 1996 Pulitzer Prize for
Explanatory Journalism, "Ebola"; Finalist, 1996 Pulitzer Prize for
International Reporting, "Ebola"; The 1996 Madeliene Dane Ross
Award from the Overseas Press Club for Best Reporting in Any
Media on the Human Condition, "Ebola"; AAAS Special Citation for
Outstanding Journalism, 1995; Alumna of the Year, University of
California in Santa Cruz, 1996; and the Peabody and Armstrong
awards. I am co-producer of a 4-hour documentary on *The Coming
Plague* for Turner Original Productions.

On a sweltering, dusty September morning in 1994 I stepped out of the
Holiday Inn in Surat, India, and signaled to the sleepy doorman. Bored
because, saving myself, there were no customers staying in the large American hotel, the Indian man had taken to counting the flies that buzzed
about his turbaned head.

"Madame is in need of assistance?" the doorman queried, careful to
avert his head slightly so that he and I did not share breathing space.

"Yes, Madame is in need of assistance. A taxi, please."

The doorman's face revealed momentary desperation. His arm swung outward in a demonstrative gesture, and he said, "But Madame can see, no taxis are working in these days."

I glanced across the expanse of cracked, flood-damaged tarmac, the unkept gardens of hibiscus and palms, and the empty street beyond. Emptiness. The entire metropolis, for as far as I could see, was abandoned. Being there was unnerving; however, this setting didn't really take me by surprise. I was here to cover a twentieth century outbreak of bubonic plague—a spreading infestation of *Yersinia pestis,* the bacteria behind the highly contagious and deadly disease. For a moment the tall Sikh doorman and I avoided eye contact, trying to conjure a solution. Then he clapped his hands together once and cried, "Madame is willing to take a rickshaw, no?"

"Sure," I said, without enthusiasm, recalling all the motorized three-wheeler rickshaws I'd seen tumble and crash in Calcutta. The doorman dashed off to a large intersection and returned 10 minutes later, bouncing in the seat of a dubious-looking rickshaw. Determining that the driver, who wore a bandanna mask, knew enough English to strike a "special plague rate" for his services, I paid him the equivalent of a week's wages ($10) and climbed aboard what was essentially a small motorcycle towing a bench that rested atop bicycle wheels.

An hour later, assuming an air of authority, I pushed past Surat Civil Hospital security and Indian army personnel armed with submachine guns, and walked into the pneumonic plague ward. The vast room housed some 100 hospital beds, evenly divided between men's and women's by a wall made of heavy cloth. Suspended from the vaulted ceiling were rows of fans that rotated furiously, creating eddying currents of warm air. The room reverberated with deep coughs, moans, and the shuffling of nurses' sandaled feet on the polished concrete floors.

At the ward's entrance, in full view of all the patients, sat a physician who wore three masks: a standard surgical tieback mask; over that, a form-fitting gauze face covering; and atop all that, a rubber fitted mask originally designed to screen out chemicals such as asbestos and paint fumes. I smiled behind my red bandanna as I greeted the agitated physician. Sweating profusely under all those layers, he described his previous two hellish sleepless days and nights of battling the *Yersinia pestis* bacteria with little more than oral tetracycline and TLC, often losing as his patients made their final gasps for air, coughing up contagious sputum and blood.

Though I have covered numerous epidemics and written a book on infectious diseases, as I stood on that ward staring into the panicked faces of plague victims, I couldn't believe that I was in the midst of an outbreak of the organism that had spawned the Black Death of the fourteenth century in Europe and the Plague that claimed nearly half of London's population 300 years later.

I also was astonished that I was alone, rather than in the company of dozens of competing science and medical reporters from throughout the world. For three days I scoured Surat for quotes and clues. How, I wanted to know, had an organism long thought to have been eradicated from the subcontinent managed to emerge in bubonic form (via, of course, rats and fleas); spread into an epidemic despite its vulnerability to antibiotics; and then make its way from a remote rural region of Maharashtra state to the northern state of Gujarat, a day's train-ride away, erupting into a pneumonic epidemic in Surat?

It was a chilling story. It was a heartbreaking story. And, from a strictly journalistic viewpoint, it was a spectacular story, replete with aspects of ecology, the greenhouse effect, basic biology, human behavior, politics, economics, and epidemiology. The Maharashtra environment, following a massive earthquake, spawned the reemergence of *Yersinia pestis* after a 30-year hiatus. The greenhouse effect is thought to have been responsible for extraordinary monsoons that immediately preceded the Surat outbreak.

Months later, operating in a far more competitive environment, I chronicled the response of an international medical team to an outbreak of the *Ebola* virus in Kikwit, Zaire. In that case reporters and television crews flocked to Zaire's capital from every corner of the planet, satellite dishes in tow. The coverage was intensely competitive and timely. But it was not executed by science reporters: Rather, it was the work of general assignment and political correspondents. As a result, it reflected obvious concerns about whether the Zaire government was maintaining proper quarantine measures, *Ebola* death tolls, and much-amplified minicontroversies over epidemic control activities.

Absent were the genuinely fascinating core issues in the *Ebola* story: Why had the virus resurfaced after a 19-year hiatus? From whence had it come? How had an individual emergence become amplified into a full-fledged epidemic? How was the social and cultural fabric of Kikwit affected by the epidemic?

Why weren't science writers there? After all, more than 10 years ago, I heard David Perlman, science editor of the *San Francisco Chronicle,* who is one of the country's top science journalists, describe infectious disease—AIDS in particular—as *the* story of the late twentieth century. In a 1983 panel discussion on science journalism, Perlman went on to explain why, in an era of nuclear weapons research, space exploration, genetic engineering, spectacular medical advances, astounding subatomic particle discoveries, and the big-bang theory, the emergence of the human immunodeficiency virus should rank number one on the science hit parade. It boiled down to surprise and contradiction, Perlman explained. Such things simply weren't supposed to happen in the modern era. AIDS forced reassessment of all the biological dogma of the previous four decades.

Science, and perhaps science writers, have been slow to accept that reality.

Our profession has failed to consistently demand proof, not only that the new innovations of biology and medicine work, but also that the old dogmas and remedies were standing the tests of time. We should always ask, "Does this old premise stand up to current scrutiny, based on advances in basic scientific understanding? If not, why not? And what are the larger implications for the field as a whole?"

Few events flesh out answers to such questions as rapidly as epidemics. The heightened emotionalism, the urgency, the make-do-with-minimal-resources science, multidisciplinary investigation, and essential gumshoe detective work make for an unusually raw environment. There is little time for peer review, bureaucratic haggling, or academic debate over long-standing biological or epidemiological theory. For the inquisitive reporter, such moments are golden, offering unusual insight into medical research in a time of crisis.

But history only rewards the well-prepared mind, and curious journalists who lack sophisticated understanding of epidemiology, microbial biology, epidemic control, and human behavior are likely to find themselves treated by scientists and local authorities as pests in the best cases, enemies and vectors of contagion's spread in worst-case scenarios. For this reason, science writers should be the first choice to cover an epidemic.

Of all sciences, epidemiology is the slipperiest. Because it appears to be mere detective work, some reporters well-versed in the arts of fact-chasing mistakenly assume that field epidemiology requires little more than sweat and gumshoe work. But unlike journalistic inquiry, which usually follows leads as they happen to emerge, epidemiology requires a strict methodology that must be adhered to if there is to be any hope that its conclusions will stand up to scientific scrutiny. When epidemiology is ignored during an epidemic, either for lack of resources or political will, nearly every aspect of the outbreak's origins, dimensions, and impact remain forever controversial.

Such is the case today with Surat's plague epidemic, the origins of the global HIV pandemic, the current spread of cholera, and hundreds of other disease emergences. Well-trained journalists can help fill in the gaps, often with surprising results. For example, the Surat epidemic and India's terrifying HIV scourge have gone virtually untouched by the rigors of professional epidemiology. But through questioning by journalists cognizant of basic epidemiology, the realities of both outbreaks are emerging in the public's consciousness, forcing political action.

The Surat plague was denounced as a "non-plague" by the Hindi language press and by scientists located hundreds of miles away from the epidemic. Independent journalistic scrutiny revealed a disinformation campaign aimed at proving that Pakistan, India's bitter Islamic enemy, had spread false word of plague in order to bring down the Indian economy. At the same time, journalists also revealed that three independent non-Indian laboratories had confirmed the presence of *Yersinia pestis*.

Similarly, politics has obscured every aspect of India's HIV epidemic. But carefully documented reporting, coupled with broad-scale blood testing, has revealed that the virus is spreading so rapidly on the subcontinent that even the World Health Organization (WHO) has predicted that India's AIDS epidemic will by 2010 outstrip the cumulative total of all sub-Saharan African cases. And that must be viewed as conservative.

There is no greater or more crucial role we members of the fourth estate can play than to demand proof. All too often, for economic or political reasons, governments—local or national—cover up or downplay microbial outbreaks. On the other extreme, there are forces that seek to exaggerate epidemic potentials, assign responsibility to scapegoats, or label diseases according to human categories (e.g., "gay plague," "Navajo flu," "Spanish influenza"). The burden for journalists is to find a middle ground in the midst of public panic, avoiding sensationalism, racism, scapegoating, or denial.

It's not easy.

But respect for the microbes, rooted in a strong understanding of their biology and ecology, can offer powerful guidance.

KNOW YOUR MICROBES

It is essential that you have a comfortable level of knowledge of microbiology. It isn't enough to know the differences between bacteria and viruses; you must have an appreciation for the ecological constraints and natural histories of the key pathogens. For most reporters, this will require a little homework. It is not necessary to memorize the life cycles of *Plasmodium falciparum* and Leishmania, the malarial and kala azar parasites. Relax.

It is, however, crucial that you acquire a comfortable, broad sense of the range of classes of pathogenic organisms, their modes of human transmission, the strategies microbes can deploy to produce illness in human hosts, the tactics used by the human immune system to counter invading microorganisms, and—where they exist—the categories of treatment.

KNOW YOUR SOURCES

Most public health scientists and physicians are wary of the media, particularly during epidemics. They've been burned. And they detest sensationalism. Trying to cultivate sources during an epidemic usually fails, compelling you to cover little more than the official story.

Probably the single most important source is your local public health officer. Take him or her out to lunch, tour the public health headquarters, get to know staff members, and develop rapport today. Don't wait for a local crisis. Similarly, you should establish close links with your state epidemiologist, toxicologist, and chief medical officer.

Nationally, the Centers for Disease Control and Prevention (CDC) is the whole ball game. Most CDC scientists are reluctant to speak to reporters—even old friends—without clearance from the extremely understaffed CDC press office. During an epidemic, that office is swamped by hundreds of queries, and yours is likely to be lost in the deluge unless press officers are familiar with you and your work. Again, developing a rapport in advance of need is advised.

Internationally, the WHO in Geneva is key. There, too, you are compelled to deal with press office gatekeepers. One shortcut, given time zone constraints, is to fax your request for an interview to the WHO press office in Washington at (202)331-9097.

Obviously you should also develop academic sources, primarily through medical and public health schools. And, finally, a good strong personal library of source books (see the suggested list in the appendix) can be the key to whether you sound like a local sports reporter ("So, could you tell me what a cryptosporidium is?") or an ace science writer ("Was this exposure due to your standard bovine transmission, fecal or water, or something new on the crypto front?")

PROPER PRECAUTIONS

The best rule of thumb is, "When in doubt, do as the scientists do." If the CDC team members are wearing latex gloves and surgical masks, you should follow suit.

You should also avoid overprotection. Wearing a mask when there is no evidence of airborne transmission of a microbe could contribute to panic among local people.

BEWARE OF INSTANT EXPERTS AND HASTY ANSWERS

Every epidemic has had its crackpots, conspiracy theorists, naysayers, shady politicians, and scaremongers. It's your job to demand a high level of scientific rigor from all sources who represent themselves as experts, whether or not they are part of the official investigation.

It is also important to remember that the official investigators aren't always correct. Toxic shock syndrome was understood by a tiny group of academic scientists long before the CDC yielded, acknowledging that the solution had been found. Prior to that, some scientists within the CDC sought to besmirch the reputations of the academic researchers.

AIDS COVERAGE

All these considerations were seen during the early years of the AIDS epidemic, and there continue to be errors, in my opinion, in reporting on that disease. The early mistakes were legion and have been described in detail elsewhere (see, for example, James Kinsella's *Covering the Plague.*) A few key points are worth underscoring.

Nearly all epidemics start small. The numbers of people afflicted are rarely the key factors likely to determine whether the microbes take hold on a large scale. But AIDS was initially ignored by most reporters in part because the first year's toll was small and scattered. Epidemics often begin among members of a distinct subpopulation of society, typically its poorest members. There is a tendency in many news rooms to say, "Yeah, that's a bummer for those people, but well, you know, it's them." Dismissing an odd microbial occurrence on the basis of who is afflicted is dangerous, as well as morally dubious.

In the case of AIDS, the *who* issue was actually critical to understanding the significance of the small numbers initially seen. Anybody who took a few minutes to discover what was going on sexually in the gay community from 1975 to 1981 instantly realized that, if the strange new ailments were due to a sexually transmissible agent, a staggering epidemic was in the offing.

The media clearly succumbed to the panic and fear response during the early days of AIDS. Reporters were afraid to touch their gay sources; camera operators refused to go on television shoots involving AIDS; some journalists reported sympathetically on vigilante actions and protests leveled by communities against gay men and children with AIDS; some reporters wore gloves during their interviews and washed up as soon as they left the rooms of AIDS patients.

Far too many general assignment reporters covered the story entirely as a sociopolitical crisis, utterly ignoring the microbe. Conversely, too many science reporters felt uncomfortable covering the social dimensions of the epidemic and resigned themselves to an endless series of test tube stories based on National Institutes of Health (NIH) research. Both extremes were a disservice to readers.

Prejudice definitely affected coverage. Homophobia, fear of IV drug users, and dismissive attitudes towards Haitians and Africans allowed some journalists to convince themselves that the story was still small, even as the U.S. death toll grew to 50,000, because the epidemic hadn't reached "the general public." It is inconceivable that news organizations would have allowed such a "general public" issue to cloud coverage of, say, 50,000 dead Americans who succumbed over a period of four years, all of whom were elderly people of Scandinavian descent.

Crackpot theories have consistently abounded—claims of cures, non-HIV causalities, treatments, vaccines, and conspiracies. Far too many reporters have been suckered in, some several times. All too often journalists have used different standards for measuring the credibility of traditional lab-based science versus maverick or quack claims.

For example, one of the most common excuses used by mavericks for lack of published evidence to support their claims is that there is a conspiracy of suppression by members of the scientific elite. There have been cases throughout science history of heretical views being quashed for years by the establishment, only to receive vindication decades later. On the other hand, feigned or delusional victimization provides a convenient out when data are absent or deficient. I have found over the years that sincere scientific mavericks have plenty of data to demonstrate their hypotheses, and are more than willing to share experimental results with a reporter and mutually agreed-on outside scientists.

It is also true, however, that by the late 1980s most science reporters were content to cover the "official story" of AIDS–related science, lending far too much credibility to a handful of well-funded labs in Bethesda, Paris, London, and so on. By 1990 a strong protest movement was developing among both AIDS activists and scientists who felt that an HIV dogma was emerging prematurely, excluding new perspectives from corners outside virology. By 1992 that dissident voice had become mainstream, and the entire NIH research effort was restructured by Congress.

REPORTERS ARE HUMAN

One facet of epidemic coverage stubbornly resists easy solution: grief. People suffer and die at the behest of the microbes, often in painful and gruesome ways. Husbands are left widowers; children are orphaned; funerals are convened; and communities are devastated. No caring human being can witness such events without experiencing wrenching emotions. If you weren't moved by the pain of others, you wouldn't be much of a human being. But if you allow that emotionalism to interfere with your ability to get the news, you won't be much of a journalist.

20

Reporting on Neuroscience

SANDRA BLAKESLEE

Sandra Blakeslee, a free-lance science writer who lives in Santa Fe, New Mexico, writes regularly for the *New York Times* science department as a special contributor and West Coast science correspondent. She also writes for numerous magazines and has co-authored three books. Educated at Northwestern University and the University of California at Berkeley, Blakeslee was a Peace Corps volunteer in Borneo before joining the *New York Times*, where she got her journalism training as a news assistant.

The bimonthly *Proceedings of the National Academy of Sciences* (*PNAS*) has just arrived on your desk. You glance at some of the neuroscience abstracts. Which is the most interesting? Which of the following would arouse your curiosity enough to pick up the phone and check out the story?

- Retrograde axonal transport of glial cell line-derived neurotrophic factor in the adult nigrostriatal system suggests a trophic role in the adult.
- Incorporation of reconstituted acetylcholine receptors from Torpedo in the xenopus oocyte membrane.
- Apoptosis and necrosis: two distinct events induced, respectively, by mild and intense insults with N-methyl-D-apartate [NMDA] or nitric oxide/superoxide in cortical cell cultures.
- Two distinct oscillators in rat suprachiasmatic nucleus in vitro.
- Intrinsic changes in developing retinal neurons result in regenerative failure of their axons.

My first choice might be the oscillators in rat brain. I've long been interested in circadian rhythms, what makes them tick. This could be a nice way to get into a story on biological clocks.

I would also check out the story on apoptosis and necrosis—two hot topics in neurobiology. The abstract also mentions NMDA and nitric oxide, which are important neurotransmitters that are implicated in numerous brain functions. While this abstract is not likely to produce a stand-alone story, I would save it in my apoptosis file for future reference. All of this, of course, depends on knowing that apoptosis refers to cell death; necrosis to tissue death; and that nitric oxide has been tentatively linked to aggressive behavior.

Obviously, to write about the brain you need to learn a huge vocabulary of specialized terms. You should be familiar with brain anatomy and know the major landmarks—the different lobes of the cortex, the cerebellum, amygdala, brainstem, hippocampus, and so on. Which of these brain regions is impaired in the various neurological diseases? Where is the damage done in Parkinson's and Alzheimer's disease, and what has gone awry in schizophrenic and autistic brains? How is the developing brain wired up, and what are the molecules that determine brain structure? How is the visual system wired up before and after birth? What are the critical periods in postnatal development?

You need to know brain chemistry, including all the neurotransmitters. The old standbys like serotonin, norepinephrine, and dopamine are being joined by new molecules like nitric oxide and even carbon monoxide.

You should know how receptors work (the old lock and key analogy) for both transmitters and hormones. And then how signals are passed via so-called second messengers from the cell membrane to the nucleus.

It helps to be familiar with all the components of a nerve cell—the mitochondria, ribosomes, the cytoskeleton, and cell adhesion molecules. How do axons fire their action potentials, and what happens at the synapse? There are transporter molecules and storage vesicles that underlie many important cognitive functions.

The brain also traffics in peptides—small protein fragments that can pack a behavioral wallop. The immune system is active with its own cast of characters that can create havoc or peace of mind.

After learning all these basic components, you need to understand how the brain is organized functionally. What regions talk to what other regions? How does the thalamus connect to the cortex, and what does this mean? What parts of the cerebellum hook up to the cortex and for what purpose? How do assemblies of cells communicate? Neuroscientists are fond of saying "cells that wire together, fire together." What role do brain oscillations play in this orchestration?

Finally, you should be familiar with neural networks and fuzzy logic. How are scientists modeling the brain and where might this lead us?

I haven't mentioned many other fascinating topics—neural plasticity, spinal cord repair, stroke, and memory, to name a few. When you write about the human brain you are dealing with dozens of specialties in medicine, psychology, basic research, and philosophy.

So where do you begin? How do you learn all this background so that your stories resonate?

I can recommend two textbooks for getting started. First is *The Principles of Neural Science,* by Eric Kandel, James Schwartz, and Thomas Jessell. It is clearly written, beautifully illustrated, and accurate. Second is *The Cognitive Neurosciences,* edited by Michael Gazzaniga. It's a compendium of current topics in cognitive research—how we know what we know, and why it matters. There's even a chapter on consciousness.

Another strategy is to attend meetings. In covering the brain, I try to attend the meetings of the Society for Neuroscience, the Cognitive Neuroscience Society, the American Academy of Neurology, and a few other smaller events.

The Society for Neuroscience is the world's largest gathering of scientists. It drew nearly 23,000 researchers to San Diego in late 1995, and it is almost impossible to cover single-handedly. But there are ways to get the most out of the meeting. First, get the abstracts early and read through them. The Society press office puts out excellent lay summaries on scores of topics. You can find good stories there.

I like to prepare one or perhaps two stories in advance of the meeting and have my paper run them concurrently with the meeting. Then I feel less pressure to deliver daily stories and can spend time wandering the poster sessions (always good for hints on upcoming news) and sitting in on half-day seminars and special lectures.

Another strategy is to take classes designed for science journalists. One of the most valuable experiences in my career was the five weeks I spent studying basic neuroscience at the Woods Hole Marine Biological Laboratory on Cape Cod. Reporters are invited to audit graduate-level biology courses; after weeks of hanging out in the basement doing experiments until two in the morning, I was accepted as one of the guys. While much of the detail was over my head, I learned to build biolayers, pull needles for patch clamping, run an oscilloscope, and dissect seaslugs.

In the process, I got a taste of bench science and a deeper appreciation of how difficult it is to do. As I left the lab, I recall asking my scientist friends, "How can you *stand* it? You run an experiment, and it fails. You run another experiment, and it fails. You run the experiment again, and it fails. You guys must be masochists." One scientist smiled sweetly and said, "It's simple. Every now and then you get data. Real data!" And suddenly I understood. It was an addiction, only instead of crack cocaine they got more data.

A good way to develop deeper understanding of topics is to befriend a few brain scientists. Get to know people who can speak ordinary English and who are believers in the importance of a free press. I call on several such experts in writing stories. They are senior people who do not mind giving credit to others, and they can explain things on deep background. E-mail is wonderful for this. I simply drop a line—"Hey, is this story worthwhile or is it dreck?"

As for journals, you should read *Science* and *Nature* and glance at a handful of specialized publications, including *Trends in Neuroscience, Brain and Behavior,* and the *Journal of Neuroscience.* Use press releases, for they can turn up good stories. For example, I saw one recently on mild traumatic brain injury—the fact that a mild bonk on the head can lead to long-term consequences. I figured that many people get bonked on the head and that most emergency rooms these days don't tell them what to expect—just to go home and take it easy for a few days. The story told readers to watch out for long-term effects.

Conducting interviews is pretty standard in the news business. But I think it bears repeating that you need to ask a multitude of questions, insisting on careful definitions of each word so that *you* understand the concepts behind it. If you don't understand it, you will not be able to write it.

I use a tactic (where I don't know much about the subject) that asks the researcher to begin with a historical perspective—starting back in the nineteenth century if need be. I do not want them to describe their current exciting finding (which is why I've called them) until I understand it in context. Starting from the beginning is a good way to get a quick overview, so that you will see where the new piece fits. Then, in writing your story, you turn the process around. You begin with the news, then tell your innocent reader the background needed to understand the news.

Brain stories are inherently fascinating. We all experience things like hallucinations, occasional depression, and bursts of emotion. People can easily put themselves or their loved ones into the story, and I often try to set this sense up in the lead (e.g., "You are walking down a dark, deserted street at night, then you suddenly hear a noise.").

Some brain stories are very complex, such as theories of consciousness and the role of experience in developing brain circuits. I assume the reader is "innocent" of the complex material and do my best to explain it. I look for powerful examples; I began a recent story on brain development with the saga of brutalized Romanian orphans.

In writing about consciousness recently, I interviewed 15 scientists and read four books, simply to prepare for the story. I asked every source for reprints or articles on their contribution to the subject. Then I digested it all and outlined the story. Had I written it at that point, it would have been 20,000 words long. Since I'm not writing for the *New Yorker*, it had to be pared down. And this is a difficult aspect of writing about brain science—or any topic. It's important to realize that what you leave out of the story is more important than what you leave in. In doing research, you are going to find out a huge number of details. Most of them will only confuse the reader. Your job is to winnow out the most salient features and put them in a clear narrative, with a beginning, a middle, and an end.

But here's an apparent paradox. It is often the little details that can make or break a story. One quote or one little example can speak volumes, making your story sing. While interviewing or reading, you should keep an eye out for these gems. Use them sparingly.

Of course your writing should be colorful and succinct, with ample use of analogies. Scientists will often provide analogies if you ask—they have spent years thinking about their subject and how to explain it. Finally, minimize technical terms. Avoid jargon—or if you have to use it, define it.

Science writing is great fun. You are getting paid to delve into endlessly fascinating subjects, to talk to really smart people, and to pass their excitement (and yours) on to the public. To me, it's the best job in the world, and I welcome you to our ranks.

21

Toxics and Risk Reporting

RICHARD F. HARRIS

Richard F. Harris has been a science correspondent at National Public Radio since 1986. He has a degree in biology from the University of California at Santa Cruz, and he started his journalism career at newspapers in California, including the *San Francisco Examiner*. His awards include a Peabody for investigative reports about the tobacco industry, two AAAS science journalism awards, an Aviation/Space Writers Association award for space coverage, and a Lewis Thomas Prize for reporting on the life sciences.

Richard was the founding president (actually "Titular Figurehead") of the D.C. Science Writers Association, which has become the largest regional science writing organization in the United States. He is president of the National Association of Science Writers in 1997 and 1998.

What do you do if your editor hands you one of these stories?

- An unusual number of children in a neighborhood seem to have birth defects and cancer. Concerned parents decide an abandoned toxic waste dump in the county is to blame.
- The local utility wants to add a new high-voltage power line along the edge of a neighborhood. Anxious citizens concerned about health effects (and property values) launch a campaign against the new line.
- County supervisors debate the installation of a trash-burning incinerator to replace the rapidly filling landfill. But the prospect of dioxin and other emissions from the incinerator stirs a public furor.

These are some of the hardest stories for a science reporter to cover. The he-said-she-said style of coverage is the easy way out, but it helps nobody. Taking the side of the little guy has obvious appeal—our first responsibility as journalists is to them, after all. But what if they're misinformed? Where's our responsibility to the truth? What is the truth?

Over the years, journalists covering stories about the environment have answered these tough questions in different ways. In the early days, it was easy to join the crusade and side with the Davids—the cash-starved environmental groups and the outraged citizens—against the Goliaths, so often industrial giants that were using everyone's air and water as their own corporate sewers.

Things aren't so simple these days. Environmental groups are now multimillion-dollar operations, searching for the next big issue to draw in more membership dollars, and not above exaggerating to make their point. Citizen groups may have more emotions than facts to back them up. Goliaths these days still have their own interests at heart, but they also argue, with some justification, that environmental regulations are costing consumers big bucks. The U.S. Environmental Protection Agency (EPA) admits that its regulations cost more than $150 billion a year—more than $2,000 for every family of four. And those costs are passed on to consumers in the form of higher prices for products. Journalists who used to ask simply whether people are being adequately protected by regulations now must ask whether society is getting the most bang for its risk-reduction buck.

To get the whole story these days, a journalist covering risk issues needs to approach the story from three different angles simultaneously: First, it's a human story involving deep-seated emotions about fear and health and society; second, it's a story about power and economics; and finally, it's a story rooted in science—and an imperfect science at that.

COVERING THE HUMAN STORY

I met Joanne Hale one day on the street where her old house used to stand, in the once-bucolic development of Love Canal, New York. Hale told a heart-wrenching story about how her family has suffered inexplicable health problems since a toxic soup leaked into her basement from an abandoned chemical dump. She recounted how she and her neighbors convinced the EPA to evacuate the neighborhood. The crusade she and her fellow citizens mounted ultimately led to the nation's Superfund law— one that has spurred the cleanup of many abandoned toxic waste sites around the country.

Two things nagged at me as Hale told her story. One was that several extensive scientific studies had failed to show that the people who lived in Love Canal were at greater risk for disease than people in comparatively clean neighborhoods nearby. How should I weigh those studies—admittedly imperfect—against the testimonial of someone who was convinced that the toxics seeping into her basement caused her family not only anguish but poor health?

The second thing that bothered me was that, throughout our interview, the smell of tobacco smoke was heavy on Hale's breath. Half of all smokers die of tobacco-related illnesses. So, finally, I couldn't resist the question that had been pounding at the back of my head. If you're so concerned about your health, I asked, why do you smoke? Her answer: Smoking is my choice; the toxic chemicals from Love Canal were imposed upon me.

Therein lies one of the truths about toxics stories: Health may be an element of them, and fear is likely to be another part of the picture, but they are also stories about justice. The first step in reporting stories about toxics is to understand these underlying issues.

Some pundits suggest that environmental conflicts arise because people have come to expect a life of zero risk. After all, we've conquered most childhood diseases, antibiotics have erased the dangers of many infections, and even something as astonishing as zinging six miles above the earth in a metal tube that's traveling at 600 miles per hour (that is, flying in a commercial aircraft) only presents about a one-in-a-million risk of death.

But zero tolerance for risk isn't the whole story. Much more often, people are intolerant of risk if they aren't getting all the benefits, too. A child living under a power line, for example, may (or may not) be at a tiny added risk for leukemia, but the benefits of those lines accrue to everyone—including houses far afield from the transmission towers. Touchier still are issues of toxic waste dumps. Chances are, they benefit some profit-making company, and bring no discernible benefit to the people who live nearby. So even if the putative risk is small, people ask why they should bear any risk at all. These inequities have given rise to the NIMBY syndrome—"not in my backyard." It's an issue a reporter must be prepared to confront.

A related phenomenon goes by the buzz phrase "environmental justice." Not surprisingly, toxic dumps tend to end up in low-rent districts. And poor people—often people of color—are more likely to live there. Robert Bullard, at the University of California in Riverside, is one of the chief proponents of the notion that the disadvantaged are targeted victims of this inequity. For an academic counterpoint to Bullard, analysts at the Center for the Study of American Business at Washington University in St. Louis argue that the decisions are based simply on economics, not racism.

Naturally, every environmental story can't plunge into these issues. But reporters covering these stories need to remain aware of their existence, and deal with them when they are key to the public debate. While a toxicologist or a project proponent may be prepared to dismiss these issues as simple emotionalism, in a democracy, emotional points of view will often carry the day.

ECONOMICS AND POWER

The easiest stories to tell have heroes and villains, victims and evil or avaricious perpetrators. Many environmental stories can be squeezed into that rubric. In fact, there's still a school of environmental journalists that believes that an environmental conflict can be explained simply by understanding the motivations (and funding) of the people on various sides. This is a convenient way of dealing with stories where the underlying facts are arcane and complex—daunting even for a reporter who has the time to study up on the issues. But simply considering the source has its pitfalls, too.

Take, for example, stories about global warming. Most scientists are reasonably convinced that manmade pollution will ultimately heat up the earth—if it's not doing so already. Likewise, most atmospheric scientists blame ozone depletion on manmade chemicals such as chlorofluorocarbons. There are a few skeptics out there, though, who don't accept the conventional wisdom. One is Patrick Michaels, the state climatologist of Virginia and a professor at the University of Virginia. Michaels makes his arguments based on archival climate data, and he has little patience for computer models that predict the future.

Scientists who disagree with Michaels have reasoned arguments, and Michaels has reasoned responses. But for reporters who don't care to understand this intellectual disagreement, Michaels has a more convenient vulnerability: He receives about a third of his financial support from industry—including coal interests—which has an obvious vested interest in the outcome of the scientific debate. Frankly, if I were the coal industry, I'd support Michaels, too, since his arguments support the industry's leanings. But should Michaels's arguments be dismissed because of this financial arrangement? He was saying these things before industry discovered him. My feeling is, reporters who understand his arguments can present them and let them rise or sink on their own merits. Saying it's a minority opinion is important, but for me, identifying his industry connection is secondary. (In fact, one can ask whether scientists funded by the EPA are truly free of economic influences, yet reporters rarely address that issue).

It would be wonderful if journalists could simply discount any scientist who has any financial stake in an issue. Unfortunately, that's a luxury we can't afford. As government funding for science stalls, more and more research is paid for by the private sector. This is particularly true in the field of toxicology, where a substantial share of academic researchers get some form of financial support from industry. And don't forget—most of the regulatory decisions about toxics in the environment are based on research that has been paid for—and often conducted—by the industry in question. Our regulatory schema says taxpayers simply can't afford to foot the bill for research that could ultimately make a private company make money.

I would argue that more important than funding, is a scientist's own personal point of view. And dealing with this can be even more difficult. For example, John Gofman from the University of California at Berkeley has long believed that radiation is a lot more hazardous than the vast majority of scientists and policymakers do today. Sam Epstein at the University of Illinois in Chicago has extreme views about the cancer-causing potential of many chemicals. Bruce Ames at UC Berkeley argues that synthetic chemicals pose trivial risks for most of the human population—a position that differs from the assumptions underlying most federal health standards, which can regulate exposures down to the part-per-billion level.

Often these points of view are either ignored entirely or given equal weight in a story. Neither solution is satisfying to me. Putting them in balance means first of all telling your readers, listeners, or viewers where an expert lies on the spectrum of opinion. More important, you should delve into the underlying scientific arguments when you can. The minority view isn't necessarily wrong—just ask Galileo.

THE SCIENCE

Underlying all these questions about money, politics, and emotion are the scientific facts about the potential hazard itself. How dangerous is a toxic waste dump? Do electromagnetic fields (EMFs) pose a real health risk? Which is really safer—a dump or an incinerator?

Answers to these questions don't come easy, either. But a reporter covering these issues can lift some of the haze over arguments down at city hall by delving into these matters. Usually, there are three different lines of evidence that help scientists—and can help the public—evaluate potential risks: epidemiological studies of human populations; animal exposure studies; and studies of the underlying biology that could explain why a substance could be harmful. Each approach has its weaknesses, so scientists usually rely on the overall picture when drawing conclusions.

When a chemical spill is found underground in a community, or when there seems to be an unusual occurrence of disease, epidemiologists are sometimes called in to investigate. Their job is to see whether there is, in fact, an excess of disease, and if it can be linked to the suspected chemical in the local environment. It's a perfectly logical request. But the history of this kind of investigation shows that these investigations rarely pay off. The federal Centers for Disease Control and Prevention has conducted more than 100 of these investigations over the years—from Love Canal to agricultural sites in California's Central Valley—but not one of them has demonstrated a clear link between a suspected agent in the environment and disease among ordinary citizens. (In contrast, investigations have found clear links between chemicals in the workplace and disease, and with personal habits such as smoking and drinking.) That's not to say the local environmental risks don't exist—just that current scientific methods aren't sufficient to find them.

Part of the reason for this failure is that most environmental risks are quite small. Former EPA administrator William Reilly inadvertently made this point as he announced that secondhand cigarette smoke was a suspected human carcinogen. He said secondhand smoke kills an estimated 3,000 people a year. To dramatize this point, Reilly said that number represents twice the number of hypothetical deaths caused by all the nation's industrial air pollution. If smokestacks account for 1,500 of the nation's 2 million deaths each year (0.075 percent of the total), it's easy to see why it's tough to identify environmentally related deaths in a study.

The other reason these studies are often disappointing is that epidemiology is actually a very blunt instrument. You wouldn't know it from reading the newspaper, but most of these studies are fraught with uncertainty—uncertainty that the reporter or the scientist may gloss over. All too often, people see that a study is statistically significant, and conclude that the effect must be real. But all statistical significance means is that if a study were repeated 100 times, it would come out the same way on 90 or 95 of those occasions. Mathematical significance says nothing about whether the study was designed well to begin with.

Epidemiologists fret about design all the time. Problems with a study's design can introduce "bias," as the experts put it. Classic examples of bias include choosing a bad comparison group. Maybe there's more disease in an "exposed" group simply because the comparison group is unusually healthy.

Bias can also be introduced when it's hard to measure a person's exposure to a potential threat. For example, studies of EMFs usually rely on a study of a home's wiring rather than the exposure to actual individuals. After all, EMFs don't leave any trace in the human body. There are many other potential sources of bias, and they are often discussed in the text of a study. It helps to read the fine print.

Because bias is such a problem, scientists usually don't draw any conclusions unless several studies find similar results. A single study carries little weight among scientists (though not necessarily in the public eye) unless the risk of disease is at least tripled. That sounds like a lot, but it's a healthy reminder that, just as you wouldn't attempt to draw detailed blueprints with a crayon, you shouldn't expect fine resolution from a tool as crude as an epidemiological study.

One of the big challenges in reporting about epidemiological studies is how to express the results accurately. A study that finds a relative risk of 3.0 for childhood cancer can be said to be evidence of a threefold risk of disease. But if the disease is rare, that may represent very few cases. In contrast, something that increases breast cancer risk by 15 percent may not seem like all that much until you consider that 180,000 women develop the disease each year. (In fact, a 15-percent increase is usually extraordinarily hard to detect with confidence in an epidemiological study.)

I like to use the raw numbers from the study to give people a better feeling for the size of a risk. For example, in the case of the Swedish study that found a threefold risk of childhood leukemia among children living near power lines, it helps to mention that the study involved half a million people over 25 years, and the triple risk reflected seven cases of childhood cancer, where two or three would be expected by chance. One lesson is: Tripling a tiny risk still leaves you with a tiny risk.

Scientists usually only feel confident about results from epidemiological studies when there are animal experiments to back them up. Power lines are linked to cancer in human beings, but animal tests with EMFs have failed to show any consistent ill effects—or plausible explanation for why EMFs might be a health hazard. So researchers are understandably more cautious about interpreting the human studies.

Animal studies have their own drawbacks, however. There's an unending debate about the best way to extrapolate from high doses in animals to extremely low doses in human beings. For chemicals and radiation that damage DNA, there's good reason to assume half a dose is half as bad, on down to zero. But biology suggests that for many hazardous chemicals that don't damage DNA, there may in fact be a threshold below which there is no effect. The toxicologist's credo is "the dose makes the poison." Identifying those thresholds has not been easy, though, so studies usually fall back on the simple extrapolations. These worst-case assumptions make sense from the standpoint of public health, but some scientists argue it's led to unnecessary alarm about chemical agents and unnecessarily burdensome regulations. That's a story in and of itself.

Ideally, scientists would like to understand exactly how a toxic material damages living tissue. The role of asbestos fibers in mesothelioma is fairly well established through studies of how these tough fibers disrupt lung tissue. Likewise, there's a lot of information about how ionizing radiation can damage DNA. But despite more than a billion dollars of research on the basic biology of dioxin, the EPA still doesn't have enough confidence in the science to base its risk assessment on this mechanistic information. So in most cases, we are a long way from having a true understanding of how a potentially dangerous substance does its damage.

22

Environmental Writing

JIM DETJEN

Jim Detjen holds the Knight Chair in Environmental Journalism at Michigan State University. He covered environmental and science topics for the *Philadelphia Inquirer* from 1982 to 1995. He has won more than 45 state and national awards for his reporting, including five Edward Meeman Awards for environmental writing. He is the founding president of the US Society of Environmental Journalists (SEJ) and is currently president of the International Federation of Environmental Journalists.

DDT. PCBs. CFCs. Dioxin. Chernobyl. Bhopal. Love Canal. The *Exxon Valdez* oil spill. Three Mile Island. Global warming. Deforestation. Overpopulation. Depletion of the ozone layer. Extinction of species.

During the past third of a century, environmental concerns have grown. In the 1960s these issues were small eddies on the edge of a river flowing through our lives and our society; today they have become one of the river's most powerful currents.

Protecting the environment has become a worldwide, multibillion-dollar industry. In field after field—from religion to law to philosophy to art and literature—subspecialties dealing with environmental issues are rapidly growing.

Poll after poll shows the American public is hungry for more information about the environment. A 1995 survey by Roper Starch found that 52 percent of the public wants more news about the environment, while only 8 percent wants less. The demand for environmental coverage is particularly high among people aged 18 to 34, the survey showed. More than 6 out of 10 people in Generation X—the demographic group that publishers and advertisers most want to reach—desire more environmental news.

As in most areas of news coverage, interest in environmental news tends to wax and wane, based on the prevailing mood in the country. During periods of economic uncertainty people focus more on jobs and the adequacy of health insurance and other financial issues. Following major environmental calamities—such as the *Exxon Valdez* oil spill in Alaskan waters or the Chernobyl nuclear accident in the Ukraine—public interest in environmental issues increases rapidly.

Overall, the media's interest in environmental issues has continued to increase since 1962, when Rachel Carson, a biologist with the U.S. Fish and Wildlife Service, first documented the perils of pesticides and herbicides in her classic book, *Silent Spring.*

One indication of this increase is the growth of the SEJ. This nonprofit organization was founded by about one dozen veteran environmental reporters in 1990. Since that time the organization's membership has climbed to more than 1,100, from throughout the United States and more than 20 foreign countries.

COVERING THE ENVIRONMENTAL BEAT

Reporting about environmental news is exciting, fascinating, and important. But it is also a complex field that is fraught with uncertainties and difficulties. To be a good environmental journalist requires substantial knowledge about scientific subjects and an awareness of complex environmental laws. To excel in this field requires a commitment to constantly read and learn.

As a reporter who has covered environmental issues since the early 1970s, I recommend that students interested in this specialty get as solid an educational background in science as possible. It's important to understand the fundamentals of chemistry, biology, physics, geology, meteorology, and ecology, as well as statistics. The more comfortable you are with the basics of earth and environmental science, the better off you will be in interviewing researchers in these fields.

But even if you haven't studied these subjects at a university, I recommend attending workshops and seminars whenever possible. The SEJ has an annual national conference and many regional conferences each year on a variety of environmental topics. More than 500 journalists from around the world attended the SEJ's fifth national conference in Boston in October 1995 to hear many top experts, including Vice President Gore, Secretary of the Interior Bruce Babbitt, EPA administrator Carol Browner, and Elizabeth Dowdeswell, executive director of the United Nations Environment Programme.

Other organizations that regularly schedule training programs for environmental journalists are the Knight Center for Specialized Journalism at the University of Maryland; the Environmental Journalism Program at

Michigan State University; the American Press Institute and Center for Foreign Journalists in Reston, Virginia; the Environmental Health Center, and the Radio and Television News Directors Foundation in Washington, D.C. The annual meetings of the American Association for the Advancement of Science also convene many panel discussions on new developments in the field of environmental science.

The fundamental concept to understand in reporting about the environment is that of an ecosystem. An ecosystem is defined as a given area in which living organisms have a stable relationship. One can refer to the ecosystem of a lake, river, forest, a large region, or the entire planet. The planetary ecosystem is sometimes called the ecosphere or biosphere.

The ecosystem concept is a reference to the close interrelationship between the parts of an ecosystem. If people remove or contaminate one part of an ecosystem—such as groundwater—it can affect or damage other parts, such as the soil or forests. It is because air, water, land, and life forms have such a close relationship that pollution in one area can affect food and drinking water somewhere else. It's important to keep this concept in mind on all environmental stories. Cutting down trees or changing the atmosphere can affect many parts of an ecosystem. Often the impacts are difficult to predict.

In reporting environmental stories, I think it's vital for reporters to go out into the field and observe things with their eyes, ears, and noses. Lots of times you'll discover things that you weren't aware of or didn't anticipate. In addition, one of the great joys of environmental reporting is getting outside—hiking through forests, canoeing on rivers, riding on research vessels that are studying the ecosystems of mountain lakes.

It's likely that you will develop sources at environmental groups, government agencies, industry, universities, and other institutions. Each time you research and write a story, catalog your sources in your card file and computer, listing their area of expertise, address, home and work phones, and e-mail address. Over time, you'll develop a valuable stable of experts to call on.

But what do you do when you must evaluate the conflicting statements of what some call "dueling experts"—seemingly credible experts who take diametrically opposed stands on issues? In general, my advice is to interview as many experts as possible and to try to identify the common ground on which they stand. The media sometimes has a tendency to look for conflict by seeking experts on the extreme fringes of issues. You'll do your readers and viewers a favor if you resist this temptation.

As you gather information, don't just rely on public relations officials from government, industry, or environmental groups. Over the years, I have found that my best sources on environmental stories are what I call front-line people—toxic waste inspectors, public health technicians, oil-spill cleanup workers, and other eyewitnesses. Cultivate these people. If they're at all interesting, consider writing feature stories about their work as a way to get them to know you and trust you. These are the people who really know what is going on, and if you treat them fairly, they will provide you with invaluable information in the future.

When I was an environmental reporter at the *Louisville Courier-Journal,* one of my best sources was a toxic waste inspector with the Kentucky state government. I regularly met with him for lunch inside his van parked behind a McDonald's restaurant in Louisville. While we munched on Big Macs and french fries, he would fill me in on the inner workings of the Kentucky Department of Natural Resources. I never used his name in my stories, but as a result of information he supplied to me, I was able to break several important environmental stories. What was in it for him? He knew that my stories had an impact on what his department did. By making good use of the information he leaked to me, I served a valuable role in prodding his agency into action.

I think it's also vital for environmental journalists to learn how to comb through the records of environmental agencies. As a result of state and federal environmental laws, agencies are required to keep on file permit applications, inspection reports, environmental impact statements, legal correspondence, and other documents. If you know what is required by these statutes and are firm in insisting that you have a right to review them, you'll collect information that most journalists never see.

And keep in mind that the same records may be in the files of competing agencies. If you are turned down by your state natural resources department for access to records on water pollution, you may be able to obtain similar records from the U.S. Environmental Protection Agency (EPA), the U.S. Coast Guard, a neighboring state agency, or a local health department.

I strongly urge environmental journalists to use state open records laws and the federal Freedom of Information Act (FOIA) to collect information. I've successfully used FOIA requests many times to obtain records from the EPA, the Nuclear Regulatory Commission, the army, and other federal agencies. It's true that it sometimes can take many months to obtain records, but many of the most important environmental stories during the past 20 years have come through FOIA requests.

One of the most difficult parts of environmental reporting is decoding scientific jargon. Your job as an environmental journalist is to take highly technical information contained in scientific reports or spoken by scientists and translate it into language understandable to the average reader or viewer. During interviews with scientists, make them talk in English. Don't be intimidated. Keep asking questions until you are sure you can explain the subject to your readers.

Describe what technical equipment looks like. Compare it to everyday items in a home. When I wrote a story about a malfunction at the Salem nuclear power plant in New Jersey, I compared the complex's faulty circuit breakers to those found in an average reader's home.

If you are writing about acid rain, don't just write that the rain in some parts of the Adirondack Mountains has a pH of 3. Translate that. Write that the rain has become as acidic as vinegar. Don't just write that X parts per million of sulfur dioxide are being released into the air. Compare these levels with those that can trigger asthmatic attacks in the sick and the elderly.

It also helps if you can assist readers in comparing small numbers such as one part per million to everyday things. One part per million (1 ppm) is about one minute in about two years. One part per billion (1 ppb) is one second in 32 years. One part per trillion (1 ppt) is one second in 32,000 years, one grain of salt in an Olympic-size swimming pool, or the width of one hair in a belt stretching around the world.

Two books I have found valuable in helping me relate numbers to my readers are *Durations,* by Stuart A. Sandow (0.002 seconds is the length of time it takes for a balloon to pop), and *Comparisons,* by the Diagram Group.

Environmental journalists must also learn how to read research papers, since many of the most important new findings about ozone depletion, global warming, the loss of wildlife, and other environmental issues are published in scientific journals such as *Science* and *Nature*. But how do you know if the research is valid?

There are no simple answers to this question, but some of the things I ask when I am evaluating a research paper are the following:

- Has it been published in a peer reviewed journal? (Peer review helps to screen out incomplete or flawed research. Be suspicious of non-reviewed studies that are being announced at a press conference.)
- Who paid for the research? (I'm far more skeptical if the study has been paid for by an environmental or industry group and not by a federal research agency such as the National Science Foundation (NSF) or the National Institutes of Health).
- How many people were involved in the research study? (Usually, the statistical validity increases with large scientific studies.)
- Who are some of the critics of the research, and what is their assessment of the new findings?

In evaluating the risks of an environmental hazard, these are some of the questions I ask:

- What are the methods of exposure to people? Plutonium inhaled into the lungs can be deadly, but it is far less harmful if spread on the skin or swallowed.
- Are there EPA or occupational health standards to compare the risks to? If so, what are these standards?
- Is the pollutant soluble in water? If so, it can pollute groundwater supplies.
- Is the pollutant soluble in fats? If so, it can build up into the food chain.
- Is the pollutant likely to become airborne? If so, it could damage the lungs. If it wafts high into the atmosphere, it could erode the ozone layer.
- How long will the pollutant take to decompose in the environment?
- What are the nonhuman impacts—on plants, marine life, and animals?
- When officials say they have no evidence of a hazard—has anybody looked?

I believe strongly in the importance of project reporting. Much of the environmental journalism found in the media is shallow and incomplete. Only by really digging into a story do journalists usually begin to understand the underlying political, legal, and scientific processes at work. One of the best environmental projects I have seen in recent years was "The Sierra in Peril," by Tom Knudson of the *Sacramento Bee,* a beautifully written and illustrated series that won the Pulitzer Prize in 1992.

But it's a difficult challenge to make a complicated story interesting and understandable to readers and viewers. One way to do this is to illustrate stories with real people. When I wrote about the complexities of cleaning up the radioactive debris at the Three Mile Island nuclear complex, I told my stories through the eyes of laborers—not just the scientists and government experts. In nonfiction, just as in fiction, strong narratives will pull a reader through complicated prose.

Sometimes you have to be imaginative to make your point. When I worked on a series of stories about the hazards of toxic chemicals in Kentucky, I wanted to show that many small landfills in rural parts of the state were routinely accepting illegal hazardous waste. The problem was that while state officials believed that illegal dumping was occurring, they had no eyewitnesses who could document this.

So my newspaper, the *Louisville Courier-Journal,* hired a news clerk to drive a pickup truck around the state. We filled up his truck with empty barrels that had the names of PCBs, dioxin, chlordane, and other dangerous chemicals stenciled onto them. Then the news clerk drove into the landfills to dump his cargo. He found that the vast majority of landfill operators never bothered to check what was being dumped. His first-person account dramatically showed the inadequacies of the state's system to regulate the disposal of hazardous wastes.

One important point worth considering in reporting about environmental issues is that very few issues are strictly local anymore. Since environmental stories frequently cross political boundaries, it's often important for journalists to pursue stories across state and national borders in order to comprehend what is going on.

Similarly, environmental stories often cross the boundaries of traditional news beats. It's not uncommon for an environmental reporter to be writing about science, public health, business, the courts, government, even religion.

Finally, it's important for journalists to follow up on past environmental stories. Environmental controversies may fade from the front page, but often the underlying problems remain. Some of the most interesting environmental stories are follow-up stories on controversies that happened long ago.

23

•••••••••••••••••••

Covering Earth Sciences

CHARLES PETIT

Charles Petit has covered science for the *San Francisco Chronicle*
since 1972, with a particular fondness for the earth sciences. He
holds a bachelor's degree in astronomy from the University of
California, Berkeley. He is a past president of the National
Association of Science Writers and the Northern California Science
Writers Association, and has taught science writing at the Graduate
School of Journalism at UC Berkeley.

It was around 9:00 A.M. on Sunday, May 18, 1980, with all signs pointing
to a blessedly pleasant, dull day at home, when the phone rang. It was
Jim Hicks, an assistant city editor. "Your mountain blew," he said. "Catch
a plane."

Mount St. Helens in southern Washington State had been steaming,
rumbling, and bulging for months. I had followed its restlessness closely,
building a supply of background material, sources, and phone numbers.
A few weeks earlier my editors, succumbing to my pleas, had sent me up
there for a story on its ominous fits of earthquakes and minor outbursts.
A photographer and I had circled its summit in a helicopter, looking at
the dark scars from steam exploding through its mantle of snow and gla-
cier ice.

Jim didn't have to identify it any further than "your mountain."

By mid-afternoon a photographer and I were in another helicopter, a
rickety little bird we rented in deadline desperation from a logging company whose number we found through a quick scour of the yellow pages
at the Portland airport. We buzzed toward one of the most amazing sights
of my life. Above the wreck of the mountain, a monstrous, pulsating, mus-
cular column of gray ash was punching straight into the stratosphere. We
flew for miles over trees laid flat by the eruption, by an immense landslide
that had peeled away half the peak. As we neared the mountain, it was
like somebody turning down the color knob on a television. The green

180

hills faded to ash gray; previously sparkling streams writhed in ugly, muddy gouts of instant snowmelt.

The radio carried reports and rumors of death. One concerned government geologist David Johnston had been observing the mountain from a cabin fatally close to its west flank. His last words to US Geological Survey (USGS) colleagues in Vancouver, Washington, were: "Vancouver! Vancouver! This is it. . . ."

This, for sure, was a big story.

Covering the earth sciences has its moments, and they sometimes arrive fast. Eruptions, earthquakes, floods, mudflows, and tsunamis tend to be surprises, freighted with drama, terror, and opportunities for human ingenuity and sometimes heroism.

Yet the earth sciences also offer some of the most sublimely ethereal and intellectually rewarding topics a reporter may encounter. In cool rocks, shimmering sheets of ice, lofty peaks, eroded plains, and ancient shorelines are the stories of the evolution of our planet, and hints to our future on it. Such fields of inquiry offer not only lodes of hard news— new discoveries, new environmental threats, new adventures—but fine examples of how scientists work.

Earth scientists are crucial players in one of the most important issues of the day: global change. Are human activities warming the planet or otherwise changing weather and climate? The men and women who study ancient rocks for the evidence of past change, who try to figure out the great cycles of gases and minerals in the air, sea, and land, and who watch for hints of new phenomena are the ones who, for the most part, will give the answers. The reporter finds high drama, and stories with real gristle. The arguments are ferocious. The people involved are colorful and passionate. The stakes are high. And—helping to assure employment for earth-oriented science writers—the issues won't be settled soon.

The economy depends in large part on earth science. Industries that extract natural resources such as petroleum, sand and gravel, metal ores, and water all employ huge numbers of geologists, hydrologists, and other specialists. Debates over offshore oil drilling, mining in national forests and other public lands, and water rights all revolve largely around the interpretations of scientific explorations. While such stories are often done by business or political reporters, the science specialist may well be called in too.

What follows are tips to preparing for such stories and gathering information in a hurry, and a few examples of what to do and what not to do.

First, what sciences are we talking about? One indicator is the list of sections of the American Geophysical Union, the umbrella professional society for earth sciences: geodesy, geophysics, paleomagnetism, volcanology, hydrology, planetology, seismology, and on and on. Earth science, as its name suggests, focuses on things that touch and significantly affect dirt.

Its practitioners fret over the structure of our planet's deep interior, the tectonic drift of continents, the meanders of rivers, the risings of mountains, the ventings of volcanic gases, the evolution of the atmosphere, and the dynamics of oceans. For perspective, they study other planets and their structures, gauge the winds blowing out from the sun, and calculate how often meteoroids hit our world and others.

To keep things manageable, I'll restrict myself here mainly to earth dirt: things that make the ground jerk, slip, spit lava, drown, or otherwise act in odd or threatening ways, plus a little bit about covering fundamental (nondisaster) earth science stories.

EARTHQUAKES

Everybody gets earthquakes, but some more often than others. Seismologists, geophysicists, and plain geologists study them, while their practical effects on human-made structures are main concerns for structural and geotechnical engineers.

An important bit of practical advice: If there is a reasonable chance of an earthquake where you work, keep your phone contact list on paper or keep up-to-date printouts of your computer's phone file. When the Loma Prieta earthquake of October 1989 cut electricity to the *Chronicle* for more than a day, the phones were working a long time before power for the computers came back. With light from candles and emergency generators, we were able to reach geologists promptly, thanks to old-fashioned Rolodexes.

When an earthquake occurs, the usual priority of questions is: Who got hurt? What broke? And last, what happened and why?

A science writer covering an earthquake solo must recognize that most editors are going to want some color, emotion, and imagery up high in the story before getting to magnitudes, fault mechanisms, and the odds for large aftershocks.

Fortunately, finding out about injuries and damage and what people thought is easy. *Everybody* who felt the thing will motor-mouth your ear off. Cold calls in search of earthquake quotes, vignettes, and other people-oriented stories are some of the easiest you'll ever make. If you can't get the police, try a cab company, or a glass company, or a hotel desk clerk, or the 7-Eleven manager. Don't be above calling a relative. My sister-in-law gave the *Chronicle* a fine quote on an earthquake swarm in the little town of Alamo about 50 miles east of San Francisco in 1990, one almost as good as a liquor store clerk.

The final category of question—What happened and why?—is where the science writer is most useful. Which fault caused the quake? What about aftershocks? Why here? After an earthquake, many people feel betrayed by the solid ground. A sense of the forces and processes at work helps them regain emotional bearings.

As with most science stories, it is important to ask simple questions and try to write a simple story. If it reads like a piece out of a journal, rewrite it.

If it is a large and damaging earthquake nearby, then a team of reporters will be at work, and the science reporter can focus on explaining what happened and why. After the Loma Prieta quake knocked out power and phones in San Francisco, I caught a ride with a friend of one of our office managers who happened to pull up in a car at the right time. We drove by back roads the 40 miles south to the local headquarters of the USGS. That was all that was on my mind: Get to some experts. And once there—where the geologists were also working by flashlight—it was a simple task to get a concise description of the big bend in the San Andreas fault where the quake had started, its magnitude, and its place in the overall seismic history of the region.

Maps are usually an essential part of the story. Reporters at daily newspapers or television stations will have to provide their graphics people with raw material early. It is not hard to get. The most obvious source is the USGS. Failing that, any good-sized research university should have a seismologist who may be helpful. Similarly, state geology departments and emergency services agencies have generalized maps of earthquake faults; often county or city governments keep them on file, too. In large communities, the yellow pages should list geotechnical engineers, who may know something about the geology of a specific news site. A science reporter in earthquake country should as a matter of course have handy in advance a few maps showing large, well-known faults.

Readers and viewers will benefit from a simple diagram of how the earthquake happened. Was it strike-slip, a normal fault, or a thrust fault that moved? These, of course, are the terms that geologists will employ. The reporter must define them simply. (A strike-slip motion means one side of the fault moved horizontally along the direction of the fault; a normal fault causes one side to slide down as the two sides are pulled apart; a thrust fault causes one side to ride up over the other as they are pushed together.) We keep diagrams of such fault motions ready on file in the newspaper's graphics computers.

Magnitudes are a vexatious problem with no easy answer. In 1935 Charles Richter of Caltech invented a scale to measure the energy release of earthquakes. It depends on a specific instrument, the Wood-Anderson seismograph, at specific distances from earthquakes. Today's magnitude scales are all calibrated to more-or-less resemble the original Richter scale, but hardly anybody still uses the Richter scale itself. At the newspaper where I work, and many others, there is a standing rule that wire stories that arrive with a magnitude "on the Richter scale" have the Richter edited out. Almost always, a reporter or editor has inserted it even though the original source did not use it. If a seismologist uses it, it may be a good idea to ask if it really is a Richter magnitude.

People tend to like the familiar word Richter. More accurate alternatives such as moment magnitude, surface-wave magnitude, and body-wave magnitude look odd on the page if left unexplained. The explanations, however, are tedious. I know no easy solution. We tend to just call it magnitude, no matter what kind it is. On all the scales, a magnitude 7 is a big dangerous quake, a magnitude 4 is a little one, and few people even feel a magnitude 2.

A common dilemma is whether to go to the quake site or to the nearest seismographic station or lab maintained by a large university or the USGS. The epicenter is exciting and provides more vivid stories. But a broad sampling of scientific data and opinion can be hard to find amid the chaos of disaster response. A part of me will always regret not going down to the Southern California desert to accompany geologists goggling in amazement over the dramatic rips in the earth where one side of the fault had lurched 20 feet along the other during the Landers Earthquake of June 1992. Yet by staying in the office and visiting the nearby USGS regional center in Menlo Park, relying mostly on phones, I got a broader factual background than any field visit could have provided.

The best solution is to have two science writers (not always an option!). For instance, during the 1994 Northridge Earthquake in Los Angeles, the *Chronicle* sent me down there, while science editor Dave Perlman remained at his desk parsing the huge flow of information available by phone, wire, and fax.

Try to illustrate the events described by scientists with concrete, vivid illustrations. A few years ago, for instance, a smallish earthquake near Cape Mendocino on California's largely rural north coast was accompanied by some of the sharpest earth movements ever measured anywhere. It was necessary to report that instruments at the site had recorded the sharpest vertical accelerations—more than the force of gravity—ever known to occur. The bookish accelerometer readings were made visceral by an eyewitness account of a bulldozer, stuck in brick-hard, dry mud for months, that popped straight up in the air and landed several feet away, amazing its owner.

FLOODS AND MUDFLOWS

Sloppy events like floods and mudflows may seem too self-explanatory to demand a science writer's touch: "Yes, Mr. or Ms. Editor, it rained hard; the creek overflowed." But there are important opportunities here. Hydrology takes a big chunk of the annual budget of the USGS. Science writers frequently must find a quick explanation for the intense weather that typically causes floods, landslides, and mudflows. Between floods, there are good stories to be written on the development and zoning of flood plains and dams and the preservation of wetlands. All entail geologists. County, state, and federal agencies are mines of information. In the Bay Area, the USGS even has a mudflow warning system that works sort of like a tornado warning.

A terminology note is in order. News reports, and most people, employ the word *mudslide* for any gloppy mess that runs down a hill. But geologists, being literal types, prefer to say *landslide,* or *mudflow* (or sometimes, *debris flow*). After all, mud does not slide. You can slide a turkey, but you can't slide the gravy. So if you interview a geologist you can show off by saying *mudflow* or *debris flow*—even if your editor insists on *mudslide.*

After floods subside (and before them, if a reporter is quite ambitious), one can write superb and useful stories about how often such events occur on average, the kinds of land-use changes that encourage or discourage floods, and the need for prudent zoning of land use.

It is also important for any reporter to separate rumors and folk tales from sensible opinion. Floods, more than most natural disasters, inspire victims to blame somebody else, usually the government, for their wet carpets. Sometimes they are right, and that's a good story. Sometimes they are not.

During heavy California floods in 1995, residents of one nearly-drowned coastal town angrily told reporters that environmental laws were to blame. Efforts to save the long-toed salamander supposedly had prevented work crews from clearing brush and other debris from a riverbed. A skeptical reporter (not a science writer) checked it out and learned that the salamander lived nowhere near the river channel. The flood control programs had been slowed for purely budgetary reasons. However, by then the episode was already fueling efforts to soften endangered species laws. A quicker bit of checking might have gotten the facts out soon enough for a more sensible public policy discussion.

VOLCANOES

For most of us, a volcano is a story we get by phone. Events such as Mount St. Helens are, fortunately, uncommon in the United States. But they are not unique. As of this writing Kilauea in Hawaii has been erupting continuously, occasionally burying homes under lava, for 15 years. Alaska, California, Oregon, and Washington also have active volcanoes.

As with earthquakes, the priority news will be: Who's hurt? What broke? and What are the authorities doing about it? But the science writer should quickly move on to the forces that made the volcano go off: Is it a symptom of bigger eruptions to come, and why? Are the gases dangerous? Can the lava be diverted? What are the underlying tectonic forces that melted the magma in the first place? What are the typical periods of dormancy between eruptions?

Find out as soon as possible what kind of volcano it is. For instance, a volcano sitting on a tectonic subduction zone, where one of the Earth's large crustal plates is sliding under the edge of another and sinking toward the semimolten mantle below, is likely to be hugely explosive, with viscous, silica-loaded magma (of forms called rhyolite or dacite) packed with dissolved gases that free themselves violently when relieved of subterranean pressures. Such violent volcanoes may have no lava at all: just super-hot ash and gas roaring from cindercones. A hot-spot volcano, like those in Hawaii, may by contrast be little but a river of glowing, highly fluid, and approachable basaltic lava flowing calmly from a vent, its gases bubbling free without fuss. Or a volcano may evolve through several phases.

Readers, viewers, or listeners are entitled to the right mental image of what is happening. Otherwise they will fall back on Hollywood sound-stage evocations of sharp cones that look like Fuji, draped in red rivers of lava. Let other reporters fire up half-baked descriptions of the eruption. If you're the science writer, get your description of the mountain right.

During coverage of the Mount St. Helens eruption, for instance, I had grabbed the chance a few weeks earlier to buy from the USGS a map- and diagram-packed bulletin called *Potential Hazards from Future Eruptions of Mount St. Helens Volcano*. After the eruption it was invaluable. Naturally, geologists cleaned the publication off the shelves. I had to keep mine in sight or secure at all times at the press center—colleagues could look it over or photocopy pages, but it was *mine*.

Don't make things any harder than they have to be: If officials spoon-feed information, open wide.

Public agencies rely on the media to get the word out. At Mount St. Helens, we (the photographer and I), trying to get great pictures, wasted an entire day renting small planes and helicopters only to have their pilots denied clearance to get over the area of worst destruction and flooding. We learned to our chagrin that other newsgroups had gotten some incredible shots by taking the seats set aside for the press in helicopters flown by the National Guard, which was eager for publicity on its rescue and reconnaissance skills.

BASIC SCIENCE

Not long ago I missed the boat on a good story, literally. A geologist at UC Davis takes his students on river-rafting trips every year to give them an unforgettable closeup look at erosion at work, and to inspect the exposures of geologic formations along rivers in the Sierra and Trinity Alps. I went on one trip, but failed to see that I could offer anything to my editors. John Cox, a *Sacramento Bee* science writer, took the exact same ride I did and produced a lyrical, intriguing profile of the river, the students, the fascinations that keep geologists going, the human history of the region, and the story in the exposed rocks. I read it and felt like a dope. The great thing about science writing is that, at almost any place in the world, there is a topic underfoot that some scholar has dissected, and that may make a fine story, if only you dig.

Basic earth science stories are everywhere. You don't need mountains or wild continental margins. The flattest plains in America contain earth science story possibilities, whether about the vast Oglala aquifer whose waters account for a good share of the nation's agricultural productivity, or the Manson Crater in northern Iowa, the 22-mile-wide, now-buried scar of a meteor strike made millions of years ago.

Even though basic science stories are often the furthest thing from breaking news, this can be their charm. Like stories in astronomy, or on fossils of prehistoric people, discoveries about the Earth's history and behavior provide for many people a welcome and invigorating break, a mental escape, from the daily diet of human disaster, political skulduggery, and crime news.

Further, basic research stories, in earth sciences as well as any other area, illustrate a particular reward of the science beat. On many other beats, reporters' best work emerges from exposing the failures, corruption, and falsehoods of others. The best science stories, by contrast, are typically about people who do things right.

24 •••••••••••••••••••

Covering Physics

KIM A. MCDONALD

Kim A. McDonald began writing about physics in the mid-1970s at the Lawrence Berkeley National Laboratory. He worked as a reporter at the *Valley Times* in Pleasanton, California, and since 1981 has been covering science for the *Chronicle of Higher Education* in Washington, D.C., as a senior writer and senior editor. He received his bachelor's degree in zoology from the University of California at Berkeley and a master's degree in journalism from Northwestern University.

Tackling a complex physics story is a daunting task for journalists, most of whom would be hard pressed to explain the difference between a quark and a muon. In fact, few science writers possess both the knowledge and skill to make physics a regular staple in their beats. But for those who do—and do it well—the personal satisfaction of covering a subject often ignored by the media is immense.

For much of my writing career, which began at a high-energy physics laboratory in the mid-1970s, I've devoted a considerable amount of time and energy learning how to cover developments in physics. Yet after all those years, physics still remains the toughest discipline in science for me to cover.

There are several reasons for this difficulty. Physics is a mature science, so most of the frontier research involves fairly esoteric problems that are far removed from our everyday experience. Physics also relies heavily on mathematical concepts that are difficult for a general science writer like myself to comprehend, much less translate accurately into prose. Then there's the common perception of physics as dry and boring. For most of us, getting readers who have long been turned off by science—and physics, in particular—to pick up and read that story on quantum field theory we labored so hard over is often the biggest hurdle.

According to Robert L. Park, a physicist who is director of public information for the American Physical Society, the scarcity of stories about physics in newspapers and magazines has contributed to a lack of public understanding about physicists and the research they conduct.

Each year in March, for example, the society holds its biggest meeting, a gathering of condensed-matter physicists. "But of the 6,000 papers that are presented," Park says, "only three are suitable for coverage. Condensed-matter physics is never covered in the press. Reporters have never heard of these things."

That's certainly not the case with astronomy. Concepts such as black holes, quasars, and the big bang have all entered the public consciousness. The extensive interest in astronomy even supports popular magazines devoted exclusively to the subject. So why do the ideas of modern physics remain so impenetrable to the average person?

"The difficulty is that there is only one language in physics, and that's mathematics," says Park. "The English language is a poor substitute." Unlike most developments in physics, discoveries in astronomy can also be easily visualized. "A new class of galaxy or the glare of matter close to a black hole can be seen in the middle of a glossy picture, usually courtesy of NASA," says Phillip Schewe of the American Institute of Physics. "In contrast, many physics stories are hard to imagine, much less image."

Journalists covering physics not only have to present complex, mathematical ideas in a readable and vivid way, to people who know little about the subject, they have to make certain the information is accurate.

Ivars Peterson, who has been writing about mathematics and physics for *Science News* for the past 15 years, says translating technical concepts in physics into everyday prose is where most of the problems occur.

"To me, the biggest thing is getting the language right," he says. "The words don't always mean the same thing to a writer as they do to a physicist."

Take "chaos," used by mathematicians and physicists to describe the behavior of systems with final states that depend so much on their initial states that they become, in effect, unpredictable. By contrast, the popular meaning of chaos is 'a mess'. "You have to be very careful in distinguishing chaos in the general sense and in the technical sense," says Peterson. Or "plasma," another troubling term that means one thing to nuclear fusion physicists and astrophysicists, but something quite different to physicians.

That doesn't mean writers should resort to using the same jargon used by their sources to convey the ideas accurately. In fact, journalists covering physicists need to be particularly conscious about resisting that urge, says Curt Suplee, who reports on physics for the *Washington Post*. "The single most common problem in physics coverage is that some of the concepts are so complex and arcane, there's enormous pressure to use jargon rather than define them," he says.

So make sure you understand what the terms mean. Look them up before you sit down to write. Or better yet, before you start the interview. "That's what reference books are for," says Suplee.

Like many other writers, I keep a number of good physics encyclopedias and reference books within reach. I use them, as well as any other background information about the subject I'm planning to write about, before starting my interviews. As Peterson points out, "Physicists never react well to someone who professes ignorance. I prefer not to have to ask the researcher the basic things. I learn as much as I can from my files first."

During the interview, pick out key points that you're likely to use in your story and recheck them with the scientist to make sure you've got the technical details right. Also make sure there aren't any nuances you've missed.

Another useful tactic I and many other physics writers use frequently is to run analogies that we're thinking about using in our stories by the physicists we're interviewing. As Suplee has often discovered, scientists are not only a great help in making the analogies more precise, but often in coming up with a better one.

"Where physics stories usually go wrong," he says, "is when a reporter fails to understand the terms, but thinks he does."

When he sits down to write, Suplee often finds it useful to think of his physics stories as narratives or murder mysteries. That gives them a structure into which he can work background or context that will make them both relevant and understandable to readers. By putting the mystery or search the same way the scientists see it, readers can appreciate the intellectual challenges and achievements that face the scientists. This approach may at first appear academic, but Suplee finds that most readers are drawn to such stories in the same way they are attracted to a good mystery novel.

"When you consider that people love to read mysteries or stories with headlines like 'Cancer Mom Says UFOs Stole My Baby,'" he says, "is it any less astonishing that two particles of the same size can have such different masses? Many of these things in physics are outright weird and fascinating. Many times we try to sugarcoat the stories by focusing on the potential applications instead of presenting it the way the scientists see it, as a puzzle or a mystery. In theory, writing a physics story shouldn't be any different than writing a UFO story. These things are weird."

Which stories can benefit from such narratives depends, of course, on the story and the amount of space a publication is willing to devote to it. "It makes the story longer," admits Suplee, "and a longer story is harder to sell to editors who might be less than receptive to a physics story in the first place. But you have to provide some background to what wasn't known, or was a mystery. If people weren't aware that something was missing, the mere fact that it was found isn't going to be interesting to them.''

Keep the ideas focused, however. You don't want to lose readers with superfluous details. Present only the relevant information a reader needs to know to understand the points you make later, since many of the physical concepts are highly technical. What details a writer chooses to focus on depends on the writer's knowledge.

Schewe, a former high-energy physicist who is a senior science writer for the American Institute of Physics, says this is what usually distinguishes the more experienced physics journalists from the less confident ones. ''The better physics journalists are generally those who know a bit of quantum mechanics,'' he says. ''This gives them the confidence to delve into the actual processes or interactions involved and translate abstruse results into terms general readers can appreciate. Less confident writers regard most physics systems as black boxes and restrict their descriptions to the most manifest aspects of the story—for example, what did the particle weigh, or can the principle be used in medical imaging?''

Don't ignore descriptions of physical units and dimensions, though, particularly when they're unusual. Doing so helps to draw readers into a story, while giving them some appreciation of some of the kinds of difficulties physicists are confronted with.

I started a story about what physicists are discovering in low-temperature experiments, for example, by trying to convey how cold the temperatures are that these researchers actually work with:

> Ithaca, N.Y.—The ice and snow outside Robert C. Richardson's laboratory here may feel cold, but cold to Mr. Richardson and his colleagues—who are creating some of the lowest temperatures in the universe—is a very relative term. This month and next, the Cornell University physicists will begin a series of experiments to determine how matter behaves when it is chilled to within 10-millionths of a degree above absolute zero.
>
> To give some idea of how cold that temperature actually is, consider this: Absolute zero, or zero on the Kelvin temperature scale, is minus 459.67 degrees Fahrenheit. Ten-millionths of a degree above absolute zero, or 0.00001 degree K, is about 10 million times as cold as the average temperature at the South Pole, the most frigid region on the earth. It is also nearly a million times as cold as the lowest natural temperature in the universe—the background radiation of interstellar space, which is 3 degrees above absolute zero, or minus 454 degrees Fahrenheit.

Viewed another way, the jump from room temperature (68 degrees Fahrenheit or 293 degrees K) to the 6,000-degree surface of the sun is less than one-millionth of the leap from room temperature to 10-millionths of a degree above absolute zero—or 10 microkelvin, as physicists put it.

Analogies are particularly useful in conveying some of the more esoteric dimensions of high-energy physics, such as the masses and lifetimes of subatomic particles. In an article about the discovery of the psi-J particle, former *Los Angeles Times* writer George Alexander used a variety of analogies to give the reader a picture of the unusual properties of the new particle:

> The mass of the psi-J particle was put at 3.1 billion electron volts (mass and energy being basically the same thing, physicists find it more convenient to express the weight of a particle in terms of its energy than to spell out its cumbersome weight). Its lifetime was calculated to be a hundred-billionth of a billionth of a second.
>
> "We talk in these esoteric terms," said Dr. Roy Schwitters, one of the experimental physicists at the Stanford Linear Accelerator Center (SLAC), "but when we go into the lab and slam a beam into something, real things come out—sparks in a spark chamber, bubble tracks in a bubble chamber, or particle tracks in a magnetic detector."
>
> Measurements in billions of electron volts seem unreal to the ordinary person, who may have difficulty comprehending the physical, temporal, or spatial aspects of commonplace objects: the size of an aspirin tablet (325 milligrams), the margin of victory in a race (frequently one-hundredth of a second, sometimes a thousandth), or the width of a human hair (about 25 microns, or roughly one-thousandth of an inch).
>
> However exotic the dimensions of the psi-J particle may be to the nonscientist, they left scientists gasping with astonishment. The lifetime was particularly striking, for it was 1,000 to 10,000 times longer than physicists would have expected for a subatomic particle.
>
> To have some feeling for this remarkable lifetime of the psi-J particle, imagine for a moment the excitement of biologists if they suddenly came across a strain of mice that lived as long as tortoises. The normal span for mice is three years, for tortoises a century. The difference in this analogy is only a factor of 33, not 1,000, yet if such mice were found, their longevity would stand the field of biology on its head.

When you're forced to talk about the dimensions of objects, which is often the case in physics, make an effort to get real-life examples that you can compare those objects to. Giving the reader a look at some of the personalities involved in the research, and introducing humor—where appropriate—are other useful ways of keeping a reader interested in an otherwise technical story. I started one story about a rather dry topic, the construction of the now-defunct Superconducting Supercollider, with a humorous lead describing the gargantuan project:

> Dallas, Texas—It is fitting that the largest, most expensive scientific facility ever started should be constructed here, in a region known for big cars, big money, and big hair.
>   Texans, as the saying goes, don't do anything small. And these days, neither do high-energy physicists.

I went on to give real-life comparisons to some of the incredible dimensions of the project, even by Texas standards:

- The collider's 10,000 superconducting magnets will require the production of 625,000 miles of superconducting cable, more than has ever been produced and enough to circle the earth more than 25 times.
- Its 12 refrigeration plants, which will cool the magnets to 4.5 degrees centigrade above absolute zero, will liquefy 2.4 million liters of helium—enough, in gaseous form, to fill more than 300 Goodyear blimps.
- Its accelerators and magnets, which will push protons to near the speed of light and guide them in opposite directions around the 54-mile-long ring, will require 225 megawatts of electricity—enough to serve the city of Dallas or the entire state of Vermont.
- Each of its two underground experimental halls is equivalent in size to Texas Stadium, home of the Dallas Cowboys football team.
- The two particle detectors that will go into those experimental halls will each weigh from 40,000 to 50,000 tons, more than an American battleship.

Visual examples are also particularly useful in illustrating ideas in physics. Suplee recommends that reporters badger researchers and their institutions for illustrations that can convey technical concepts more accurately and efficiently than prose.

Making a story as simple and appealing as possible to the reader is especially important at general interest publications, where physics can be a particularly hard sell. At those publications, it's important to pick your stories carefully.

"Pick your targets, choose your subjects carefully. You need a definitive result," says Suplee, who waits until a long line of research culminates in an actual result before writing a story. "Don't do a story at the point when the result is almost there. Do it when it's there."

If a story is extremely technical, consider running the parts you're unsure about by someone knowledgeable about the development. I do this, and I've found I can greatly improve the accuracy of my stories without compromising their integrity. The key is to just read them the paragraphs you're unsure about (while a lot of scientists will ask, don't give them copies of your story) and pick the right person to call (usually someone who is both knowledgeable about his or her field and how the media operate). This person might be a reliable source, someone with a good overview of the field whose name you get from the American Physical Society or the American Institute of Physics, or a program manager overseeing that area of physics at the National Science Foundation.

Getting a second or third opinion from a trusted source also helps a reporter put a story in the proper context. This is particularly important for developments about which there are a wide variety of opinions or even a dispute among physicists.

"A Ph.D. in physics," says Park of the American Physical Society, "is not an inoculation against insanity.

"There aren't any exclusives in science," he adds, "so if you're getting the story exclusively, you've got to wonder why."

Like Suplee, Park thinks more journalists need to cultivate physicists as sources. "You need to develop a set of contacts of scientists whose judgment you trust," says Park.

Physicists who have their ear to the ground about developments in their subdisciplines can be a good source for generating physics stories. Another is the American Institute of Physics, which sponsors a variety of meetings during the year devoted to various subdisciplines. The group runs seminars for reporters in Washington, puts out tip sheets for reporters by e-mail, and has a public information staff that identifies and translates important papers that appear in *Physical Review Letters,* the premier publication for physicists to announce their discoveries.

Don't forget the Internet as a source, either. Discussion groups on the Internet devoted to particle physics, nuclear fusion, and physics are good places to start. I learned about the details of the discovery of the top quark more than a week before the official announcement at Fermilab because of a graduate student who posted the details of a seminar he attended on the discovery in a physics discussion group.

Many people, in fact, expect the Internet to play an increasing role in the communication of physics results, from World Wide Web pages to online physics journals. And many physicists, like Robert Park, say they increasingly prefer to deal with reporters by e-mail. "The advantage of e-mail is that the quality of the response is so much better," he says. "A person doesn't just answer off the top of his or her head."

True, reporters lose some of the spontaneity of a telephone interview, but I've often found that scientists in disciplines like physics that frequently communicate by e-mail write in a conversational style that allows me to easily quote them. Some reporters may object to the fact that the scientists are editing their responses, but in a discipline where accuracy is paramount, I consider that a distinct plus.

In fact, I believe that those science reporters who believe they can get all of their source material by mail, phone, and a fax machine will be at a distinct disadvantage if they continue their archaic ways. If you want to communicate with physicists on a regular basis, make sure you have an e-mail account. Like it or not, this is the future for physics reporting.

25

Writing About Astronomy

MICHAEL D. LEMONICK

Michael D. Lemonick is a senior writer at *Time,* where he has worked since 1986. He has written 19 cover stories, on a wide variety of scientific topics, including supernovas, superconductivity, particle physics, Egyptology, and cosmology, and has twice won the American Association for the Advancement of Science–Westinghouse Award for science writing. Lemonick graduated from Harvard College in 1976 with a bachelor's degree in economics, and received a master's degree in journalism from Columbia University in 1983. He began his career at *Science Digest* magazine, and served briefly as executive editor of *Discover* magazine. He has written free-lance pieces for *People, Science 83, American Health, Audubon,* and the *Washington Post.* He is also the author of *The Light at the Edge of the Universe,* a book about the frontiers of cosmology.

Astronomy is the only branch of science where the questions are literally cosmic. Its practitioners are trying to answer the most profound questions imaginable, the same questions that philosophers have been wrestling with for millennia. How big is the universe? How old is it? What is it made of? How did it begin? How did it come to look the way it does today? And how will it end?

None of these questions has yet been answered in any definitive way. Astronomers know, for example, that the visible stars and planets are made of ordinary chemical elements, mostly hydrogen and helium, with a smattering of other things like carbon, iron, oxygen. But they also know that there is some sort of mysterious dark matter, never observed directly but weighing in at 10 times the mass of the stuff they can see. It may be composed of black holes, dark stars, or even some new type of matter altogether; the search for dark matter is a major focus of modern astronomy.

Astronomers are also facing a growing crisis in understanding how old the cosmos is. Based on the universe's current expansion rate, it must be somewhere between 8 and 12 billion years old. Yet there are stars in the Milky Way that are at least 14 billion years old. That clearly can't be, yet nobody has come up with a satisfying solution. Unraveling this paradox will take years or even decades.

Closer to home, astronomers are on the verge of finding planets that orbit nearby sunlike stars. Everybody assumes they must exist—there is no reason to think our solar system is unique, and there is circumstantial evidence to support the possibility. Yet nobody had found a single planet before October 1995, when Swiss observers found evidence of a Jupiter-like planet circling the star 51 Pegasus, about 50 light-years from Earth. Since then, evidence for at least half-a-dozen more planets has been reported. Over the next decade, astronomers will almost certainly start to find alien planets in abundance, perhaps even starting to study their chemical composition. That will dramatically bolster the argument that life must exist on other worlds (for which the existence of other worlds is the minimum requirement), and give renewed energy to the astronomers who are now searching for signals from alien civilizations.

There are plenty of other questions as well: What supplies the energy that makes starlike quasars outshine an entire galaxy? What powers the bursts of gamma rays that go off at random like cosmic flashbulbs? What happens when a star explodes, when galaxies collide, when a black hole evaporates? Astronomers are wrestling with these and dozens of other mysteries every day at observatories and in front of computer screens, and meeting with each other all the time to discuss (and frequently fight over) the latest evidence.

It may be possible for the discerning reader to guess that I have more than a passing interest in astronomy. It isn't just a beat for me. I am completely in love with the subject, and always have been. My father is a physics professor, and from the time I was very young he would tell me stories about the stars. My vigil for Halley's comet began in about 1960, when I was seven years old. (It wouldn't arrive for another 26 years, and then it was as a huge disappointment.) I checked every book on astronomy out of the library, and was constantly frustrated when most of them spent the first 15 chapters recapping the history of stargazing from the Greeks onward; I wanted the really new, exciting, just-out-of-the observatory stuff—the big bang, the quasars, the possibility of life on other worlds— and they never got to that until the very last chapter.

I was transfixed in the early 1960s by the first closeups of the lunar surface, photographed by the *Explorer* probe in the seconds before it crashed (on purpose) into the Moon; you could actually make out craters three feet across, though they were badly out of focus. The idea that we'd be looking at razor-sharp images of a human moonwalker's footprints less than a decade later was inconceivable, no matter what President Kennedy had told us.

It wasn't until several years after I'd graduated from college, though, that it finally got through my skull that somebody actually wrote those astronomy articles and books I devoured—and that maybe I could do it too.

Faced with the prospect of trying to break into professional science writing at the advanced age of 27, I realized I needed some sort of credential. So in 1982, I went back to graduate school to study journalism—fully aware going in that I eventually wanted to cover whatever was going on from about 100 miles above the Earth's surface to the edge of the universe.

Luckily for me, I had chosen an area of science reporting that terrified even most professionals—a fact that remains true. Most science journalists are interested in medical and health reporting; they want to talk about touchy-feely subjects like the immune system and cholesterol, not bizarre, counterintuitive things like black holes or neutron stars or Einstein's theories of relativity. That, I gradually realized, was why I was so graciously received when I arrived at my first job as an assistant editor at the late and not especially lamented magazine *Science Digest;* I was immediately assigned to edit the astronomy column, and then, when the outside columnist was let go as a cost-saving measure, to write it.

I was immediately plunged into an environment that seemed almost like heaven. For one thing, I was now being paid, in part, to do what I'd always done for pleasure: read everything I could find about astronomy and space. This reading was suddenly much more important, since I had to understand the science and the major issues deeply enough to be able to restate them in my own words, clearly and accurately. Concepts like the inflationary universe, cold dark matter, nuclear fusion, the curvature of the universe, and angular momentum, which I'd always just accepted, now had to be part of my working vocabulary. It was like learning a foreign language after getting along in a pidgin version for years.

And just as is the case with learning a language, the only way to absorb these ideas was through constant repetition. Unlike Bill Gates of Microsoft, who once told me that he never attended college classes, read the text the night before the exam, and then invariably got an *A,* I need to hear something 20 or 30 times before I truly, intuitively grasp it (well, sometimes only two or three). So I read everything I could get my hands on: newspapers with good astronomy writers (the *New York Times,* of course, the *Washington Post,* the *Boston Globe,* the *Los Angeles Times,* and the *San Francisco Chronicle,* fine examples among big-city papers; the *San Jose*

Mercury News and the *Sacramento Bee;* other popular science magazines, including *Discover, Science News,* and the now-defunct *Science 83 (84, 85...* the name changed every year, which staffers found to be a huge pain in the neck); specialty astronomy magazines like *Sky & Telescope* and *Astronomy,* which covered many more areas of space and in greater depth than we could; and the more technical magazines and journals, including *Scientific American, Science, Nature,* and the *Astrophysical Journal* (mostly Greek to me).

I also read plenty of astronomy-related books, including Tim Ferris's *The Red Limit* and Steven Weinberg's *The First Three Minutes* (both still very useful, though getting dated). I urge people to read Marcia Bartusiak's *Through a Universe Darkly,* Dennis Overbye's *Lonely Hearts of the Cosmos,* Ken Croswell's *Alchemy of the Heavens,* and Alan Dressler's *Voyage to the Great Attractor.* Stay away from Stephen Hawking, though: his *A Brief History of Time* was falsely advertised as being comprehensible. (Eventually, I wrote my own book on cosmology: *The Light at the Edge of the Universe.*)

But like all professional astronomy writers, I relied, and I still rely, on the preselection process performed by astronomers, university public relations officers, and editors at the major broad-spectrum science journals. They are the ones who see thousands of astronomical reports every year and decide which ones to promote. Both *Science* and *Nature* magazines, for example, accept only the most significant of the papers they receive. Both send an extra signal, a sort of raised editorial eyebrow, when they think an article is especially interesting by publishing an accompanying news story. (It's usually more comprehensible than the original paper.)

Similarly, press officers send out press releases only on the stories they think are most important at their institutions. It's in the nature of their jobs that they tend to err on the side of being too liberal about the meaning of "important," but there is often gold mixed in with the iron filings, and it pays to be attentive.

In astronomy, moreover, unlike the situation with some other branches of science, the American Astronomical Society, the professional association that most of the scientists belong to, has had an unusually effective press officer for the past decade. Steve Maran, an astronomer himself at NASA's Goddard Space Flight Center and also a talented science writer, is among the best in the business at spotting major stories. He stages press conferences at the association's two big meetings each year, puts reporters in touch with astronomers, and helps explain a report's significance.

Most important of all in developing stories, though, is to cultivate relationships with the astronomers themselves, so that you can find out what they're doing that's newsworthy before it gets as far as a press release or a journal paper. You may not be able to print what you learn right away.

Astronomers, like all scientists, generally prefer to let their discoveries appear in the popular press only after they've been formally reviewed by colleagues and published in a journal or announced at a meeting. But reporters who have established their trustworthiness will often be given an interview in advance—a great help, since it eliminates the need to try and rush a complex story into print or broadcast.

How do you cultivate such relationships? It takes time, but it isn't especially complicated. The basic requirement is common sense. An astronomer is almost indistinguishable from a regular person; he or she is almost always happy to try and help you (and therefore your readers) understand what a particular observation or theoretical breakthrough is and why it's important. All they ask in return is that you do your best to get it right. That generally involves asking questions, and not being afraid to ask dumb ones. You don't want to be too dumb if you can help it; that's why constant reading is important. It's okay to ask what a quasar is, if you really don't know—but even a novice astronomy reporter should know.

However, most scientists don't expect you to know their fields thoroughly at first; if you don't ask questions when you don't understand something, you'll earn a reputation as someone who doesn't really care—or, what's just as bad, as someone who can't tell the difference between grasping a concept and missing it entirely. In general, an astronomer would rather that you ask a question three times to make sure you've got it than have you ask just once and print a lot of garbled nonsense.

Again, though, common sense should prevail; if the scientist is late for a meeting, don't push it; just ask if you can do a follow-up interview later. In other words, don't be obnoxious. I generally raise the possibility of a follow-up interview anyway. Even after a decade of experience, I sometimes get back to the office, start writing my story, and discover that I've failed to ask a crucial question. I find that it helps to have asked the scientist in advance if I can call back later; in fact, I usually acknowledge up front that I'll undoubtedly think of something after the interview is over. Astronomers being human, they know how it is. And since I may find myself baffled after working hours, I always get both an office and a home phone number (and permission to use the latter), plus an e-mail address.

I also warn my sources in advance that I might be asking them to look at all or part of the story before it goes to press. This is still considered anathema to some reporters, and rightly so in political or investigative reporting where you're making an accusation or uncovering some unsavory facts; but when you're explaining why astronomers believe they've found a giant black hole at the core of a distant galaxy, the risk of coming under political or legal pressure not to publish pales beside the risk of printing a garbled story. I don't believe in false professional pride; I explicitly tell astronomers that I may well end up getting something confused in the writing, and that I'd like their help in straightening out the kinks. They appreciate my honesty and my obvious desire to get it right.

All these good intentions don't count for much if the story that appears in print isn't any good, and it's possible to achieve that dubious distinction if good reporting is not conveyed in good writing. It is not as rare as it should be to see a story in which all the facts are correct but where only someone who already knows a lot about astronomy can put together what you're actually talking about. The rules for good science writing are the same as those for good writing in general: Be clear; structure your story so that it flows logically and so the reader really wants to look at the next paragraph; use too few adjectives rather than too many to avoid sounding gushy. Here's an example that I hope illustrates this point, taken from a 1995 cover story on the age of the universe I wrote for *Time:*

> Astronomers have known since Hubble's heyday in the 1920s that you need only two pieces of information to deduce the age of the universe: how fast the galaxies are flying apart and how far away they are. The ratio of these two numbers tells you how fast the cosmos is expanding (a rate known as the Hubble Constant; it's expressed, for those who insist on the proper terminology, in units of kilometers per second of recessional speed per megaparsec of distance). A simple calculation then tells you how long it's been since the expansion started. "There are these two loopholes, though," notes University of Oklahoma astrophysicist David Branch. "What's the right distance, and what's the right speed?"
>
> These loopholes are big enough to drive the Starship Enterprise through. It's terrifically hard to measure how far away galaxies are. If they came in a standard brightness, like 100-W light bulbs, the astronomers could just figure that a dimmer galaxy was more distant than a bright one. Unfortunately, they don't. Edwin Hubble himself didn't realize this and triggered an earlier "age crisis" in the 1940s when he announced that the universe was 2 billion years old. Geologists already knew that Earth was older than that.

It's also important to define your terms when necessary, judging from experience what that means. Thus, you don't have to tell readers what a star or a planet is. But you might have to tell them what a galaxy is, depending on the audience. You almost always have to define a black hole or a quasar, at least in passing. You're remiss if you don't define the cosmic microwave background or the redshift whenever you use them.

Finally, you have to learn what to leave out. Just about everyone has had the excruciating experience of listening to an inept raconteur telling an endless story full of unimportant details. It's hard to extract the signal from the background noise. Science writing is analogous, though not precisely the same. There are few if any unimportant details in a piece of scientific research. But some facts and logical steps and concepts are more important than others—and if you include everything, the average lay reader is going to end up hopelessly confused.

Since that's the opposite of what we want to achieve, good science writers do leave out lots of the details, and leap over three steps in the deductive process in order to get to a fourth. We know we're doing it, and the scientists understand that we have to. The best science writers come out of this balancing act—between drowning the reader in facts and oversimplifying to the point of inaccuracy—with a story that is both accurate and readable. This difficulty is one reason why people with scientific training sometimes make terrible science writers; they simply can't judge how much to leave out. If I have any doubts about whether I'm striking the right balance, I try and explain the story to an acquaintance who doesn't know much about science, and also to a scientist.

If I've done my job right, I'll end up writing a good, newsworthy story. If I do it over and over, astronomers will know they can trust me, and they'll begin calling me, volunteering information about work in progress, about stories coming up that I might want to cover. They'll also be receptive when I call them and ask what's the most interesting or exciting thing they've heard on the astronomical grapevine lately. Almost everything worth talking about has been discussed at length among astronomers before it's made public. You might as well know what they've been discussing.

Finally, while it's very satisfying to come upon a piece of breaking news long before it breaks, it's even more satisfying to detect a trend well before it happens. That's where a serious basic interest in the subject—and a layperson's sense of astonishment at the mind-bending phenomena the universe conceals—come in handy.

When I heard someone speak at an astronomical conference in 1983 about something called gravitational lensing—a cosmic optical illusion formed when a nearby galaxy's strong gravity creates a double image of a more distant quasar—the concept itself struck me as being so strangely cool that I sold my editor on a feature story. It turned out to be one of the first on what has become, more than a decade later, one of the hottest fields in astrophysics.

26

Technology Writing

JON VAN

A science writer for the *Chicago Tribune* since 1977, Jon Van joined that paper as a general assignment reporter in 1973. Previously, he covered local government for the *Des Moines Register* from 1968 to 1973. He earned master's and bachelor's degrees from the University of Iowa. Van is past president of the National Association of Science Writers.

In the 1990s, American policymakers periodically set about adding the words "and technology" to official references to science in the nation's laws. Some even favored changing the name of the National Science Foundation to the National Science and Technology Foundation. The idea was to stress the goal of converting scientific discovery into practical application that creates new industries, markets, and jobs.

Technology is central to most news stories about science and is, in fact, the engine driving modern economies, but even so, many people appreciate it poorly. Even well-informed, thoughtful people may have a vague notion that science is somehow "pure," an enterprise pursued by high-minded truth-seekers out to answer questions that interest them without regard to practicality.

Once scientists make discoveries, others may apply them to commercially valuable questions, producing technology, in this view. Such a notion of technology and its relation to science isn't really wrong, but it is simplistic and incomplete. While technology does, indeed, depend on scientific research and discovery to prosper, the reverse is also true. Science and technology are tightly intertwined, usually so much so that it is difficult to see where science leaves off and technology begins. Just as early astronomers owed a huge debt to telescope builders and often made telescopes themselves, progress today in fundamental research often requires devising better technology.

High-energy physicists who investigate subatomic particles and the basic forces that control them spend much of their time designing and building new tools that enable them to recreate and observe conditions mimicking those of the earliest moments of the universe's birth. They are limited by the reach of their technology and seek always to extend it. On the other hand, engineers who design new telecommunications systems for the commercial market may encounter the limits of scientific understanding of physical phenomena in their quest to improve efficiency and reduce the costs of their systems.

Rather than trying to separate science and technology into two distinct categories, I find it more useful to adopt a model suggested by Burton Richter, longtime director of the Stanford Linear Accelerator Center. He proposes that the double helix of DNA is the ideal metaphor when considering science and technology. In this view, science comprises one strand in the double helix and technology the other. The two are inextricably linked, and neither can advance without the other.

My point is that anyone who writes about science will inevitably find himself or herself writing about technology as well. Those who write about technology, on the other hand, may ignore the science woven through their topic, but they do so to their own detriment and that of their readers.

Having said that, one can acknowledge that writing about technology can pose challenges that are different from those encountered when writing about scientific research. For instance, when you write about some new technology, such as coating a material with a thin diamond film to improve its durability, it is important to address the question of whether something that is theoretically possible does, indeed, work in the laboratory and in field testing. Other important questions concern the cost of doing something and the need for it. In the case of thin diamond films, researchers have demonstrated their ability to coat cutting tools with these films, but that doesn't assure an industrial success. Diamond-coated cutting tools must be inexpensive enough to produce and to compete with other cutting tools and must show significantly better performance to gain the attention of the people who design, make, and use industrial cutting equipment.

A rule of thumb is that a technologic innovation should be a factor of 10 better than existing equipment at making things faster, cheaper, and with greater potential to succeed commercially. This doesn't mean you shouldn't write stories about innovations that may be only incrementally better than existing technology. The chief criterion for writing a story is whether readers may find it interesting. But to avoid appearing naive, the writer must discuss the marketplace hurdles a technologic innovation faces.

Indeed, it is fine to openly question whether any given innovation will make its way out of the laboratory. Innovations that never make it into commerce may still give researchers the foundation for future success. The first computers offered to the commercial market were, after all, money losers, due mostly to market forces, not lack of intrinsic value. But when someone writes a story about a new discovery regarding songs learned by birds, there is no need to raise questions about practical applications. A story about how materials scientists have developed a new form of plastic that is both sturdy and flexible, as well as being able to conduct electricity, lacks context without reference to the market value for such stuff.

Because technology is so central to modern commerce, newspaper writers who cover it often work for the business desk rather than for the national, features, or city desks. At the *Chicago Tribune* where I work, the technology beat was staffed by business writers for several years before I took it over. Having spent many years covering medicine and science for the *Tribune,* I brought a decidedly different perspective to the beat.

Whereas my predecessor's approach to covering telecommunications, for example, centered on marketing strategies and profit margins, mine has focused on photonics and digitization. Because my editors on the financial desk have a strong business news orientation, there are pressures to consider such things as profits and market share when writing stories, but I haven't found this difficult. My own bias is that it is easier for someone who is comfortable discussing basic technology with engineers to also talk to marketing and financial people than it is the other way around. The market forces rocking today's communications industry are basically generated by advancing technology.

For instance, telecommunications was once considered a "natural monopoly," with excellent reason. At the dawn of this century, as the telephone industry was getting its start, competing phone companies meant a hodgepodge of poles and tangles of wires in cities. But if someone you hoped to call didn't use your phone company, you couldn't dial him or her up. Businesses that wanted to be accessible to customers by phone had to get a line from every competing phone company. This mess led to granting a monopoly to one company, A T & T's Bell Telephone, for most urban areas and a collection of independent monopolies in rural America. Bell and these independents cooperated to interconnect and were regulated by federal and state authorities.

The system made sense for several reasons, but chief among them was the standardization it brought to our telephone industry in the United States. As the one big gorilla of telecommunications that owned and ran the biggest networks and also manufactured the equipment they used, Bell imposed standards throughout the country and built the most advanced and universal phone system in the world. But after several successful decades, this system was undermined by advancing technology.

As a monopoly, Bell's interests lay not in embracing the newest and best innovations but rather in upgrading the system slowly and deliberately, getting maximum use out of existing equipment before replacing it.

But Bell's monopoly didn't extend to ideas. Engineers outside the Bell system, as well as those at Bell Labs, were finding new and different ways of sending messages. One group in Chicago set up a system of microwave radio towers along the highway between Chicago and St. Louis to give truckers a means of staying in touch with their home office while on the road. Eventually these innovators, who called themselves Microwave-Communications, Inc. (MCI), decided they could provide long-distance phone service between Chicago and St. Louis using this microwave system and make a profit charging business customers less than the Bell system.

While most of MCI's battle with A T & T played out in the courts, it was a technologic innovation that sowed the seeds for what led to the breakup of the Bell system in 1984 to accommodate full-fledged competition for long-distance phone service. These days, further innovation in the use of light traveling over strands of glass and digitized radio signals traveling through the air have undermined the monopolies in local phone service created in 1984.

The standards imposed on telephone communication by the Bell system produced a marvelous system, but once it was in place, it was vulnerable to improved technology that no single company could hope to monopolize. Understanding the technology is invaluable to comprehending what is happening to an industry.

Another basic marketplace truth is that having the best technology never guarantees financial success. But no one in business can afford to ignore new technologies, and that provides a ready audience for stories about technologic innovation.

Some of the stories I have the most fun reporting and writing are those that combine university research with field applications. The study of chaos, which looks for patterns in events that occur in a nonlinear, seemingly random fashion, provides an example. In one story on chaos I described studies by Northwestern University scientists concerned with the best way to thoroughly mix a batch of chemicals in the most efficient fashion. Failure to mix substances completely can cause explosions in toxic waste holding tanks, and chaos theory can inform scientists as to how, even with vigorous stirring, some islands of chemicals in a batch may be left unmixed. But instead of limiting the story to work done by university scientists, I also included the work of Richard Morley, chief executive of Flavors Technology Inc. of Amherst, New Hampshire, a firm that develops hardware and software platforms for industry. Morley puts chaos theory into everyday use for manufacturers in a way readily understandable to a reader.

"Chaos allows us to change our thinking and take advantage of the world as it is," Morley told me. Instead of trying to rigidly control all the processes in a factory, his approach is to give robots throughout the factory a few simple rules to follow and then turn them loose.

A system Morley set up for a major automaker gave seven robotic painting stations the same simple rules to follow: first, do what's easiest; second, do what's needed; third, do something. Following these rules, a robot loaded with black paint will search among vehicles lined up to be painted seeking any scheduled for black because that's the easiest thing to do. If no black paint candidate is found, the robot will search for a vehicle with a red tag, indicating it should receive priority, and then purge its black paint and load up with whatever color the high-priority vehicle needs, because that follows the second rule, to do what's needed. If no priority vehicles are found, the robot picks a car at random and paints it the desired color, because that obeys the third rule, to do something. When one of the seven robotic painters in the system breaks down and quits painting, which happens regularly, the flexibility and self-correcting nature of the system enables the other six to take over the work of the seventh smoothly, Morley said. By combining Morley's application of chaos theory with cutting-edge university research, I tried to give readers a greater appreciation of the reach and depth of chaos theory on technology.

Here is how I led into the chaos story:

> While a lot of people may think there's already too much chaos in their lives, that making things more orderly and predictable would be better, that's only because they don't understand chaos, say researchers.
>
> It may be unpredictable, they say, but chaos can be controlled. And it can be far more useful than bland, orderly systems.
>
> Chaos theory offers a variety of new processes and products that range from more effective ways of mixing chemicals to more efficient satellite communications systems to cardiac defibrillators that use subtle electrical signals instead of massive voltage to stop irregular heart rhythms.

Using similar approaches, I've described how fuzzy logic and neural networks can make computers less literal and more useful in applications that range from scanning airplane wings for serious cracks to making automobile airbag systems work better.

Even though technology stories generally focus on cold hard equipment, software, or concepts that intrinsically have little of the traditional elements of a human interest story, it usually isn't hard to find something in the story that will grab a reader's interest. This might include a person's motivation for pursuing a particular line of inquiry.

In one story I did about the quest for "smart" hearing aids that could filter out noise and amplify only the sounds of interest to people, one man was working on this problem solely because his mother, who wore a hearing aid, said, "Enough already with all your fancy research, why don't you do something useful like inventing a hearing aid that I can use?" Some of my favorite technology stories are those that focus on innovators and the process of innovation rather than any specific technology. It was in doing just such a story that I learned, from the man who invented the first usable remote control device for television sets, that he and his colleagues at Zenith were literally ordered to develop a remote-control clicker because the man who founded Zenith, Eugene F. McDonald, personally couldn't stand television commercials and thought that his customers probably couldn't either, so he wanted some way to quickly and easily tune them out.

As much as I enjoy learning about new technology and describing innovations to my readers, my best advice to writers is to remain skeptical. The enthusiasm of engineers for their technology is infectious and seductive, and it is all too easy to become a cheerleader instead of a critical reporter.

The fact is that even successful new technologies such as color television, video players, and fax machines took a decade or more after their introduction to become widely accepted. It could well happen that people will someday watch some video shows on their laptop computers and conduct two-way communications on their television sets, but if that does happen, the nature of that communication will likely be very different from today's conventional phone call or television show.

People have a way of adopting new technology in ways that developers of that technology mostly failed to anticipate. In the 1980s experts predicted that home computers would become widespread. People would use them to run their homes, went the thinking, getting up in the morning to coffee and toast whipped up by the computer and coming home at night to hot meals and cold drinks served by robots. Almost no one suggested that people would use their computers to create and publish documents or spend hours playing games on them.

Likewise, when it became possible to use computers to keep track of products as they were being manufactured, many touted the notion of automated inventory control for factories, and that was widely implemented. But what manufacturers learned, after wasting billions of dollars, was that keeping track of a large inventory is the wrong problem. The right problem is keeping inventory extremely small and using information technology to make product and get it out the door far more quickly than was traditionally thought possible.

The savvy writer will remember that when it comes to technology, even those bright and eager engineers who develop it aren't really experts on how their technology will be used or its impact on society. A good reporter who spends time talking to people who actually use new technology may spot trends or countertrends that will be far more interesting to people than the commercial blather from marketing people who work where the technology is being developed.

When doing a story on telecommuting, you can get oodles of stuff praising the concept from phone companies and equipment makers, and it may be difficult to locate anyone forced to work at home by a boss who didn't want to pay for office space, but getting at the dark side of the trend is what can make the story really worth reading. One story I did was touted as an example of our brave new age of telecommuting: a man who continued to hold his job in Chicago while riding his bicycle across America. When I asked the cyclist how well his cellular phone, pager, and laptop computer were working for him out there in Wyoming, he had to concede that once he left California, he didn't seem to be within the range of any reliable wireless communication at all, and half the time the wire-line network of rural phone companies wouldn't enable his laptop to link up to the home computer in Chicago. Even though independent rural phone companies serve less than 20 percent of America's customers, they cover more than 80 percent of the nation's territory, a lesson worth passing along to readers who expect that the communications service they get in Chicago, Dallas, or San Francisco will be available everywhere else.

One last point about how technology can differ from science, from the reporter's perspective, concerns that icon of modern America, the professional meeting. When attending the annual meeting of physicists or chemists, a reporter will find the event consists of numerous presentations of research results by scientists. To assist reporters, the association staff will probably have picked out certain sessions thought to be of general interest and have written press releases explaining them. They may also arrange for press conferences. At meetings of engineers, the emphasis may often be on new products and processes. The press room may be filled with press kits prepared by companies to promote their newest products. These events may have some interesting speakers and research presentations, but they are usually overshadowed by the emphasis on the meeting as a trade show. For reporters covering these affairs for general interest media, it may take more preparation than covering a meeting where academically oriented researchers predominate. You'll have to read through programs in advance and talk to people organizing the trade show to get an idea of who'll be there and what things of interest they might have to say. This advance work is often worth the effort. At one gathering of manufacturing engineers in Chicago, I was able to discover and tell my readers of the feverish research underway to discover substitutes for such environmentally damaging products as freon.

In summary, the main skills one needs to write about technology are very similar to those needed for covering science or medicine. The added dimension one needs to provide for technology coverage is a perspective that conveys some understanding of the marketplace and historic trends. I contend that it is easier for a science writer to acquire the business perspective to do this than it is for a business writer to become comfortable delving into the guts of what makes a technology work. But, in truth, a lot of business writers do a grand job covering technology. The main traits needed, curiosity and skepticism, are actually the same things any good reporter covering any beat has got to have.

PART FOUR

Working Outside the Media

●●●●●●●●●●●●●●●●●●●●●

27 • • • • • • • • • • • • • • • • •

Introduction

CAROL L. ROGERS

Carol L. Rogers currently teaches at the College of Journalism at the University of Maryland at College Park, and is doing research there for her doctorate in mass communication. Previously, she spent 14 years as director of communications for the American Association for the Advancement of Science (AAAS). On leaving her job there, the National Association of Science Writers bestowed on Carol its first-ever award for outstanding professional service.

Carol continues her ties to AAAS as a fellow and as secretary of the AAAS's Section on General Interest in Science and Engineering. She is a member of the board of the Council for the Advancement of Science Writing and of the D.C. Science Writers Association. She was a longtime member of the board of the National Association of Science Writers, and served on the board of the University of Missouri Science Journalism Center.

Carol also conducts seminars for both journalists and scientists. She is co-editor of *Scientists and Journalists: Reporting Science as News*, and is a senior contributing editor for *Science Communication*.

If a guide to science writing had been produced fifteen years ago, it's likely that this section wouldn't have been included at all or would have been relegated to a single chapter—a footnote, as it were, to a discussion of "real" science writing. Its existence attests to two significant changes—the increasing numbers of science information people and their accompanying visibility.

If any single concept could be used to represent science writing activities in nonmedia organizations, it would probably be variety. I was asked recently by a student to describe a typical day in my career as a science information officer. Not only was I unable to reconstruct any typical day, I was unable to define any typical job. Similarities existed—both across days and across jobs—but it was the differences that tended to define the jobs.

Some science information officers find themselves primarily writing—press releases, news and feature stories for magazines, speeches, exhibit copy, radio or television reports, and the like. And others find themselves writing rarely—their days are spent handling media relations, for example, initiating and responding to inquiries from reporters. Most information officers, however, regularly juggle many of these tasks.

If you want a job that is interesting and challenging, provides professional growth opportunities, offers a good salary, good benefits, and a good working environment, and has a significant impact on people's lives and our society—a science information job might fill the bill. Further, more jobs actually exist in science information than in the mass media. With cutbacks and consolidations and closures, mass media jobs are in short supply.

The very resource problems encountered by mass media organizations often provide opportunities for other institutions. For example, as television stations face cutbacks, they are more likely to welcome well-done video news releases (VNRs) to provide their viewers with good stories they are unable to cover themselves.

At the same time, organizations are increasingly recognizing how important their various constituents are to their own well-being and survival. So they develop special programs and publications—research magazines, newsletters and newspapers, brochures—to keep those constituents informed about their activities and to generate interest and involvement. All of these activities can provide opportunities for science writers.

You can prepare yourself for these opportunities in a number of ways. Some of the most skilled and successful practitioners in the field came into it from careers as working journalists. Other highly skilled professionals came into it, as I did, with science backgrounds. Still others followed different routes. No one formula seems to work for everyone.

Science information work is not for the fainthearted. One of the hardest parts of the job is staying on top of things—your organization (its history, programs, principal people, interests), your specialty area (physics, engineering, microbiology, psychology), your key constituents (reporters, members, legislators), and your communication techniques (VNRs, desktop publishing, Web Home Pages). Keeping up in your specialty area can be an especially daunting task. The chapters earlier in this book can be as instructive for a science information officer as for a mass media science writer. In fact, the levels of knowledge and understanding required for the two jobs are virtually indistinguishable. So you need to employ some of the same strategies that journalists use—read the major publications in your field, as well as interdisciplinary science publications and mass media accounts of science. Attend scientific meetings—not just those for which you are managing a news room—and meetings designed for science writers.

In addition, as several authors in this section point out, science communicators have to consider many different audiences that might vary considerably in such factors as age, education level, knowledge of or interest in the topic, and need for the material. In several of these types of positions, one day or week you might be writing a news release for reporters, followed by a VNR script for a mass audience, followed by an article for your association's members or your university's alumni.

Strategies that help you get to know your audiences better include going to the meetings they attend, reading what they read, and making an effort to know them individually and as a group.

And then, keeping up with the changing communications landscape can be one of the hardest tasks of all. The world was simpler, although not necessarily easier, a few years ago. News releases were printed and mailed, radio and television programs were taped and mailed on cassettes or reels. The rapidly escalating pace of technology has changed all that. Computers and satellites have provided numerous opportunities to communicate in real-time across the world. At the same time, cable and CD-ROMs have made it possible to target very narrowly specialized audiences.

Along with the opportunities these technologies provide come new challenges. Not only does one have to be on the cutting edge of these new developments, but also one needs to keep them in perspective, recognizing their limitations as well as their possibilities. One of these limitations is access. Many of these new technologies enable us to deliver our information directly to key audiences without having it filtered through the lens of others—of the media, for example. But we need to remember that access—while growing significantly—is still quite limited. Large segments of the population will probably never see a Web page, interesting and appealing and informative as it might be. Attending to such audiences in the face of these technologies might be an especially difficult task.

Finally, no introduction to the realm of science information would be complete without some attention to the professional tensions that exist for people who choose these careers. Several chapter authors mention them in passing or address them in some detail. At least to some extent, I believe that some of the tensions exist because no single philosophy unites the field. For example, do practitioners see their role as promoting their institutions, providing information to general and selected audiences, helping an organization recognize and respond to the needs of its constituents, none of the above, all of the above, or some combination of the above?

Many institutional science writers regularly take on each of these roles, shifting between them as the situations warrant. But those shifts can have an impact on the writer's credibility. For example, when the role assumed is one of promotion, relationships with reporters may be altered.

More tangibly, tensions can exist between the science writer and the scientists with whom they work. Scientists usually have little understanding of how the media or institutional science writers operate. They often see science information people as representing the interests of mass media reporters, rather than the interests of individual scientists or of the scientific community, as if the two are necessarily in conflict.

At the same time, mass media reporters often view institutional science writers as representatives of their home institutions, granting them little credibility or professional status and often failing to acknowledge their own reliance on the assistance these other professionals provide them.

In the past, I have referred to this particular set of tensions as those of the practitioner in the middle—balancing somewhere between their home institution and the mass media—partly at home in both places, but maybe never completely at home in either.

If the challenges inherent in these science writing careers are so great and the tensions likely to last indefinitely, why would you want to choose such a career? The chapters that follow give you lots of answers to that question. Where else can you deal with major issues that are at or near the top of the public agenda—issues such as AIDS or global climate change or how humans develop and learn? And in what other professions do you get to develop and perfect skills in so many different areas?

Exactly what opportunities will be available in the future is difficult to predict. But they are likely to require the same types of qualifications we see reflected in the best practitioners today—good written and oral communication skills, flexibility, adaptability, versatility and a commitment to the highest ideals of journalism and public responsibility.

28

Colleges and Universities

DAVID F. SALISBURY

David F. Salisbury has been a university science writer for 10 years, first at the University of California, Santa Barbara, currently at Stanford University. Before that he wrote about science and technology at the *Christian Science Monitor* for more than 12 years. He studied physics at the University of Washington, obtaining a bachelor of science degree, before pursuing science writing as a career. As a reporter, he received a number of awards, including the National Association of Science Writers Science-in-Society Award, the Aviation Space Writers Association Award, and the National Society of Professional Engineers Technology Writing Award. As a university science writer, his work has been recognized by several awards from the Council for the Advancement and Support of Education. He has also written articles for a number of publications, including *New Scientist, Popular Science, Technology Review,* and *Outside* magazines. He is the author of *Money Matters: Personal Financial Decision Making with the Pocket Calculator.*

The announcement of an unusual archaeological dig in Peru gave me one of my most dramatic firsthand demonstrations of the difference between writing newspaper science articles and university news releases.

It was January 1985. I worked for the *Christian Science Monitor* and was based in San Francisco at the time. The University of Colorado at Boulder announced an upcoming news conference. The subject was an agreement with the Peruvian government to begin a major dig at a remote site called Gran Pajaten, which contained the ruins of a major Incan city in the type of mountainous, cloud-forest jungle setting that had long been discounted by archaeologists. In addition, the site, described as rivaling Macchu Pichu in extent, closely resembled the descriptions of the legendary lost city where the Inca kings supposedly secreted the last of their treasure!

It sounded like a good story. So I put it together with some other ideas

217

that I could pursue in the area and got my editor's approval for a trip to Denver. As a result, I was one of the few representatives from a national publication at the news conference. But a number of reporters from papers such as the *New York Times* and the *Washington Post* covered the story by telephone and news release.

Only later, after reading some of these other articles, did I realize that there had been a failure in communications. Several of the other reporters had described the story as the possible discovery of the lost city of Incas, which it wasn't. The site had been discovered in 1963, as the university's five-page release and four-page backgrounder pointed out, and was fairly well known.

Shortly thereafter a member of a New York explorers' club, who had visited the site previously, raised a ruckus and forced the *New York Times* and some other papers to run corrections. As was all too human, some of the reporters accused the university, unfairly in my view, of misleading them.

In pondering what went wrong, I have concluded that the university science writer involved underestimated the power of strong cultural images like the lost city of the Incas. In retrospect, the lead of the news release—"Exploring one of the legendary 'lost cities of the Andes' will be a major focus of a comprehensive research program to be undertaken by the University of Colorado, Boulder"—was ambiguous. Enough so that even experienced science writers, under deadline pressures and working by phone, jumped to the conclusion that it must be a discovery story.

The lesson for university science writers is that accuracy alone is sometimes not enough for a news release. Particularly with major stories, you must do everything possible to minimize misinterpretation. Sometimes this demand can take some of the fun and creativity out of the writing process. Clever leads and literary allusions are often prone to misinterpretation. As a result, I often begin the first draft of a story with my cleverest lead and then delete it on the second draft.

The primary imperative of science reporting is readability. The science reporter is always trying to make his or her stories as interesting as possible to editors and readers. Sometimes accuracy suffers. But, as long as the errors are minor and infrequent, they do not harm the reputation of the reporter. On the other hand, an error, or even a misinterpretation like that which occurred on the Gran Pajaten story, can seriously injure the reputation of the university science writer.

In many ways, the two jobs of science reporter and university science writer are very similar. Both require similar abilities to comprehend technical subjects readily and explain them clearly. But, as the Gran Pajaten case illustrates, there are some important differences.

The experienced university science writer places a higher priority on clarity and accuracy than on readability in his or her writing; works closely with university scientists; responds to media requests for experts; keeps track of the beats and interests of science reporters; advises scientists how to deal with reporters; and copes with the pressures from academic and administrative politics.

A MULTIPLICITY OF AUDIENCES

Normally, science reporters write each article for a single audience. Although the readership of a given publication may have a distinct range of tastes, educational levels, and interests, there is still an "average" reader whom reporters learn to write for. The situation is more complicated for university science writers.

The primary readers of university science writers are reporters and editors. But, you must bear in mind the very different levels of knowledge and sophistication of those in different branches of the media, ranging from trade publications, newspapers, and magazines and wire services to television and radio. Then there is the campus community. Faculty members, in particular, put a high premium on factual accuracy. Finally, there are alumni. Frequently, science writers write specifically for alumni publications, or their stories are edited for this purpose.

AN UNCEASING SEARCH FOR GOOD STORIES

Tracking the research of hundreds of scientists at a major campus is another critical part of the university science writer's job. As a science reporter at a major national newspaper, I found that a good proportion of story ideas came to my attention through news conferences, important events like space missions, papers appearing in *Science* or *Nature,* and news releases and queries. My major problem was usually choosing the most important or interesting story to pursue at a given time. As a university science writer, on the other hand, fewer stories come to you. You generally have to go out and find them.

Of the total number of researchers on campus, a certain number are pursuing potentially newsworthy projects. But to identify them you must build and maintain an extensive personal network of faculty contacts. Today's major research university is not a slow-paced, deliberative place. Successful university scientists are busy and entrepreneurial. They often work 60, 70, even 80 hours per week, travel frequently, and can be difficult to contact, particularly on short notice.

Scientists live in a different "time zone" from reporters. They work on projects for months and years, so a paper that has been out for six months can still seem new to them. Conversely, in some fields it takes six months to a year for a paper to appear in journal, and by then the scientist has moved onto another topic and considers the paper old news. Because scientists' time frame is so different, they are unlikely to contact the news office at a journalistically appropriate time.

Introducing yourself to a scientist once is seldom enough. When I find an interesting piece of research in progress, I normally check in every month, quarter, or half-year, depending on the state of the research, until it reaches a point where it can be written up. Thank goodness for computer calendars! There is no central office or database on a university campus that contains information useful for this purpose. So it is extremely important to locate these knowledgeable scientists and build a strong personal relationship with them.

SCIENCE WRITERS FUNCTION LIKE MESSENGER-RNA

At a party, a NASA biologist once told me that he thought science writers performed a job analogous to that of messenger-RNA, the ribonucleic molecule that conveys the information from DNA that is translated into the structure of a particular polypeptide. Using this analogy, a university science writers is like a specialized form of messenger-RNA that, first, locates newsworthy projects from the large body of research produced at its institution and, second, translates it into a form that the news media, and other audiences, can use.

Translation entails parameters beyond comprehending the research and clearly describing why it is important or interesting. Scientific research is an ongoing process. True breakthroughs are extremely rare, and frequently not recognized at the time they are made. The news media, by contrast, is event-driven. So part of the writer's job is to find appropriate events, such as the publication of a paper, the presentation at a meeting, or the issuance of a patent, that enhance the news value of a given piece of research. Also, the media is obsessed with superlatives: the first, fastest, smallest, hottest, coldest. Many scientists resist such characterizations. So it is frequently up to the science writer not only to identify any such superlatives that apply, but also to convince the scientist that they should be used.

DUCK! INCOMING!

Another major element of the university science writer's job is to respond to media requests for information and experts. Depending on the size and reputation of the research university involved, dealing with incoming requests for information can take up from a very little to a major portion of your time and energy. At Stanford, it can take as much as 20 percent of my time in any given week. Such requests vary all over the map. They can be as general as "Do you have any hot research projects I can write about?" or as specific as "I need somebody who knows about Dr. X's recent paper and can comment on it." Calls come not only from print publications, but also television and radio programs. Not only is it important to know what various research projects are about, but also how they look and sound.

Reporters have the luxury of concentrating on a few stories at one time. After a story is written, they can generally put the subject out of their minds and go on to the next one. That is not the case for university science writers. Researching and writing a story is just the beginning, not the end of the process. You must keep the basic details of a number of research projects continually in mind, making the job much harder on one's long-term memory than reporting!

PLACING SPECIAL STORIES

Some stories obviously will generate widespread media interest. A new study on the amount of damage from a major earthquake is one example. But there are dozens of good stories with a more limited market. In these cases, having a sense of which science publications, programs, or individuals are most likely to be interested in the specific topic can be the key to placing the stories. Given the rapidity with which beats change and people move, this is as big a task as tracking scientists.

Carol Cruzan Morton at UC Davis is particularly good at matching writers with unlikely stories. The key, she says, is paying attention to different writers' style and interests and finding the source of conflict that makes a good story. While one person may prefer writing about personalities, another may specialize in pure science, and a third may concentrate on public policy.

An example of her matchmaking: Davis geneticist John Gillespie had developed a new mathematical theory to support the punctuated equilibrium theory of evolution. In the course of interviewing, Gillespie happened to mention to Morton that a Japanese scientist who is a leading proponent of steady-state evolution had called him "the evil scientist from America." That interesting angle allowed Morton to pitch the story successfully to Deborah Blum at the *Sacramento Bee*.

JOURNALISTIC VERSUS SCIENTIFIC COMMUNITIES

In addition to the functional differences between university science writing and science reporting, there are important differences in basic loyalties. Science reporters owe their primary allegiance to their readers and rightly consider themselves members of the journalistic community. The allegiance of university science writers, by contrast, is first to the institution where they work and second to the scientific community.

This gap is not as great as those that exist between reporters and sources in many other fields. The scientific and journalistic communities share two defining values—a skeptical approach to information and a devotion to discovering the truth—that make them in many ways natural allies. In fact, as Marcel LaFollette, research professor of science and technology policy at George Washington University, has pointed out, the fourth estate and the scientific community, which has been termed the fifth estate, have worked together quite congenially in the past. In the 1920s, for example, mass-market magazines like *Collier's Weekly* and the *Saturday Evening Post* drew heavily on reports of exciting scientific discoveries to help expand their circulations. At the same time, leading scientists saw the mass media as a way to attract political and economic support for research. During this period science journalism became recognized as a legitimate specialty within the field, and scientists' participation in public communication was legitimized.

Despite the values that the two estates share, there are many differences. To scientists, the devil is definitely in the details, while journalists are interested primarily in the big picture. To scientists, disputation is part of the process of advancing understanding ever closer to truth; to journalists conflict is the source of drama that adds zest to a story. Scientists are continually trying to build consensus, while journalists focus on the drama of pro and con. To scientists, peer review is an integral part of a process designed to reduce errors. To most journalists, allowing sources to review material before publication is an unacceptable ceding of editorial independence. To scientists, technical terms provide added precision and clarity to discourse. To journalists, technical terms constitute a jargon that obfuscates science and makes it incomprehensible to the general reader.

MEDIA COVERAGE BRINGS RISKS AS WELL AS BENEFITS

Many reporters feel that they are doing scientists a favor by covering their research. In some cases they are. Publicity can help attract outside funding for research, provide ammunition for getting increased resources from the university administration, sometimes even help a scientist explain to spouse, children, and neighbors what he or she does for a living. Increasingly, coverage can also catalyze useful interdisciplinary collaborations by bringing research to the attention of scientists in different fields.

But there are significant risks for scientists as well. A case in point is what happened when the media covered an article by UC Santa Barbara anthropologist Napoleon Chagnon that appeared in *Science* magazine in 1988. It dealt with the question of why the Yanomamo Indians, who live in the remote jungles of the Amazon, practice blood feuding. Chagnon reported data showing that men who killed members of neighboring villages while defending their homes or revenging the death of kin had more wives and children on average than men who did not. He used this data to support the hypothesis that the reason for blood feuding was competition for reproductive resources.

Both the article and the news release that we prepared carefully avoided using culturally laden terms such as killers or murderers. But in the extensive coverage that followed such distinctions were lost. The *Los Angeles Times* headline was "Homicidal Streak in S. American Tribe Studied by Anthropologist," while a Scripps Howard's story proclaimed that "murder and violence were common in primitive societies, making heroes out of killers and explaining some of modern culture's fascination with military leaders." The temptation to interpret Chagnon's research in American cultural terms was apparently irresistible and overshadowed the scientific significance of the work.

As a result of the coverage, a group of Brazilian Marxist anthropologists denounced Chagnon to the American Anthropological Association, not so much to challenge his research as to complain that the resulting negative portrayals of the Yanomamo threatened efforts to protect their lands from the gold hunters who were moving aggressively into the area. Chagnon was able to fend off this attack, but it took a toll in time, energy, and emotion. It's not clear to me whether all the publicity hurt or helped the Yanomamo. What is clear, however, is that few of the science reporters or editors who did the story gave serious thought to the impact that their articles would have on Chagnon or his subjects.

Enough scientists feel they have been burned by reporters that university science writers frequently find themselves in the position of defending the media. Part of the job involves persuading scientists that the overall benefits to the science community at large are worth the time, energy, and risk involved in dealing with reporters. Dennis Meredith at Duke University has developed four time-tested techniques to encourage reluctant faculty researchers to work with the media:

- Point out to faculty members that surveys have shown that the majority of responses faculty receive as a result of publicity are not from the public, but from colleagues in either their field or related fields.
- Emphasize that carefully prepared news releases actually protect the faculty member from any charges that he or she may have overstated or misrepresented the research.
- Point out that news releases are sent not only to the lay media, but to specialty and professional magazines such as *Science, Nature,* and *Scientific American,* which faculty consider important outlets for news of their work.
- Point out that, by working with the media, faculty can assure that stories will be more accurate.

DEALING WITH SCIENCE AND CAMPUS POLITICS

Generally, university science writers do not cover science politics. But that doesn't mean they can safely ignore them. Academic politics can be every bit as vicious as what takes place in city hall or on Capitol Hill. Ignorance is an invitation to the less scrupulous to use you for their own ends.

Proponents of a research project or program that is in trouble may turn to the campus news office for publicity to help their project out. If the research involved is solid, this can be an opportunity, because the researchers involved have a strong motivation to work with you. On the other hand, it can be a sign that the effort has some deeper problems. To determine which is the case, you need to know what is really going on. This is another reason why maintaining a strong faculty network is so important.

In cases where you have some doubts, one protection is to insist that anything you do be tied to publication in a peer reviewed journal. But this raises a philosophical point for which I don't have a good answer. University science writers must continually make decisions on whether or not to publicize research on what are essentially journalistic grounds. When a given piece of research would make a good story, to what extent should a science writer act as a gatekeeper on scientific grounds? I'm not comfortable with the proposition that we should refrain from publicizing work that is controversial or politically incorrect. When we do so, however, it is important that we tell our news media colleagues and other readers that the work has strong detractors. On the other hand, I have no desire to promote flawed science. Unfortunately, there will always be cases where it is extremely difficult for university writers, like reporters, to tell the difference.

All but the most fortunate university science writers sooner or later face pressure from administrators to publicize certain projects or put some questionable spin on certain stories. The most egregious cases are when the administration encourages its scientists to "publish in the press" before the research has been peer reviewed. The most notorious case of this sort in recent years was the cold fusion controversy ignited by the University of Utah. But there have been a number of other less-publicized cases.

Difficult as it may be, university science writers have a responsibility to oppose this kind of pressure. Usually, reminding the administrators and researchers involved of the ultimate bad press that have accompanied similar instances can be very effective, because administrators are notoriously risk averse.

LOOKING INTO A CRYSTAL BALL, DARKLY

Until now, I have been discussing the job of the university science writer as it exists today. But the times definitely are changing. New telecommunications technologies, such as the growth of the Internet and the World Wide Web, are forcing major changes in the form, if not the substance, of both the news media and media relations. We are currently caught in the painful transition into the electronic information age. No one knows exactly how it will all turn out. But it is likely to cause a fundamental change in the relationship between university science writers and science reporters. If the emerging information infrastructure allows universities to deliver information directly to its various publics, as appears likely, then the importance of dealing with media gatekeepers will decline, and university science writers will be competing with their journalistic colleagues as much as working with them.

29

Government Agencies

RICK E. BORCHELT

Rick E. Borchelt is special assistant for public affairs in the Executive Office of the President at the White House. He handles media relations on science and technology issues for the White House, and writes speeches and background papers for senior White House staff. He has been a press secretary for the Committee on Science, Space, and Technology of the U.S. House of Representatives, director of media relations for the National Academy of Sciences, and associate editor for public information at the University of Maryland.

A naturalist by training, Rick is still an avid hiker and outdoorsman who actively free-lances on natural history topics and teaches science and nature writing at the Writers Center based in Bethesda, Maryland. He is a member of the board of the National Association of Science Writers, and a past president of the D.C. Science Writers Association.

The turning point for me came one hot summer at the Smithsonian Institution's National Museum of Natural History. As part of my graduate work in systematic entomology, I was working as a curatorial assistant in the museum's butterfly and moth collection in a cubicle about eight feet square, surrounded on all sides by trays and boards and boxes filled with dead insects a quarter-century old. The ventilation wasn't great: two ducts running up through the floor from the office and exhibit areas below.

As it happened, one of the ducts originated in the Insect Zoo, an exhibit of live insects in realistic environmental settings. It had all the usual denizens of insect petting zoos—Madagascar hissing cockroaches, giant walking sticks, leaf-cutting ants, a cloud of cabbage butterflies in a flight room, scorpions, and tarantulas. At eleven and two o'clock each day, the air vent closest to my desk would erupt with children's screams and oohs and ahs as the Insect Zoo staff hosted feeding time. And questions—the kids had hundreds of questions, from the mundane to the esoteric. Does it bite, does it sting, is it poisonous? Why is it pink? Why does it have six legs, eight legs, hundreds of legs?

The other vent into my room came from one of the museum's entomology department offices. The questions that floated up through the duct were equally telling: Are you sure the cladogram resolves on that trait? What kind of predation could drive this behavior? Is that a homologous character?

That summer pointed out very clearly the disconnection between a society filled with the most basic questions about natural history, and the inability of most scientists to communicate the answers to those questions in ways intelligible to a lay public. At the end of the summer, I'd made up my mind to be a translator of sorts—a communicator of technology and science. Instead of *doing* science, I'd *write* about it.

This job of science communicator has taken me from a research university, to the National Academy of Sciences, to Congress, and to the White House. And I still sit at the table during staff meetings, wondering who has the better questions—the public or the scientists—and how to get the scientists to talk to the public in ways they both understand.

THE FEDERAL ROLE IN SCIENCE AND TECHNOLOGY

Today, Congress spends about $40 billion each year on civilian science and technology programs, ranging from the space program to health sciences to weather forecasting. That's in addition to another $30 billion or so spent by the military on research and development. That's why many of these agencies hire science writers—either as full-time employees or as free-lancers on assignment—to help explain what they do to the taxpaying public.

A science writer in federal employ typically writes more about science policy than science itself, although a good writer can use science to generate interest in the more abstract policy decisions that are the bread and butter of most federal agencies. In this regard, it's useful to think of two kinds of science policy: science for policy, and policy for science.

In science for policy, most regulatory agencies (the Environmental Protection Agency, or EPA, for example) conduct extensive research to determine what kinds of regulations would work best or what critical information needs to be obtained before effective rulemaking can begin. When the EPA makes a decision to ban a pesticide like DDT from the market, it must first determine what the health effects of the pesticide are, weigh them against the potential damage to agribusiness, and figure out if there are alternative ways to control what the pesticide controls. A science writer at the EPA, then, might need to translate this information into readily understood prose to help policymakers and voters make an informed decision about regulating the pesticide.

A hot topic for government science writers today is ozone depletion in the upper atmosphere. Science writers from a host of agencies all struggle with how to help policymakers and the lay public better understand the chemistry behind ozone depletion, what human activities contribute to it, the likely medical and environmental impacts of increased ultraviolet radiation reaching the earth's surface, and what governments and individuals can do to help stabilize the earth's protective ozone layer.

These issues and others came to a head in a recent congressional hearing in which some members of Congress testified that they believed the science behind ozone depletion was tainted by liberal politics, and produced their own set of witnesses to question the severity and extent of the "ozone hole" and what it means for public policy. Science writers and public affairs offices on both sides of the issue scrambled to produce factual, easy-to-understand press releases, briefing papers, and issue briefs for representatives that told their version of this debate—a debate that died down considerably the following week with the awarding of the Nobel Prize in chemistry to the researchers who first brought the ozone depletion problem to public attention!

Policy for science, on the other hand, is more concerned with budgets and resources for the conduct of science than it is with the science itself. The National Science Foundation (NSF) which funds most civilian nonmedical basic research, employs science writers who can write well both about the science that's being conducted with NSF funds and about the impact of budget shortfalls on how much and what kind of research is likely to get done. The same is true of the National Institutes of Health (NIH).

As you might guess from these descriptions, by far the greatest number of science writers in the federal government are employed as public affairs officers of one kind or another, working to help reporters, policymakers, and the public understand and appreciate research that the government supports. There are also science writers with few or no public information responsibilities. At the NIH, for example, these science writers write pamphlets and background papers for physicians and the public on medical subjects such as lupus, gene therapy, AIDS treatments, arthritis, neurological diseases, and other topics.

Both kinds of government science writers should be concerned with clear and truthful accounting of how taxpayer dollars are used to fund important scientific research.

One of my greatest frustrations as a government science writer has been the difficulty of praising in print policies or programs that I personally disagree with. During the transition from my job as a committee press secretary in the House of Representatives to my current job with the White House, I took a week of vacation to volunteer at the White House to help "roll out" the president's 1996 budget for science and technology. On alternate days—depending on whether I was at the White House or on Capitol Hill—I characterized the budget as either woefully inadequate or just right, and provided the very same reporters with ammunition for both sides of the story. I got lots of ribbing from reporter friends who followed this particular game of political volleyball.

One last source of tension for government communicators is the pervasive sense of secrecy that shrouds some government research. Lots of government scientific work is classified; many writers need top-level security clearances to be able to write unclassified summaries of classified documents. And many scientists in the federal government, especially, are—intellectually, at least—products of the Manhattan Project and the Cold War. Openness with reporters or the public is a foreign concept.

The job of a science writer when confronted with unnecessary secrecy is to wheedle, cajole, and coerce greater openness. Often, this means demonstrating the positive impact of good press. I recall one scientific meeting in particular, a workshop of herpetologists discussing why frogs, toads, and other amphibian populations across the world were declining precipitously. Workshop organizers adamantly refused to allow reporters to listen to the discussions—too preliminary, the scientists feared, and the presence of reporters in the room would inhibit the free and open sharing of scientific data if the scientists feared public ridicule or the premature reporting of an untested hypothesis. Government writers and public affairs folks hear this excuse a lot.

It seemed too interesting a story to let go, so after much discussion and arm-twisting, I managed to get the workshop opened to a maximum of six reporters. I spent hours with the workshop leaders, going over how one deals with reporters in a public setting. And I spent a good deal of time translating the technical papers that were the basis of the workshop into lay-language documents, as well as rounding up good color slides of some endangered amphibians. The result was a great meeting: The interplay between reporters and the scientists was productive, and the resulting stories—in *USA Today,* the *New York Times,* the *Los Angeles Times, BioScience,* and elsewhere—sparked a story that still generates dozens of articles every year.

WRITING ABOUT GOVERNMENT RESEARCH

Research and development funded by federal dollars is a gold mine of interesting science and technology for the science writer who is willing to be a team player in an agency's communications office or a hired pen for a government research effort. Here are some of the ways the best federal science writers find to write interestingly and provocatively:

Write for People, Not Personnel

As in many public affairs offices, government writers often have a hard time figuring out exactly who is their audience. Is it the assistant secretary of the agency? The senior member of the Senate appropriations committee? The scientists whose work you're writing about?

Of course, your audience includes all of these people, who have different levels of scientific and technological literacy. But a government science writer's primary audience is the general public—the taxpayer. And a piece of science writing that is crisp enough, clear enough, and interesting enough to hold the attention of a lay audience will also be understood by your other audiences.

Start with the most basic information you can. Given the way review works in most federal offices, you'll have plenty of chances to add the things that each set of reviewers thinks is critical. It's much harder to strike things once they're in the draft; you don't want to create expectations on the part of some readers that will ultimately be unfulfilled by the final piece.

A former director of the news office at the National Academy of Sciences would start each major writing project by looking out her window and focusing on the first person walking by on the way to the Vietnam Memorial. She'd ask herself, What does that person need to know about this report? How will it affect him and his family? What would it take to make this issue relevant to him? In the White House, we call this the Joe Six-Pack Rule—write a piece that would be interesting if it were read on television at half time for the Super Bowl.

Do Periodic Reality Checks

There's a reason why most newspapers have guidelines against one-source stories: It's too easy to get caught up in the private agenda of individual researchers and lose the perspective of the research field as a whole. This poses a particular problem for the government science writers who profile the work of researchers at an agency. You want to make the researcher's work appear important, even critical. And you don't want to interject any doubt into the story by quoting scientists outside the agency who may disagree with the researcher's work or findings.

Even if the agency isn't interested in a balanced portrayal of scientific controversy that involves one of its researchers, as a writer you need to be aware of where the research findings you're writing about fit in the scientific scheme of things. When interviewing the researcher, ask: Are there people who would discount or disagree with your findings? Are there other researchers whose work doesn't bear out these findings? A good scientist won't be defensive about these kinds of questions.

You may find that your researcher is out on a scientific limb. Then you need to alert agency management—perhaps you really don't want to raise the visibility of this issue until there's better corroboration. Or maybe the work is so new and revolutionary that it needs to be reported right away. Either way, you need to be aware of the scientific context in which your writing fits.

Spend Time in the Field

Most government science writing is done from your desk in the bowels of an agency somewhere—you're lucky to have a window, let alone a chance to interview researchers in the laboratory or in the field. But the best science writing is done—and the best interviews are given—when the science writer goes to the scientist's home base.

When I travel on official business, I always look for a story I can write along the way, or gather material for a speech or background paper. Sure, I could get the same basic information over the telephone—but there's no substitute for seeing the research you're writing about. It often means the difference between a dull and lifeless narrative and a piece of writing that sings.

Coping with Editing

More than anywhere else—academia, the press, trade associations, industry—a government writer's work is scrutinized, reviewed, and often denatured to the point that it seldom resembles the original work product. Multiple layers of review for a given piece of writing are the rule rather than the exception. All along the tortuous route to publication, different political sensitivities are at play, each seeking to minimize any potential negative reaction by a member of Congress, the White House, or an affected industry or trade group. The result too often is the government writing product we all know—obtuse, unclear, and uninformative.

The first rule in coping with agency editing is never to get personally invested in anything you write. Nine times out of 10 you may not recognize it again when it comes out of review. But there are ways you can minimize the gap between your final draft and the agency's final product.

First, float an initial outline to likely reviewers or editors. Get approval in advance for the major components of the story before you get down to wordsmithing—it will make it much easier to gain concurrence down the line.

Second, offer to incorporate comments on the draft yourself rather than letting someone else work over the piece. Talk over the changes with the person who suggested them; the biggest single failing of most writers during the editing process is to assume that every mark on the draft needs to be made without question.

One of my hardest recent tasks was writing a speech for the president on science policy. It's not something he talks about often, so every agency under the sun wanted to make sure he took this rare chance to mention the work it was doing. And there was pressure from program officials who were facing possible budget cuts in Congress to make sure the speech was hard-hitting and partisan. Industry wanted to hear some mention of initiatives favorable to business; universities were expecting a speech that stressed the vital role of university research; technology agencies wanted a technology speech; and the basic science agencies wanted a strong endorsement of fundamental science. One senior administration official even demanded that the president hold up her agency's recent report during the speech and say what a good job it was!

The speech took nearly five weeks to write. Three outlines were discarded before one finally got approved, and 17 drafts later each of the major science agencies had signed off on a speech that was almost ready for the president to deliver. It was a good speech; a few more days of polishing, and it was a major policy address on science and technology, a speech that everyone who'd had a hand in it liked—including me.

The night before the speech, a senior official in the White House—who was not a science writer—rewrote it as a brief set of remarks about the marvels of science that gave us the ultrathin diaper and the glue on Post-it Notes.

You win some, you lose some.

One final thought—never throw away a good draft. The vice president later used the original speech.

WHERE THE JOBS ARE

Most of the agencies that receive federal funds to do scientific or technological research hire science writers. Here's a partial list:

The NIH. Comprising a dozen or so separate institutes, each with its own budget, the NIH is home to some 200 science writers and public affairs personnel. Most of the institutes have newsletters and other publications that describe their activities; most also write tip sheets, background reports, and news releases for reporters who cover health and medical research. The focus of these writers usually is on medical research and health care policy.

The National Institute of Standards and Technology (NIST). The former National Bureau of Standards employs writers who explain the technological advances and materials research for which NIST is responsible.

The National Aeronautics and Space Administration (NASA). From a state-of-the-art television studio to supercharged computer graphics, NASA is a high-tech communications environment. While agency downsizing is likely to pare many of the science writing jobs at NASA, communicating science is likely to remain a high priority for the agency.

The Smithsonian Institution. In addition to the National Museum of Natural History, science writers and public affairs officers work at the National Museum of American Life, the National Air and Space Museum, and at the Smithsonian's National Zoo. The magazine *Smithsonian* features excellent writing—much of it free-lance—on science and technology, and many of the individual museums also publish magazines.

United States Department of Agriculture (USDA). This agency employs a substantial cadre of writers and editors at its Washington headquarters, but many USDA science writers are scattered across the country in the nation's far-flung system of Agriculture Experiment Stations and Agricultural Research Service (ARS) offices. Since the primary mission of the experiment stations is to develop new agricultural technologies and communicate them to farmers at the local level, communications functions permeate the entire USDA infrastructure. ARS publishes its own magazine.

National Oceanic and Atmospheric Administration (NOAA). An agency of the Department of Commerce, NOAA hires science writers to help it communicate research in weather forecasting, marine biology, and global climate change.

National Science Foundation (NSF). The premier funding source for most federal basic research, the NSF employs a number of writers, editors, and public affairs specialists who discuss and write about the research done by the scientists who receive NSF grants.

The White House. Science writing jobs at the White House are scarce, but there are some: mostly in the Office of Science and Technology Policy, the Council for Environmental Quality, and the Office of Media Affairs, which has a specialty press officer whose duties include science and technology trade press relations. Almost all of these jobs—for which the competition is keen—are best described as press secretary.

Congress. Both the Senate and the House employ public affairs officers and press secretaries. Only occasionally do these people have expertise in science and technical writing, but a science writer with a political bent may well find job opportunities on Capitol Hill.

In some instances—especially for the science-related committees, such as the House Science Committee—the press secretary is a science writer by training. Members of the House whose district includes high-tech industries are also likely to have a press secretary who understands and can write about science and technology. The narrow skills of science writing are seldom sufficient to gain the attention of the hiring authorities—successful candidates also will have a familiarity with legislative process, law, campaign finance, and a host of other special skills.

This is not an exhaustive list of federal job opportunities; you'll also find science and technology writers employed at the Department of Energy, the Department of Defense, the Environmental Protection Agency, the US Information Agency, the Department of State, and many other federal agencies both in Washington and around the country.

Nor is government science writing the exclusive domain of the federal government. While federal employment in general has actually declined over the past four years, overall state and local government employment has tripled since the 1970s. Many states and, increasingly, counties and other governmental entities have similar agencies that hire science writers, especially in health and environmental issues. State and county employment offices are your best source of information on these other government science writing jobs.

30
● ● ● ● ● ● ● ● ● ● ● ● ● ● ● ● ● ●

Non-Profits, Small Research Laboratories, and Museums: Non-Profits

PHIL KIBAK

Phil Kibak received a B.A. in biology from State University of New York College at New Paltz, but he was determined not to attend graduate school to specialize in a narrowly defined field of study; instead, he entered scientific publishing as a production editor. After six years of this, he entered graduate school, but not in ecology, which had been his original plan; he received a graduate certificate from Polytechnic Institute of New York, Brooklyn, in 1982 in science and medical journalism.

After brief stints in medical advertising and medical reporting, Kibak became a media relations officer with the Johns Hopkins Medical Institutions in Baltimore in 1985. He moved to Texas in January 1990, to join the health and science news division (now the news media relations division) of the American Heart Association National Center, where he is health and science editor.

Thankfully, for those of us who have never aspired to working on a daily newspaper, there are opportunities for science writers in the many scientific and medical nonprofits.

The mission of the American Heart Association (AHA) is to reduce death and disability from cardiovascular disease and stroke; partly this is done by educating the public and health care professionals about heart-healthy habits and therapeutic and research advances. The science writers and media relations officers who work for such non-profit organizations—and there are quite a few of them—reach the public through the media. Successful organizations achieve their goals by anticipating and serving journalists' needs.

At the AHA, we do this by issuing news releases on reports published in our scientific journals; promoting research presented at our scientific meetings via news releases and news conferences; and responding *promptly* to media inquiries. One staff person interacts solely with broadcast media and is responsible for overseeing the production of 12–15 video news releases annually.

When a "hot" issue appears in the news, we line up some of our scientific volunteers to give the official AHA response. We also may prepare a written statement.

Sometimes, though, efforts can backfire. In March 1995 at our annual meeting on cardiovascular disease epidemiology, Dr. Bruce Psaty of the University of Washington presented the results of a study that suggested that people taking a class of drugs called calcium channel blockers (CCBs) to control high blood pressure had a higher risk of heart attack. His presentation was of great media interest, and we pulled him into the news room for an ad hoc news conference.

We were hardly prepared for the blitz that followed. Although Dr. Psaty stated that the *relative risk* of a heart attack in patients taking calcium channel blockers was 60 percent higher than in patients taking other drugs, he strenuously emphasized that this was comparable to 16 out of a thousand patients on CCBs versus 10 out of a thousand patients taking other classes of drugs.

Unfortunately, the 60-percent increase in relative risk was what made it into the initial news reports. Many people taking these drugs panicked. Some decided on their own to stop taking their medication and landed in emergency rooms with spiking high blood pressure. Many did what they should have—consulted their doctors—which caused us to be inundated with calls from irate physicians. We also had to deal with numerous media calls.

To deal with this problem nationally we prepared a media statement and sent it to our mailing list. And the AP reporter who had done the initial story wrote a follow-up article to quell the public uncertainty the original article had spawned.

More often than not, however, we are able to be the conduit through which necessary information about cardiovascular disease and stroke reaches the world. An example of this is the news operation we run at the AHA's Scientific Sessions, which in 1995 attracted about 430 media representatives from around the world.

Planning for this annual November gathering begins early in the year with developing budgets and logistical information.

We also produce an extensive news packet. This begins in August, when we receive the abstracts (distilled summaries of the scientific presentations prepared by the researchers). For the 1995 Scientific Sessions we waded through all 3,874 abstracts in the following way: the five members of the news media relations staff and three free-lance science writers each read about 480 abstracts. Each person then selected the ones he or she thought were most newsworthy and presented them to the other readers, as well as to members of the AHA's Office of Science and Medicine.

Once we decide which presentations to publicize, we contact the researchers to see if they will cooperate. (Usually there is no problem, but sometimes researchers will not want media attention because they think it may affect their ability to publish in certain journals.) Once we have approval, we farm the work of writing the releases out to free-lancers. The releases then undergo a rigorous editorial and approval process that involves our office, the scientific affairs office, the AHA statistician, and, of course, the researcher.

Free-lancers don't write all our news releases, but we rely on them for the Scientific Sessions simply because our normal operations do not cease at this time—we're still turning out two news packets per month on our journal materials, responding to media inquiries, and dealing with material for other meetings and projects, such as our quarterly newsletter Heart*Style* (which I wrote and produced for five years).

For the 1995 Scientific Sessions we produced 12 news releases (about two to three pages each), 10 news "briefs" (one-half to one page) and a few pages of shorter news "tips" (two to three sentences).

Simultaneously, we plan a series of news conferences on newsworthy and interesting topics presented at the meeting. Last year, such topics included: minimally invasive bypass surgery, cerebral angioplasty, and late-breaking clinical trials.

One of these trials was the West-of-Scotland study, which suggested that the use of a specific cholesterol-lowering drug could significantly reduce the risk of primary heart attack in men with high blood cholesterol but otherwise good health. Prior to the meeting we received a call from the study's principal investigator, who wanted us to hold a news conference on *only* this study. He also requested interactive audio and video links to beam the news conference back to his Scottish colleagues (and media).

We anticipate that this practice will be standard in the future; but we did not have the budget to accommodate this request. We communicated this to him. His response was: "No problem. My university will pick up the tab."

Our antennae rose immediately. It has been our experience that universities are generally economically strained. We interpreted his statement as actually being, "No problem. The pharmaceutical company that makes this drug will pick up the tab." This placed us in an uncomfortable position. We have tried to run news operations free of interference by companies trying to sell their products. But the fact of the matter was that this procedure would help us get necessary information out to our client base—the public.

So we compromised: This researcher was one of several at a news conference talking about the results of their clinical trials on the therapeutic effects of different drugs; we allowed the scientists to beam the news conference to Scotland via a hired video production crew (and it was not interactive); and we allowed them to use our facilities for a "satellite tour" (a remote feed allowing broadcast stations to interview the researcher from their home base). The result: The researchers were happy, the public got some useful information, and the AHA got some great visibility.

Our latest efforts involve the development of a web site, where journalists can view our news releases and other information.

But our most regular activity is a biweekly news kit featuring news releases and news "briefs" about information published in the AHA scientific journals—biweekly because our flagship journal, *Circulation*, is published every two weeks. Therefore, we spend a good bit of time reading galleys to find research to publicize. About 70 percent of the material in our news kits is written by free-lancers. (By the way, any free-lance writer is welcome to contact us about work availability.)

Free-lancers also find work at the AHA in other departments in which projects need writers to produce papers, brochures, scripts, and other material.

But the public knows us through the media, which knows us through our news releases. And sometimes we get to be creative. In one study, scientists subjected chickens to secondhand tobacco smoke and investigated the ensuing cardiovascular complications. I led the release with the sentence, "Foghorn Leghorn, that blustering cartoon rooster, would be mortified." The researcher hated it! But after I explained to him the merits of various literary devices, he conducted an experiment. He showed the release to about 15 people in his own and neighboring labs. Everyone else loved it, so he withdrew his objections.

Sometimes the magic works.

● ●

Small Research Laboratories and Museums

CATHY YARBROUGH

Cathy Yarbrough is manager of News Media Relations for the American Heart Association, headquartered in Houston. When she

wrote this chapter, she was public affairs chief of the Yerkes Regional
Primate Research Center, of Emory University in Atlanta, Georgia.
An Atlanta native, Yarbrough has spent almost 20 years in medical
and scientific communications. Among her professional awards are
an Atlanta International Association of Business Communications
"Silver Anvil," awarded for the Yerkes Center's Sixtieth anniversary
report. For her volunteer work as associate producer of a video
about Jerusalem House, a home in Atlanta for people with AIDS, she
was honored by the Georgia Public Relations Society of America.

When he saw the Associated Press photograph that gave the impression
that I was kissing an orangutan—on the lips—the then director of the
Yerkes Regional Primate Research Center did not respond (as my mother
had), by saying, "Oh, how cute!"

No, his first reaction lay somewhere between dismay and anger.

The photo was part of a series—proposed by me—about the way institutions care for young apes. On the day of the photo shoot, several Yerkes
primate caretakers were ill; the remaining nursery staff members were
overwhelmed with work. They were delighted when I offered to stand in
with the photographer—and I was delighted to play with the occupants
of the nursery.

Soon after I began holding him, the little orangutan turned his face
toward me, and I puckered my lips and made kissing sounds—a favorite
game. The animal puckered back. I didn't see the photographer snap the
moment, but the resulting photo was the most widely used one in the
entire series.

Smooching with a nonhuman primate is definitely taboo, because it is
a health risk to both parties. So the photograph conveyed a message that
we were acting irresponsibly.

"I wasn't kissing him," I said, defending myself to the director. "I would
have known if our lips touched."

"Well it looks to me like you're kissing the orangutan," he said, pulling
a magnifying glass from his desk drawer. To my relief, his close examination of the photo proved my innocence—and added to my reputation
for honesty, a must in this kind of job.

Dr. Frederick King, the then director, created my position in 1979, despite the objection of several faculty members. The center had already
suffered too many "monkeying around at Yerkes" newspaper headlines.
With a public relations person on board, many scientists seemed to believe
that it would become our slogan. They wanted to be taken seriously—they
wanted the center to be taken seriously.

The orangutan photo was definitely a setback in convincing them otherwise. But 17 years later, I remain chief of public affairs at Yerkes, and during that time, many scientists have worked with me, repeatedly, in communicating to the public through the media, presentations to civic and school groups, and tours.

The challenge of enlisting scientists to take time from their schedules for public relations—and the absolute necessity for credibility in the workplace—unite science writers at small research institutions, and science museums. In both environments, we are often the sole interface between highly reluctant, busy researchers and the public, particularly the mass media.

Still, news media coverage is essential to the survival of museums but not the Yerkes Center and many other small research centers. Museums depend on coverage to bring visitors to exhibits and to encourage contributions from the public.

They need visibility. At Yerkes, by contrast, we seek visibility because the current director, Dr. Thomas Insel, regards communicating the results of our work to the public as an obligation, since taxes fund most biomedical and behavioral research in this country.

SMALL RESEARCH INSTITUTIONS

Dealing with the news media is one of many aspects of my job. I'm also responsible for our employee bulletin, *Inside Yerkes* magazine, and other publications for the public; community relations, including speeches to civic groups and tours; and short-term but often time-consuming projects such as our Home Page on the Internet (http://www.cc.emory.edu/yerkes).

For most publications, I'm a one-person production shop. Not only do I write (and edit) my text, I create the layout, using Pagemaker computer software, and illustrate it with photographs that I've taken. I recently used these same skills to create, at Dr. Insel's request, a lobby display about the history of Yerkes to answer the frequent question, "Who or what is 'Yerkes'?"

My courses in journalism at the University of Georgia, from which I received a bachelor's degree almost 30 years ago, taught me the theory and tools of public relations, but not how to produce a magazine or a lobby display. So I've taken noncredit classes in photography, design, and desktop publishing, as well as several college courses in the sciences.

When I discovered my passion for science almost 20 years ago, I read as many science and medical books as I could find at the local library. My favorite quick reference is Dorland's *Illustrated Medical Dictionary*. I keep it at my side at work—closer than *Webster's*—because without it, my chance of writing an understandable news release or *Inside Yerkes* is minimal.

Because I have yet to read a satisfactory lay description prepared by a scientist, I do not ask researchers to write one for me. If their versions of lay descriptions do not suffer from superficiality ("This project will investigate a possible treatment for cystic fibrosis. Cystic fibrosis is a fatal disease. More effective treatment will extend life."), they are so technical as to be meaningless to the general public.

Asking a scientist to write a lay description and then rewriting it (after the scientist has agonized over the text for hours if not days) is not recommended as a relationship builder. When interviewed for my current position, I met with a group of scientists whose major complaint about the Emory publicity office was that it asked them to prepare lay descriptions of their studies.

"I spent the entire weekend writing a description," one exasperated researcher said. "And it was completely rewritten by that PR person."

Probably it was rewritten not only to translate those technical words that the researcher had forgotten to explain, but to convert the scientist's document into a news release style. I suspect that he had written a narrative that began with the history of the problem under study, followed by a description of the research protocol, the methods, the experiments, and finally the conclusions. The publicist probably reversed the order—to the scientist's dismay.

Public relations officers at small research centers want to avoid alienating scientists. At a large research university, such as Stanford, there are many more fish in the pond. At Yerkes, there are relatively few: 170 scientists. It's like a small town.

Still, in both a small research center and a large one such as Stanford, the public relations professionals are more effective if they're regarded by the scientists as a colleague. This relationship is built over time and on trust and a track record of good work.

Trust is built by being honest with scientists about the potential positives and negatives of whatever I'm asking them to do, whether it be a media interview, a speech to a civic group, or a VIP's visit to the lab.

I tap into that trust, particularly in media relations. Many Yerkes scientists have given extensive interviews and spent a lot of time with news media organizations that they did not know because I've said, "This reporter is excellent," or "This is a superb television program for children. You ought to do it."

When such relationships exist, the public relations staffer can also be ahead of the curve, aware of research that promises to become a great story. And even before media release, such knowledge keeps my tours fresh and interesting. In describing a particular study, I can say: "Dr. Kim Wallen just told me that he was finding that prenatal hormone exposure influences gender identity in the most remarkable way."

My newspaper background, as a reporter for the *Atlanta Constitution* in the 1970s, has proved invaluable in media relations. In educating scientists about the demands on a reporter, so that they will cooperate with and understand the journalist better, I can speak firsthand about the pressure of deadlines. I can respond with authority to scientists who respond to a request for an interview: "Why can't the reporter just use the interview that I gave to that other reporter yesterday?"

Working at a research institution has also allowed me to view journalists from a different perspective. Some years ago, a reporter asked to interview Dr. King for a story on the new animal welfare regulations, requiring labs to take into account the "psychological well-being" of primates. Unlike some labs, Yerkes has maintained an open-door policy on journalists covering the issue of animal research. So we don't enter a "crisis communications" mode when reporters ask to visit or interview Yerkes officials about this issue. A meeting for the reporter was scheduled.

Often when reporters first meet with us to ask questions about this issue, their manner is noticeably cool, as if they expect scientists to fulfill the image that animal rights activists portray of them.

But this particular reporter's dislike was intense from the beginning and only increased during the three and a half hours of his interview. When Dr. King, a neuroscientist with a Ph.D. in physiological psychology from Johns Hopkins University, explained a study related to epilepsy, the reporter sarcastically questioned Dr. King's credentials to judge such research, since he was "just a psychologist." As a former reporter, I was embarrassed. As the public relations officer, I was concerned.

After the reporter finally left, Dr. King and I discussed our options. My newspaper training had convinced me that complaining to editors in advance of a story was a waste of time. Editors routinely support their writers against such gripes. So we waited until the story was published and responded with a letter, detailing its inaccuracies.

It did not mention the reporter's attitude—since we could not prove he was rude. Neither the reporter nor I had taped the interview. Some of my public relations colleagues avoid writing letters to the editor about inaccuracies or unprofessional behavior because they fear that the news media organization will put them on a blacklist.

But I do it, when appropriate, because, as I noted, we don't depend on the media for survival, and an editor's attention should be called to reporters who are biased and sloppy in their work. (I also wish that more journalists complained to the bosses of unprofessional public relations people.)

A BRIEF NOTE ABOUT MUSEUMS

The writing and public relations skills required at a museum differ sharply from those needed at research institutes. I was recently reminded of how different these jobs are when Sci-Trek, Atlanta's science and technology museum, asked me to provide a draft text for a display on the scanning electron microscope.

My draft began:

> Using a computerized digital light microscope, Rob Apkarian of the Yerkes Primate Research Center of Emory University was able to detect evidence of atherosclerosis (blockage of the vessels that can lead to heart attacks and strokes) in the inside wall of a human blood vessel. The two dimensional image, shown on the video screen and in the photograph at right, magnifies the surface of the wall 1,200 times. The image shows early atherosclerosis—as indicated by the white blood cells (dark colored pimple-like structures) stuck to the wall of the vessel.

The Sci-Trek writers changed my text, making it more dramatic and fun to read:

> THE CRIME—TRESPASSING IN THE BLOODSTREAM. A mob of trespassers have clogged a major artery, blocking the flow of important traffic. This dangerous condition, called atherosclerosis, may lead to heart attack or stroke.
>
> THE DETECTIVE. THE GAME IS AFOOT! Rob Apkarian uses a computer-controlled light microscope to examine the scene of the crime: the inside wall of a human blood vessel.

Mary Miller, at San Francisco's user-friendly science museum, the Exploratorium, explained that museum science writers must always remember that people read their work while standing up. The text must cut to the chase.

Yet Miller emphasized that she does extensive background research before writing a simple text: "I have to have a level of understanding that is three times deeper than what I'm expressing."

To encourage the public to visit their science museums, public relations staff promote new and current exhibits in the same way that I promote Yerkes research—by news releases, personal contacts with reporters, and publications. They also stage special events and are constantly looking for fresh ways to present science.

Kathleen Neal, director of public relations and marketing at Sci-Trek, hired an Elvis impersonator to attract media attention to the opening of an exhibit on music. As a result of the television coverage, 700 visited the museum the next day. Normally, 150 people attend an opening.

Neal and David Shaw, manager of the public information office at the California Academy of Sciences (whose museum offers everything from an aquarium to an interactive exhibit on evolution), agreed that news media coverage is key to attracting visitors to their museums. And that their effectiveness in gaining media coverage for their museums has been helped by their own backgrounds in journalism.

"It prepared me well to help promote the academy," said Shaw, formerly a reporter at the *San Francisco Bay Guardian*. "You need to know how a news room works—to see what kind of deadlines reporters have, the type of information that they need. As a result, when I telephone reporters, I'm really direct, give them what they need, and don't waste time."

31

Business and Industry: Drug Industry and Other Medical Business

CANDACE S. GULKO

Along with another medical writer, I founded and now run NCM Publishers, a medical education and communications company. Cardiology and psychiatry are my main areas of expertise.

I've written and produced numerous medical education programs in both print and broadcast media for major pharmaceutical sponsors, including Eli Lilly and Company, Glaxo Wellcome Inc., Lederle Laboratories, and the Upjohn Company. My medical education videotapes have received several national and international awards, including CINE Golden Eagles, the Chris Plaque from the Columbus Film Festival, and Cum Laude award from Medikinale International Parma Rassegna Internazionale del Cinema Medico Scientifico.

Before forming NCM, I wrote medical articles for general consumer publications, including *Family Health* and a supplement to the Sunday *New York Times*.

Almost no one sets out on this path. People detour to medical education and communication companies from careers in journalism, or they seek refuge here from jobs in academia. Such refugees may be Ph.D.s disappointed by the lack of grant money or just disillusioned with research, those with a master's degree in the sciences who changed their minds about medical school, or had it changed for them, and the occasional physician who now wishes he or she hadn't attended medical school.

Some of the pioneer companies were started by disaffected socialists black listed during the McCarthy era. These idealists thought that using pharmaceutical industry funds to develop educational materials for doc-

245

tors was the perfect merger of capitalism and social responsibility. In addition, they provided employment for many creative associates who lost their original careers during that period of paranoia. Ironically, and to the embarrassment of many of the original entrepreneurs, the companies became extremely lucrative enterprises.

Like many of our predecessors, my partner and I, who co-own our company, are writers, and we hope this helps us foster a stimulating, rewarding work atmosphere for other writers. But medical communications companies now probably represent as many different backgrounds and philosophies as any other business. Some have been started by marketing executives, some by scientists or doctors, some by ad agencies. And in this competitive marketplace, all are high-pressured, fast-paced, and cost-conscious, regardless of their underlying philosophy.

So what exactly are these companies? Medical education and communication companies—sometimes called med ed houses or project houses—serve pharmaceutical companies the way an ad agency serves a corporation. The strategies we suggest, however, and the programs we produce are for medical or public education rather than promotion. The pharmaceutical company usually wants to make physicians, nurses, pharmacists, patients, or the general public more aware of a particular disease or mechanism that causes a disease. Thus they fund quality educational programs; but at the same time, these programs set the stage, or lay the groundwork, for a promotional and advertising campaign. Ideally, these motives blend together to the benefit of health professionals, the public, and the pharmaceutical company. But they can also form an uneasy alliance that doesn't do justice to any party.

The initial marketing strategy for Prozac is an example of good blending. Contrary to some of the media attention—the glowingly positive reports from some overzealous reporters and the unfounded negative stories from a few ill-informed writers—Eli Lilly and Co. simply viewed their new antidepressant as a drug equal in efficacy to its predecessors but without the troubling side effects and complicated dosing regimens that had limited their use. Lilly knew that before Prozac, most people on antidepressants stopped the drug before it helped them because they couldn't tolerate the side effects. They felt Prozac's blockbuster potential lay in its tolerability, simplicity, and safety. (It's pretty hard to kill yourself with Prozac; people have failed even when taking 37 times the maximum dose.)

Much work needed to be done, however, before Lilly could begin to market its drug. Lilly's market research department discovered that misinformation and myths about depression were rampant among both primary-care physicians and the general public. Physicians and patients alike confused major depressive disorder—or clinical depression, as it is often called—which is a medical syndrome, with the "blues" that everyone complains of at one time or another.

Patients were ashamed of a perceived weakness, so they tried to hide their symptoms, and physicians didn't know enough about the illness to recognize its varied presentations. Consequently, most people with clinical depression went undiagnosed and untreated, resulting in a cost of over $31 billion a year in reduced worker productivity, increased absenteeism, and suicide.

In an effort to destigmatize depression, Lilly contracted with my company, NCM Publishers, to produce *Moving Back into the Light,* a video to make the public more aware of depression and to help new patients understand their illness. We also produced several educational videotapes for physicians, with dramatic patient vignettes to help them recognize depression and expert commentary to teach them current treatment principles. Accompanying monographs were written to impart more in-depth information and to provide a vehicle for testing and subsequent continuing medical education credit. Slide/lecture programs were developed for use by psychiatrists when lecturing primary-care physicians.

Lilly's funding of these programs and others, many of which contained no mention of their drug, is a noteworthy example of what a pharmaceutical company can do to serve the public health interest.

It isn't always this noble. When you're providing educational materials to support a "me-too" product, many pharmaceutical companies will try to split hairs in an effort to make a minor difference seem earth-shattering. This probably isn't inherently wrong. It's just advertising. A fine line distinguishes medical writing sponsored by a pharmaceutical company that is nonetheless medical writing from advertising copywriting. And herein lies perhaps the root of the ethical conflicts that plague us (or should).

Although we may question its existence, professional ethics lead us to at least search for the "truth." Depending on the type of publication, we may be subject to journalistic ethics as well, as in the case of a sponsored but independently produced news publication. Scientific integrity must always be considered. Inaccurate or misleading writing can have both research and clinical consequences.

What do you do when a client's strategy conflicts with your professional ethics? I try to demonstrate the advantages of taking the high road. I explain that an unbalanced, misleading piece will be perceived as such by many physicians (or other audiences), and that once a physician becomes suspicious about one item, he or she becomes wary of everything else in that publication, and future publications. Sometimes you can show how an unbalanced story can backfire. Isn't it better to make someone aware of the problems with your product than to let them find out for themselves? Once burned, nary a physician will return to a drug unless there is no other choice. But forewarned, the clinician can prepare to avert or deal with potential complications. Finally, quality and integrity are great selling tools. They sell the company that makes the product.

When all this fails, as it occasionally does, my solution is an escapist one: I bow out. To me, it isn't worth endless battles and compromises. There are other clients who'll appreciate quality writing and sound advice. You can do this if you're a free-lancer or if you run the company. If you're a full-time employee, you'll have to make your case as best you can, try to give your boss ammunition to convince the client, and then decide whether you have the support you need or whether you should be looking to move on.

While pondering our writing ethics, however, we can't forget the basic work ethic. The pharmaceutical company is paying for this project, and they have a right to market their drug. Their objectives must be met, or we're not earning our salaries. The trick is to achieve that aforementioned blending of their marketing objectives with your professional ethics.

The Prozac story is an example of the types of editorial work available at medical education and communication companies: video scripts, audio scripts, interactive laser disks and CD-ROMs, and a vast array of publications and slides. Publications include:

- Monographs. These single-topic publications are targeted toward one or more professional groups, usually physicians in a particular specialty, nurses, or pharmacists. They generally focus on one disease or aspect of a disease, or on a particular drug, and can run anywhere from 8 to 96 printed pages. One we did evolved into a 200-page hardcover book. Usually, the medical writer interviews an expert in the field, does a literature search (via Medline or Grateful Med, for example), and writes a manuscript from the interview and medical literature. The manuscript is sent to the expert physician (or nurse or pharmacist) for approval, and the printed piece usually bears that person's name. Many monographs contain quizzes in the back and are approved for continuing medical education. They can stand alone as a continuing education program, and they often accompany videotapes or audiotapes. The writing style ranges from the feature style found in magazines to the scientific writing common in scientific journals.
- Ongoing newsletters. These brief publications used to be the backbone of this industry before "special projects" took hold. These publications fall into the realm of journalism. Although the pharma-

ceutical company pays for this publication, its only involvement is to submit an advertisement. The newsletter is published independently by the medical education company, and is prepared by medical writers with the same journalistic integrity as a general circulation newspaper. A predetermined format usually includes a combination of news stories and a clinical feature. Depending on the newsletter's style, writers may or may not receive bylines or masthead credit.

- Journal papers. Pharmaceutical companies often ask writers from the medical education company to assist researchers in preparation of papers from their studies. A lot of ethical questions have been raised about this type of "ghost" writing, and the peer review journals usually publish some guidelines. To me, this is ethical if the pharmaceutical company is paying you to provide support to researchers who don't have the time to do first drafts themselves. It is not ethical if the company is trying to put words into the mouth of the researcher. The physician author should be someone who was involved in the study and who has reviewed the data. The writer should interview this researcher so that the paper reflects his or her interpretation of the data. The paper is then written from a study report or, in the case of a review article, from a compilation of the scientific literature. Generally, a few drafts will go back and forth between the writer and researcher to make sure the researcher's views are reflected accurately.

The opportunity to work in different media has always been one of the draws of this industry. While graduates of video schools struggle for career opportunities, experienced medical writers can often find a mentor to teach them scriptwriting.

Boredom is unlikely in a busy med ed company. In one month, you might write a newsletter, script and produce a videotape, edit an audiotape, write a monograph, and prepare slides for a medical lecture.

These companies also offer writers the opportunity to work in many different clinical areas. Depending on the company's clients, a writer might produce a videotape on depression, a monograph on hypertension, and a newsletter on cancer in the same month.

Anyone considering this kind of writing should also consider the downside, however—the ethical conflicts just discussed, and the stress. The stress factor comes from the fact that medical education companies are service companies and must respond to the demands of their pharmaceutical client in much the same way as an advertising agency. A client call at 4 P.M. can mean rewriting till midnight and sending the manuscript via an air courier service at 6 A.M. You're usually working on several projects simultaneously, and you rip up your schedules almost as fast as you write them. The need for physician and client approval on almost all programs strips you of any control over your own time. Independent newsletters are the exception.

If you want a saner, but less varied and probably less lucrative, job in industry, consider working directly for a pharmaceutical company. Most employ medical writers to work on new drug applications, to help researchers write scientific papers, and to produce posters and abstracts for scientific meetings.

There are many opportunities for employment and for free-lance work in this field. Some writers free-lance for both medical education and communication companies as well as pharmaceutical companies. There are staff positions available at many independent med ed houses and at med ed houses owned by advertising agencies.

Networking is the best way to enter this field. But if you don't know anyone, you might start with the Pharmaceutical Marketers Directory (PS Communications, Inc., Directories Division, 7200 W. Camino Real, Suite 215, Boca Raton, Fla. 33433; phone: (407)368-9301; fax: (407)368-7870). Probably as many med ed companies choose not to list themselves here as those that do, but it's a place to get started. The Continuing Medical Education section includes over 100 companies ranging in size from 1 person to over 100; the one-person companies are generally independent free-lancers, but they might be able to help you network for a job. Some companies are listed under Alternative Media, and over 90 newsletters are listed. The directory also includes all the drug and device companies and their advertising agencies.

I miss journalism, and I hope to return to magazine writing someday. I'd caution anyone interested in med ed writing to consider the ethical conflicts and the stress. But if you feel you have the personality to withstand the pressure, the field offers endless opportunities for learning and challenge. The constant exposure to different areas of medicine and different media can stave off boredom for many years. And the money's not bad either.

● ●

Technology Companies

MICHAEL ROSS

While pursuing a master's degree in materials science and chemistry at Rice University in Houston, Michael Ross covered three *Apollo* moonwalk space missions for the campus radio station and became interested in pursuing a career in science writing. He joined the staff of the Lawrence Livermore National Laboratory's public information office in California, where for 12 years he covered such high-energy topics as nuclear weapons design, magnetic fusion, and the so-called Star Wars antimissile defense research. In 1988, he traded terawatts for nanometers when he moved to IBM's Almaden Research Center in San Jose, California, where he is staff communications specialist.

Many billions of dollars are spent each year on fundamental and applied research at university and government laboratories. But with few exceptions, it is a private company that actually turns a new technology into a product people can buy.

At many places along a high-tech product's path from laboratory to store shelf or specialist's catalog, a science or technology writer working for a company (or for an advertising or public relations agency hired by a company) can find excellent opportunities for interesting and influential work. Few developments will receive national newspaper attention, but well-crafted writing in a well-timed news release can help make the company or its products a success.

News releases, fact sheets, marketing documents, trade journal features, and—for internal use—lists of expected questions and suggested answers are the most commonly assigned publicity writing tasks in a company. Each document has its own requirements, but since the quality of writing is most critical and highly leveraged in the news release, I'll concentrate on that form in this short chapter.

Aside from demonstrating basic science writing skills, I think the high-tech news release writer benefits greatly by demonstrating the following qualities with honesty and integrity: being realistic in expectations for the release and aiming it at the correct audience; being accurate but creative in descriptions and analogies; and being visual when possible.

Be realistic and aim for the right audience. Before you even start writing a news release, you should make a critical assessment of the newsworthiness of the milestone or achievement and determine its most important audience. Corporate management should be comfortable with your judgment and your expectations for the story's use.

Reporters make similar judgments every day in deciding which of many potential stories they will spend their time writing about. Science writers working for a publication can have a distinct advantage over the corporate writer: They know exactly who their audience is. You'll gain reporters' respect if you do, too.

Knowing the intended audience's familiarity with the subject matter of the news release will determine the tone and level of detail I use. If the news has a chance of being used by a wire service or a newspaper reporter, I'll begin the release with a "hard-news" lead and continue with an inverted-pyramid, wire-service-style form. At the end, I'll often include a "technical details" section that gives more facts that would be useful to the specialized trade media. Inevitably, even general reporters who are interested in the story are eager to have these technical details. But you don't want to bog down the initial flow of your release with them.

How many details should you include? I try to include those that answer most of the reasonable questions I expect reporters to ask. But beware of trying to answer every question. Such releases can become too long and disjointed. They also leave little room for a journalist's initiative. It's good practice to save some attractive but nonessential details for reporters who call for more information or for an interview with your experts. An alternative is to issue separate releases, each tailored for a different audience. But this will work well only if the burden of managing multiple versions is not too great for you or your staff.

I'd love for every reporter on my distribution list to revel in the newsworthiness and significance of each dispatch I send. But get real! Each day, a typical technology reporter at a big-city paper's business section may write one or two stories, but receives at least a foot-high stack of mailed news releases. Moreover, hundreds more stream daily to the business desk from private wire services such as Business Wire, and fax machines crank out still dozens more. And these public relations missives are in addition to the ready-to-use stories that journalists at various wire and syndication services provide daily. One consequence of this torrent of information is that many reporters don't even open much of their mail. They decide to throw many letters away unopened just by looking at the return address.

To be successful, a public relations writer must have a sufficient reputation for quality that reporters will at least open the mail you send them, read your faxes, and return your phone calls. You get this reputation by sending reporters only well-written releases on subjects that are likely to interest them.

If you expect that a technology or product will interest only a narrow group of potential customers, it may prove more productive to aim your news release not at newspapers but at some of the nearly 10,000 trade magazines or newsletters in the United States, and the industry analysts who cover technology. Readers of these publications are more likely to be potential customers. For these audiences, you can consider using a more technical lead, including more details and even providing diagrams. And it's not uncommon for a story in a respected trade magazine to stimulate subsequent coverage by high-circulation newspapers.

Also, don't ignore media abroad. Many U.S. trade publications have locally influential counterparts in Europe, Asia, and Latin America, and the economies of many emerging countries are growing very fast.

Be accurate but creative. It's sad but true that many people feel intimidated by science, mathematics, and technology. As the power and capabilities of today's technologies increase, surely more attention will be paid to their ease of use. But most achievements that companies publicize will still be perceived at first as being arcane and of little interest to the general public. Your writing—especially your lead and analogies—will often make the difference between a reporter using your release or adding it to the huge paper-recycling pile. Of course, the lead should tell all the five Ws (who, what, when, where, and why) right away. And if it's not obvious, emphasize the development's importance (the why).

Describing technology inevitably requires using analogies that the nonexpert can understand. The best analogy will give a correct impression without also giving an incorrect impression. As many of our technologies grow both more powerful in function and more microscopic in size, some pretty fantastic comparisons result.

At Lawrence Livermore National Laboratory, we referred to the world's most powerful laser as producing light that has the "power" of all the country's electrical generating capacity (and it's probably increased to several times that now). But since the laser pulse's duration was very short—several billionths of a second—its "energy" was only that consumed by a 100-watt light bulb in a few seconds to minutes.

At IBM, our new magnetic hard disk technologies are leading to a 60-percent annual increase in the amount of data that can be put on a disk. Until recently, I compared the capacity of disk drives to the height of a stack of double-spaced, typed paper containing the same information. But when the stack representing a 10-billion-byte (gigabyte) hard drive reached more than three times the height of the Washington Monument, the analogy began to lose its relevance. Who has or can relate to *that* much paper?

The analogies I have the most difficulty with are the "small" ones. Once you get smaller than a human hair (about 50 to 100 micrometers in diameter, 2- or 2 to 4-thousandths of an inch), there's not a lot a person can relate to. Benchmarks for smallness can include the diameters of a red blood cell, a virus, and a single atom, or the wavelengths of various colors of lights. But when I say that the recording heads on today's disk drives fly above the spinning disk at a height less than one-tenth the wavelength of green light (i.e., 50 nanometers or billionths of a meter), I can't expect general readers to have a precise grasp of this distance. Rather, I just hope they think, "That's darn small!"

Be visual. In addition to visual analogies, real images, such as photos, diagrams, and—in this multimedia world—video and computer-generated animations, are often welcomed by reporters and editors. I try to produce and distribute at least one cover-quality photo for every major release. Why? Because newspaper and magazine stories with photos are generally longer and placed more prominently than text-only reports. A good photo is attractive (a subjective judgment, admittedly), is realistic, and conveys a sense of at least one feature of the technology. In promoting our first "multilevel" optical disk, which stores information on both the top and bottom surfaces of several disks stacked on top of each other, I included three colorful photos. The story received wide attention, but the photos (and a diagram) boosted that considerably. Shortly after he filed his story, a local correspondent for a national newspaper told me, "My editors in New York love your art [photos]. They're going to play it big." "Big" turned out to be text and photo on the front page of the business section. A French magazine used one photo on its cover and all four images as part of a two-page spread.

A photo and caption alone can often be as good or better than a release that's just text. Every day, Associated Press sends out several business-related photos-with-captions that are quite popular with editors nationwide. Some are provided by companies. The photo has to grab a viewer's attention. It also helps to craft a short, Wirephoto-style caption with a catchy headline. And don't forget the trade journals. One photo I produced in 1991, showing intersecting red laser beams to illustrate our testing of materials for future holographic data-storage devices (headline: "X Marks the Spot"), has been used frequently—including on three magazine covers in 1994–95.

Finally, a few words about publicizing corporate technology with the honesty and integrity I recommended at the beginning of this chapter.

No one likes bad news. But private companies dislike it even more than other institutions. Bad news may cause customers to delay or even stop purchasing a company's products. Without sales, no company can survive, so it's understandable that corporate public relations managers would prefer no news to bad news. To some, this situation might also be an invitation for dishonest exploitation: deception in the face of bad news or spreading lies about competitors. Although competition is fierce in most industries, dishonesty is rarely productive over the long run, however, because that is the worst bad-news story of all. I'm proud that IBM believes in honest public relations. To those who are not persuaded by mere morality, I would argue that being deceitful in technical public relations is especially unwise because getting caught is so likely: The facts are usually clear, and significant errors would surely be corrected quickly and publicly either by the media or by scientists sending e-mail over the Internet. Such was the case in late 1994 when Intel initially downplayed the significance of calculation errors by the first models of its Pentium microprocessors. When faced with a mistake or bad-news situation, I recommend admitting and fixing any error promptly. The public usually appreciates such candor, especially from a company with an established reputation for honesty, which remains—no surprise—the best policy.

We end this book with the same theme that began it: Getting Started! If you are a student expected to go out and get a story as though you were a working reporter, if you are newly assigned to a job covering science, or if you write from your home office without the support services of a major news organization, you may feel overwhelmed. If you're just getting started, you don't yet have a list of sources you've developed. Where do you turn to find experts? To get story ideas? To schmooze with colleagues and meet new sources? To keep up with topics you need to understand and write about?

What follows should help you a lot. We do caution, however, that this is not intended to be an encyclopedia of all sources of information that could be helpful to science writers. It is a collection of very practical places to turn to—supplied by veteran science writers, science communicators and academics who themselves find the resources helpful, and think that you will, too. They are: Sandra Blakeslee, Frank Blanchard, Deborah Blum, Rick Borchelt, Jim Detjen, Sharon Dunwoody, Laurie Garrett, Candace Gulko, Richard Harris, Mary Knudson, Rich Monastersky, Carol Morton, Kim McDonald, Elizabeth Pennisi, Charles Petit, Boyce Rensberger, Carol Rogers, David Ropeik, Phil Schewe, Tom Siegfried, Meredith Small, Janice Hopkins Tanne, Jon Van, and Patrick Young.

We at NASW wish you the very best in your career as a science writer or communicator. We leave you with these last words of advice:

Seek the truth.
Treat people with respect, and hold the power you will have as a writer or editor gently in the palm of your hand.
Understand what you write before you write it.
Tell your story in language your readers will understand.
Dare to write differently and interestingly.
And, have fun doing it!

GENERAL SCIENCE INFORMATION

- The National Association of Science Writers (NASW) is the leading professional organization in the field. It publishes a quarterly review, *ScienceWriters*, which addresses issues in the profession. NASW has an inexpensive guidebook,

Communicating Science News: A Guide for Scientists, Physicians, and Public Information Officers. The NASW also has a members-only Internet site on CompuServe's JForum. Dues are $60 a year. For more information, write Diane McGurgan, P.O. Box 294, Greenlawn, N.Y. 11740; e-mail: 71223.3441@compuserve.com; phone: (516) 757-5664; fax: (516) 757-0069.

- The American Association for the Advancement of Science (AAAS) is the largest general science organization in the United States. Its annual meeting is held in February of each year. The AAAS also publishes an excellent directory, *Science Sources*, listing science press contacts at many universities, government agencies, and research institutions. AAAS, 1200 New York Avenue, NW, Washington, DC 20005; fax: (202) 789-0455.

- "New Horizons" is the annual briefing held each fall on cutting-edge science topics arranged by the Council for the Advancement of Science Writing, P.O. Box 404, Greenlawn, N.Y. 11740.

- Many universities publish "experts lists" that contain the names, telephone numbers, and sometimes e-mail addresses of faculty members grouped by their disciplines.

- A number of government agencies and scientific societies specialize in specific sciences and can sometimes help you. (Examples: the National Oceanic and Atmospheric Administration on weather and oceanography; the American Astronomical Society on astronomy and space sciences; the National Institutes of Health (NIH) on just about anything medical).

- The public affairs offices of professional, nonprofit, and academic groups often serve quite effectively in locating researchers for writers. If you don't know where to look, ask a local reference librarian or see *Science Sources.*

- The independent Media Resource Service, used by writers of all experience levels, has a list of scientists willing to discuss their specific fields: (800) 223-1730; inside New York State: (212) 268-5279.

- ProfNet, the "Professors Network," is a cooperative of more than 2,100 public information officers representing 800 colleges, universities, corporations, governmental offices, and nonprofit organizations in 17 countries. Requests for help go directly to ProfNet participants and almost inevitably get results within two or three days, sometimes on the same day. You can reach ProfNet via CompuServe: 73163,1362; the Internet: profnet@vyne.com/profnet; fax: (516) 689-1425; or phone: (800) 776-3638, which spells out (800) PROFNET. You might want to call the first time, to get the specifics on how best to submit your query.

- "Communicating University Research" conferences for university information officers are held approximately every 18 months by the Council for the Advancement and Support of Education, 11 Dupont Circle, Washington, D.C. 20036.

- The American Society of Journalists and Authors, Alexandra Cantor Owens, Executive Director, 1501 Broadway, Suite 302, New York, N.Y. 10036; phone: (212) 997-0947; fax: (212) 768-7414; e-mail: CompuServe: 75227.1650@compuserve.com.

- The Authors Guild, Paul Aiken, Executive Director, 330 West 42nd Street, New York, N.Y. 10036; phone: (212) 563-5904; fax: (212) 564-8363; the Internet: authors guild.org. For general information: authors@pipeline.com or info @authors guild.org. To contact a staff member: staff@authors guild.org.

- The National Writers Union, 873 Broadway, New York, N.Y. 10003; phone: (212) 254-0279; fax: (212) 254-0673; e-mail: NWU@netcom.com.
- The National Union of Journalists, 314 Grays Inn Road, London, England WC1X 8DP; phone: 0171-278-7916; fax: 0171-837-8143; e-mail: the.journalist@mcr1.poptel.org.uk.
- The Society of Authors, 84 Drayton Gardens, London, England SW10 9SB; phone: 0171-373-6642.
- The Writers Guild of Great Britain, Alison V. Gray, General Secretary, 430 Edgware Road, London, England W2 1EH; phone: 0171-723-8074; fax: 0171-706-2413.
- Periodical Writers of Canada, 54 Wolseley Street, Toronto, Ontario, Canada M5T 1A5; phone: (416) 504-1645; fax: (416) 947-0159; e-mail: PWAC@cycor.ca
- The National Association of Government Communicators is the organization of many of the federal government's science writers. It annually grants "Blue Pencil" awards for outstanding examples of government writers' work. Address: 669 S. Washington St., Alexandria, Va. 22314; phone: (703) 519-3902.

ASTRONOMY
Organizations

- The American Astronomical Society is the major professional organization for astronomers in North America: 2000 Florida Avenue, Suite 400, Washington, D.C. 20009; phone: (202) 328-2010; e-mail: aas@aas.org; World Wide Web: http://www.aas.org
- The International Astronomical Union was founded in 1919 to provide a forum for international cooperation in astronomical research. It is the sole authority for designating names of celestial bodies and their features: Institut d'Astrophysique, 98bis, bd. Arago, F-75014 Paris, France (33) 143258358; e-mail: liau@iap.fr; World Wide Web: http://www.lsw.uni-heidelberg.de/iau.html
- The Astronomical Society of the Pacific is an international scientific and educational society for professional and amateur astronomers, educators, and interested laypeople: 390 Ashton Avenue, San Francisco, Calif. 94112; phone: (415) 337-1100; e-mail: membership@stars.sfsu.edu; World Wide Web: http://www.physics. sfsu.edu/asp/asp.html
- The Space Telescope Science Institute is responsible for scientific operations of the Hubble Space Telescope: 3700 San Martin Drive, Baltimore, Md.; phone: (410) 338-4514; World Wide Web: http://www.stsci.edu/stsci.html
- The National Aeronautics and Space Administration (NASA) is the U.S. space agency. Links to information that includes the shuttle mission schedules, Hubble images, and press releases on breaking news: phone: (202) 358-0000; World Wide Web: http://www.gsfc.nasa.gov/NASA homepage.html; TODAY@NASA: http://www.hq.nasa.gov/office/pao/NewsRoom/today.html

Meetings

- The American Astronomical Society holds two yearly meetings, usually in January and June.
- The American Astronomical Society's Division of Planetary Sciences meets annually in the fall.

- The International Astronomical Union General Assembly meets every third year.
  - The Astronomical Society of the Pacific holds an annual meeting, usually in June or July.

Key Journals and Magazines

The Astronomical Journal
The Astrophysical Journal
Monthly Notices of the Royal Astronomical Society
Sky & Telescope
Astronomy

World Wide Web

- Internet Astronomy Links
  http://marvel.stsci.edu/net-resources.html
- World Wide Web Astronomy Pages
  http://www.stsci.edu/astroweb/net-www.html

A very comprehensive listing of pages about astronomy including astronomy research centers.

BIOLOGY

Much of the writing about biology now deals with cell and molecular biology, genetics, and biotechnology. Serious biology writers who did not get courses in the new biology in college will want to return for a few courses, or at least get good texts and reference books for your personal library. Here are a few.

Books

- *DNA Science: A First Course in Recombinant DNA Technology,* David A. Micklos and Greg A. Freyer. Cold Spring Harbor: Cold Spring Harbor Laboratory Press and Carolina Biological Supply Company, 1990.
- *Molecular Biology of the Cell,* Alberts et al. Garland, 1994.
- *Molecular Cell Biology,* James Darnell, Harvey Lodish, and David Baltimore. New York: Scientific American Books, 1995.
- *Molecular Biology of the Gene,* James D. Watson, Nancy H. Hopkins, Jeffrey W. Roberts, Joan Argetsinger Steitz, and Alan M. Weiner. Menlo Park, Calif.: Benjamin Cummings, 1987.
- *Life: The Science of Biology,* Purves et al. Sinauer/Freeman.
- *Human Physiology: The Mechanisms of Body Function,* Arthur J. Vander, James H. Sherman, and Dorothy S. Luciano. New York: McGraw-Hill, 1985.

Organizations and Meetings

- American Society for Cell Biology, 9650 Rockville Pike, Bethesda, Md. 20814-3992, holds the biggest meeting of basic researchers in cell and molecular biology.
- American Anthropological Association, 4350 N. Fairfax Dr., Suite 640, Arlington Va. 22203. Their meeting contains lots of social science, and usually good story material on human evolution.

- American Society for Microbiology, 1325 Massachusetts Ave. NW, Washington, D.C. 20005. This group deals mainly with bacteria and the diseases they cause.
- Society for Neuroscience, 11 Dupont Circle, Suite 500, Washington, D.C. 20036. Good source for brain research.

World Wide Web

- National Institutes of Health home page—www.nih.gov
- Harvard's list of evolutionary biology links—golgi.harvard.edu/biopages/evolution.html
- The Tree of Life—phylogeny.arizona.edu/tree/phylogeny.html
- Grateful Med, the National Library of Medicine on the Internet. You need an account to access this, but public pages will tell you how to sign up. It's the premier search engine for basic and clinical biomedical sciences—igm.nlm.nih.gov:80/index.html
- Dictionary of Cell Biology—www.mblab.gla.ac.uk/julian/Dict.html
- Cell and Molecular Biology Online—www.tlac.net/users/pmgannon/cool.html

CHEMISTRY

Too few science writers understand the beauty of a chemistry beat. They think of testtubes and chemical formulas and forget that almost everything, from cooking to nuclear waste containment, from paper production to black stars, from buckyballs to antibiotic resistance can fall under chemistry's rubric. Writing about all of science from a chemical perspective is a way of resisting the temptation to be corralled by traditional discipline—or beat—boundaries. Here are a few tips on where to go for chemistry news and information.

Organizations

- American Chemical Society, 1155 16th Street, NW, Washington, D.C. 20036; phone: (202) 872-4600. With 149,000 chemists and chemical engineers as members, the American Chemical Society ranks as one of chemistry's largest organizations. It maintains an online database of its many chemical journals, has a media office, awards an annual science-writing prize, and has committees that deal with many of the issues important to chemists.
- Materials Research Society, 9800 McKnight Road, Pittsburgh, Pa. 15237; phone: (412) 367-3004. Its purpose is to bring together materials scientists, engineers, and other professionals interested in all aspects of materials, with the goal of fostering interdisciplinary approaches to the understanding and use of all types of materials. Its MRS Bulletin, twice-a-year meetings, and media office are useful sources for ideas about stories involving materials.
- American Ceramic Society, 735 Ceramic Place, Westerville, Ohio 43081-8720; phone: (614) 890-4700. Members include engineers, scientists, and other professionals interested in glass, cement, nuclear ceramics, structural clay, and electronics. The society sponsors technical meetings and provides technical information. It's a useful resource because the materials this group focuses on are such a big part of people's everyday lives, and these folks are the ones who are shaping the future of those products.
- American Crystallographic Association, P.O. Box 96, Ellicott Station, Buffalo,

N.Y. 14205-0096; phone: (716) 856-9600. Its members are interested in determining the arrangements of atoms in materials of all kinds. Toward this end, the society was established to promote the development of both knowledge and techniques such as x-ray and electron and neutron diffraction. More and more crystallography—the elucidation of structure—is seen as critical to understanding not just inorganic materials, but also proteins, drug compounds, and other biological substances that many lay readers want to know about.

- American Institute of Chemical Engineers, 345 East 46th Street, New York, N.Y. 10017; phone: (212) 705-7660. This group emphasizes education, curriculum development, and placement services, and it sponsors workshops, particularly in petrochemicals and refining. It is a useful resource when doing stories about manufacturing processes that have an applied focus.
- American Society for Biochemistry and Molecular Biology, 9650 Rockville Pike, Bethesda, Md. 20814-3996; phone: (301) 530-7145. This is an organization of some 9,000 biochemists and molecular biologists who do biology with a chemical bent. The society tends to include researchers who are doing work on the cutting edge of interfacing biology with chemistry. Often its journal and meetings provide innovative story ideas.

Journals

General journals such as *Nature, Science, PNAS*
Chemical and Engineering News
Journal of the American Chemical Society
Physical Review Letters
MRS Bulletin
Journal of Biological Chemistry
Angewante Chemie

World Wide Web

(These will link to many other sites.)

- http://hackberry.chem.niu.edu/Infobahn/Paper38/ (Given as a paper at a scientific meeting.)
- http://www.rpi.edu/dept/chem.cheminfo/chemres.html (Rensselaer Polytechnic Institute)
- http://www.acs.org (The American Chemical Society Website; look under meetings section for a list of meetings.)

Meetings

- American Chemical Society (two national per year)
- Materials Research Society (two national per year)
- CLEO—Conference on Lasers and Electro Optics
- American Physical Society (March Meeting—condensed matter physics)

EARTH SCIENCES

Organizations

- The largest international organization for earth sciences, with many technical subsections, is the American Geophysical Union (AGU), 2000 Florida Avenue

N.W., Washington, D.C. 20009; phone: (202) 462-6900. Its information office is a good source for phone numbers, full names, and professional associations of earth scientists. Its two annual meetings, in Baltimore in late May or early June, and in San Francisco in December, are rich mines of both basic science and policy stories. The AGU can lead reporters to specialty groups, such as those concerned with tsunamis, oil exploration, or climate change.

- More focused on geology is the Geological Society of America, 3300 Penrose Place, Boulder, Colo., 80301; press contact: (303) 443-8489. The annual meetings are good sources of up-to-date, practical, or breaking news.
- National Oceanic and Atmospheric Administration, 14th and Constitution Ave., N.W., Washington, D.C. 20230; public affairs: general: (202) 482-6090; weather: (301) 713-0622. This agency includes the National Weather Service, the Environmental Research Laboratories, the Climate Analysis Center, and other offices studying oceans, tsunamis, tornadoes, hurricanes, general weather, and climate.
- The United States Geological Survey (USGS), 12201 Sunrise Valley Drive, Reston, Va., 22092; public affairs: (703) 648-4460. This is the leading U.S. agency for basic earth sciences and natural hazards including earthquakes, volcanoes, floods, and landslides.
- National Center for Atmospheric Research, P.O. Box 3000, Boulder, Colo. 80307; public affairs: (303) 497-8607. A university consortium operated under NSF contract, NCAR has many authorities on global warming, El Nino, and weather oddities. Its public affairs office has prepared concise phone guides to experts for a number of such topics.

Books and Periodicals

The magazine *Earth* is a good popular barometer of hot topics in earth sciences. The AGU publishes a somewhat more technical weekly, *EOS Transactions,* The Newspaper of the Geophysical Sciences, that can lead to good stories. Have on the shelf a few basic earth science textbooks. Make sure at least one has a simple guide to the geological ages, epochs, and eons, so you can look up the difference between Miocene and Mississippian. A time-honored example: Press, Frank, and Raymond Siever. *Earth.* New York: W.H. Freeman, 1985. An example of the many good, general guides to earthquake science: Bolt, Bruce. *Earthquakes.* New York: W.H. Freeman, 1993.

ENVIRONMENT

Organizations

- The Society for Environmental Journalists: For the $35 annual membership fee ($30 for students) you will get a subscription to the quarterly newsletter, *SEJournal;* access to the SEJ Forum available through America Online; the annual membership directory; and other information. For more information about SEJ, contact Beth Parke, SEJ's executive director, P.O. Box 27280, Philadelphia, Pa. 19118; phone: (215) 247-9710; e-mail: sejoffice@aol.com; Home Page: http://www.tribnet.com/environ/env_site.htm
- The Environmental Reporting Council is an activity of the Radio and Television News Directors Foundation: 1000 Connecticut Ave., N.W.; Suite 615, Washington, D.C. 20036; (202) 659-6510.

- For those interested in international environmental issues, there is the newly established International Federation of Environmental Journalists (IFEJ), a nonprofit umbrella group that links together environmental journalist organizations and environmental reporters around the world. For the $25 annual membership fee you will receive an international directory, a newsletter, and access to the IFEJ computer listserv, which sends e-mail to reporters worldwide. For more information about IFEJ, write to the organization's North American office: 341 Communications Arts Building, Michigan State University, East Lansing, Mich. 48824-1212.

- Poison control centers: Most local or regional governments have a poison control center, typically housed at a local hospital or equipped with an 800 number. These folks are on call 24 hours a day, and they have lots of information at their fingertips. When reporting about a specific chemical, this is a great place to start.

- The U.S. Environmental Protection Agency (EPA) maintains several useful databases, including a list of known or suspected carcinogenic chemicals, and the Toxic Release Inventory, which details the emissions from individual plants around the country. Call the EPA at (202) 260-4355 for the list of carcinogens. The Toxic Release Inventory is available via Telnet: Telnet RTKNET.ORG.

- The National Toxicology Program (NTP) at the National Institute of Environmental Health Sciences, P.O. Box 12233, Research Triangle Park, N.C. 27709, is responsible for maintaining an official list of carcinogens—different from the EPA list. The NTP list is supposed to be updated every two years. Twenty-four agents are listed as known human carcinogens, and dozens of others are on the lists of probable and possible carcinogens.

- The National Institute of Occupational Health Sciences (NIOSH) has a compact guidebook of industrial chemicals with thumbnail sketches of their toxic properties. NIOSH is part of the federal Centers for Disease Control and Prevention (CDC) in Atlanta. To order the *Pocket Guide to Chemical Hazards*, phone: (800) 35NIOSH or write NIOSH Publications Dissemination, 4676 Columbia Parkway, Cincinnati, Ohio, 45226.

- The Agency for Toxic Substances and Disease Registry (ATSDR), also at the CDC, is another source of toxicology information. The registry has an Internet site loaded with information about toxics, including health effects reports and detailed information about individual Superfund sites. The address: http://atsdr1.atsdr.cdc.gov:8080.

- For information about radiation, try the Health Physics Society: (703) 790-1745. It can help you get in touch with a local expert on radiation effects. Hospital radiology departments can be another useful source of information about the health effects of radiation. There's also good information about radiation on the Internet: http://www.umich.edu/~bbusby.

Key Books and Periodicals

- For general information about thousands of chemicals, look into the *Merck Index* (as opposed to the medically oriented *Merck Manual*). You can use the CAS Registry numbers from the *Merck Index* to look at more specialized databases, for example Toxline on Dialog.

- The Federation for American Communications and the National Sea Grant College Program have produced a small volume called *Reporting on Risk,* which is a useful primer. It is distributed by the Annapolis Center, a nonprofit educational organization: 47 State Circle, Suite 203, Annapolis, Md. 21401, phone: (410) 268-3302; fax: (401) 268-4953. Its bibliography lists many other good sources of information.
- Useful periodicals include: *Science; Chemical and Engineering News; WorldWatch: the High Country News; Earth; Science News; Outside; Audubon; Sierra; Environment;* and *E Magazine.* Reporters can obtain a free subscription to *Environment Writer,* a very useful monthly newsletter published by the Environmental Health Center; address: 1019 19th St., N.W., Suite 401, Washington, D.C. 20036; phone: (202) 293-2270, ext. 6271.
- Another valuable source of information is the photos taken by *Landsat* and other satellites. These photos have dramatically shown the fires in Yellowstone National Park, the flooding of the Mississippi River, and the *Exxon Valdez* oil spill. They can also vividly illustrate long-term trends such as the spread of urban sprawl around Los Angeles, deforestation in the Amazon rain forests, and the spread of deserts in North Africa. For more information, contact the public information office of the Earth Observation Satellite Company, 4300 Forbes Boulevard, Lanham, Md. 20720, phone: (800) 344-9933.

HEALTH AND MEDICINE
Key Books

- To learn about an illness, start simple and broad and progress to the more sophisticated. Start with the *Merck Manual of Diagnosis and Therapy,* Robert Berkow, M.D., ed. Rahway, N.J.: Merck Research Laboratories, 1992. Or read about the illness in a book written for the lay public such as the *Mayo Clinic Family Health Book,* David E. Larson, M.D., ed.-in-chief. New York: William Morrow, 1990. Then turn to a standard medical textbook, like: *Harrison's Principles of Internal Medicine,* Eugene Braunwald et al., eds. New York: McGraw-Hill, 1987. For more detailed information, progress to a text in that specialty. Once you have a basic understanding of the illness, do a Medline search for current areas of research.
- A good start-up library for reporting on infectious diseases might include: Wilson, Mary. *A World Guide to Infections.* New York: Oxford University Press, Benensen, Abram. *Control of Communicable Diseases in Man.* American Public Health Association, Mann, Jonathan, Daniel Tarantola, and Thomas Netter, eds. *AIDS in the World.* Cambridge, Mass.: Harvard University Press. Watson, James, *Molecular Biology of the Gene.* Nancy H. Hopkins, Jeffrey W. Roberts, Joan A. Steitz and Alan M. Weiner, eds. Menlo Park, Calif.: Benjamin Cummings, 1987. Morse, Stephen. ed. *Emerging Viruses.* New York: Oxford University Press, 1993. Joshua, Lederberg, and Robert Shepe. *Emerging Infections.* Washington, D.C.: Institute of Medicine, 1992. Oaks, Stanley, Violaine S. Mitchell, Greg W. Pearson, Charles J. Carpenter, eds. *Malaria: Obstacles & Opportunities.* Washington, D.C.: Institute of Medicine, 1991.

Lappe, Mark. *Evolutionary Medicine.* San Francisco: Sierra Club Books, 1994.

Bloom, Barry. *Tuberculosis.* Washington, D.C.: ASM Press, 1994.

Dubos, René. *The White Plague.* New Brunswick: Rutgers University Press, 1992.

Wilson, Mary E., *Disease in Evolution.* [Annals of the New York Academy of Sciences Vol. 740 (entire volume).] Richard Levins, and Andrew Spielman, eds. New York: New York Academy of Sciences, 1994.

Meetings

- If you're writing a lot about a particular subject, it's helpful to attend the primary medical meetings about it, such as the annual national meetings of the American Heart Association, the American Psychiatric Association, or the American College of Obstetrics and Gynecology. Check the *Encyclopedia of Associations* in the library or *Science Sources.* Some organizations, including the American Cancer Society and the American Heart Association, hold annual meetings for science writers about new and recent research.
- For brain function and neurological diseases, contact: The Society for Neuroscience: 11 Dupont Circle, N.W., Suite 500, Washington, D.C. 20036; phone: (202) 462-6688. The Dana Alliance: (212) 223-4040.

General Medical Information

- The National Library of Medicine (NLM) offers easy, relatively inexpensive computer access to its vast store of books, abstracts, journal articles, and other bits of medical and health science information, as well as entree to several other useful sources. These include a National Cancer Institute database with a directory of physicians and TOXNET, a group of toxicology databases. Tapping into NLM's data trove requires a users code and Grateful Med, a $29.95 software package; for more details, call (800) 638-8480. Also, see our listing in this appendix under "Internet Resources."

INVESTIGATIVE REPORTING

Organizations

- Investigative Reporters and Editors (IRE) is an association that holds both national and regional meetings every year. Membership is $25 for students, $40 for working journalists, and includes a bimonthly journal. Box 838, Columbia, Mo. 65205; phone: (314) 882-2042. Internet address is http://www.IRE.org. or http://www.reporter.org/IRE.
- The Center for Investigative Reporting has a research library and holds meetings, seminars, and workshops. 568 Howard Street, Fifth Floor, San Francisco, Calif. 94105-3008; phone: (415) 543-1200.
- The Reporters Committee for Freedom of the Press publishes a detailed guide to using public records. The booklet, *How to Use the Federal Freedom of Information Act,* costs $3, plus $1.50 for shipping and handling. Address: 1735 I St., N.W. Suite 50W, Washington, D.C. 20006, phone: (202)-466-6313.
- The best collection of investigative science writing can be found in: McCourt, Rick, and Ted Anton, eds. *The New Science Journalists.* New York: Ballantine, 1995.

PHYSICS

It's the kind of challenge that can be fun. Nevertheless, physics is a difficult enough subject to write about—from nuclear fusion, the process that heats the sun and stars, to nuclear fission, the process that powers nuclear reactors; from explaining what provoked the Big Bang, to telling people why things they come in contact with every day move as they do.

So surround yourself with basic, ready reference material. No science writer's desk should be without a copy of *The CRC Handbook of Chemistry and Physics,* a book of chemical and physical science data, published each year by CRC Press Inc. in Boca Raton, Florida. Out-of-date editions can usually be purchased for a discount.

Another useful reference is a chart of the Standard Model of Fundamental Particles and Interactions. It lists many of the major elementary particles and forces. Handy stuff for covering high-energy physics. It can be obtained from the Contemporary Physics Education Project, MS 50-308, Lawrence Berkeley Laboratory, Berkeley, Calif. 94720.

A good reference book on physics is the *McGraw-Hill Encyclopedia of Physics,* published by McGraw-Hill.

Organizations

- American Physical Society is the leading organization of physicists worldwide and publisher of the top physics journals, *Physical Review, Physical Review Letters,* and *Reviews of Modern Physics.*
  One Ellipse Circle
  College Park, Md. 20740-3844
  (301) 209-3200
  World Wide Web: http://aps.org
- American Institute of Physics is an umbrella organization encompassing several physics and physics-related societies, including, among others:
  Acoustical Society of America
  American Astronomical Society
  American Geophysical Union
  American Physical Society
  American Vacuum Society

  One Physics Ellipse
  College Park, Md. 20740-3843
  (301) 209-3100
  Contact: Phillip Schewe (301-209-3092) or Ben Stein (301-209-3091)
  fax: (301)209-0846
  E-mail: pfs@aip.org
  World Wide Web: http://www.aip.org/aiphome.html
- Materials Research Society is an organization dedicated to goal-oriented basic research on materials of technological importance.
  9800 McKnight Road
  Pittsburgh, Pa. 15237-6006
  (412) 367-3004

E-mail: info@mrs.org
World Wide Web: http://www.mrs.org

Meetings

- The American Physical Society has two national meetings each year, usually in March and April. The March meeting focuses on condensed matter physics, materials science, and biological physics. The April meeting includes astrophysics and nuclear and particle physics.
- The Acoustical Society of America holds two meetings annually, one in the spring, one in late fall.
- International Conference on High Energy Physics is held every other year.

Key Journals

Physical Review Letters
Nature
Science
Physical Review (in five separate versions, labeled A–E)
Reviews of Modern Physics

Magazines

Physics Today
Physics World
About Physics
Discover
New Scientist (UK)
Science News
Scientific America

A good weekly summary of science-policy news of interest to physicists is *What's New*, by Robert Park of the American Physical Society. It can be obtained electronically. To subscribe, send an e-mail message to listserve@aps.org. In the body of the message, type "sub whatsnew".

A good weekly summary of newsworthy research developments in physics is Physics News Update, by Phillip Schewe of the American Institute of Physics. To subscribe to the electronic version of the update, send a message to listserve@aip.org. Leave the subject line blank and in the body of the message, type "add physnews".

World Wide Web

The Physics News Update and other information of value to physics reporters can be obtained from Physical Science News Sources: http://www.aip.org/aip/physnews.html

A good list of physical-science resources on the World Wide Web can be obtained from http://www.aip.org/aip/physres.htm

Other Important Websites

- American Physical Society: http://aip.org
- American Institute of Physics: http://www.aip.org/aiphome.html
- Physics-Related Resources on the Internet: http://aps.org/phys.html

- AIP World Wide Web Links and Pointers: http://aip.org/aip/wwwinfo.html
- The World-Wide Web Virtual Library: Physics: http://www.w3.org/hypertext/ DataSources/bySubject/Physics/Overview.html
- Physics Today calendar of physics meetings worldwide—www.aip.org/pt/callist.html
- Library of physics preprints at Los Alamos—http://xxx.lanl.gov
- The Internet Pilot to Physics, numerous physics services—www.tp.umu.se/TIP-TOP

Physics Organization Homepages

American Institute of Physics—www.aip.org
American Physical Society—www.aps.org
Acoustical Society of America—asa.aip.org
American Astronomical Society—www.aas.org
American Crystallographic Association—www.hwi.buffalo.edu/ACA
American Vacuum Society—www.vacuum.org
American Geophysical Union—earth.agu.org/kosmos/homepage.html
Materials Research Society—www.mrs.org

TECHNOLOGY

Because technology permeates American life, reporters can find sources almost everywhere. Trade and professional organizations as well as academic institutions all abound in expertise, depending on the topic of interest. The same is true of specialty publications and journals.

Here is just a sampling of the organizations and journals where reporters can find sources who can explain and comment on various types of technology.

Organizations

- Electrical Power Research Institute, P.O. Box 10412, Palo Alto, Calif., 94303; phone: (415) 855-2413; fax: (415) 855-2900.
- National Academy of Engineering, 2101 Constitution Avenue, NW, Washington, D.C., 20418, phone: (202) 334-2138.
- Institute of Electrical and Electronics Engineers, 445 Hoes Lane; Piscataway, N.J., 08855; phone: (908) 562-6823; fax: (908) 981-9511; e-mail: r.barber@ieee.org
- Consumer Electronics Manufacturers Association, 2500 Wilson Blvd., Arlington Va., 22201-3834; phone: (703) 907-7674.
- American Chemical Society, 1155 16th Street, NW, Washington, D.C., 20036; phone: (202) 872-4600.

Journals

Technology Review
IEEE Spectrum
Chemical & Engineering News
Bulletin of the Atomic Scientists
Physics Today

Key Books

- Lederman, Leon M., and David N. Schramm. *From Quarks to the Cosmos: Tools of Discovery.* New York: Scientific American Library, 1989.
- Taubes, Gary. *Nobel Dreams: Power, Deceit and the Ultimate Experiment.* New York: Random House, 1986.
- Pierce, John R., and A. Michael Noll. *Signals: The Science of Telecommunications.* New York: Scientific American Library, 1990.
- Brand, Stewart. *The Media Lab: Inventing the Future at MIT.* New York: Penguin Books, 1988.

Science Communication Courses and Programs in the United States

There are science writing programs and courses at over forty colleges and universities in the United States. A 1996 directory compiled by Sharon Dunwoody, Elizabeth Crane, and Bonnie Brown of the University of Wisconsin-Madison lists details about 43 science communication courses and programs. To order the directory contact:

Center for Environmental Communication and Education Studies
School of Journalism and Mass Communication
University of Wisconsin-Madison
821 University Avenue
Madison, Wisc. 53706
Phone: (608) 263-3389
Fax: (608) 262-1361
E-mail: dunwoody@facstaff.wisc.edu

Some of the better known programs found in the directory are listed below:

Boston University
Program in Science Journalism
College of Communication
Boston University
640 Commonwealth Ave.
Boston, Mass. 02215
Phone: (617) 353-4239
Co-Directors: Ellen Ruppel Shell, Douglas Starr
E-mail: dstarr@acs.bu.edu or eschell@acs.bu.edu

Columbia University
Graduate School of Journalism
Columbia University
New York, N.Y. 10027
Phone: (212) 854-4718/4150
Fax: (212) 854-7837
Contact: Kenneth K. Goldstein
Phone: (212) 854-4718
E-mail: kkgl@columbia.edu

Indiana University
School of Journalism
Ernie Pyle Hall
Indiana University
Bloomington, Ind. 47405
Phone: (812) 855-9247
Director/Contact: S. Holly Stocking
Phone: (812) 855-9828
E-mail: ogan@indiana.edu or stocking@indiana.edu

Iowa State University
Journalism and Mass Communication
114 Hamilton Hall
Iowa State University
Ames, Iowa 50011
Director/Contact: Jane W. Peterson
Phone: (515) 294-4340
E-mail: jpeterso@iastate.edu

The Johns Hopkins University
The Writing Seminars
Gilman 135
Johns Hopkins University
Baltimore, Md. 21218
Phone: (410) 516-7563
Director/Contact: Barbara J. Culliton
Phone: (410) 516-7714

Lehigh University
Department of Journalism and Communication
29 Trembley Drive
Lehigh University
Bethlehem, Pa. 18015
Phone: (610) 758-4180
Fax: (610) 758-6198
Director/Contact: Sharon Friedman
Phone: (215) 758-4179
E-mail: smf6@lehigh.edu
homepage: http://www.lehigh.edu/injrl/semenu.html

New York University
Department of Journalism and Mass Communication
Science and Environmental Reporting Program
10 Washington Place
New York University
New York, N.Y. 10003
Phone: (212) 998-7970
Director/Contact: William E. Burrows
Phone: (212) 998-7970

Northwestern University
Medill School of Journalism
1845 Sheridan Road
Northwestern University
Evanston, Ill. 60208-2101
Phone: (708) 491-5228
Director/Contact: Jon Ziomek
Phone: (708) 491-5228
E-mail: medill-admis@nwu.edu

Texas A&M University
Department of Journalism
230 Reed McDonald Building
Texas A&M University
College Station, Tex. 77843-4111
Phone: (409) 845-4611
Director/Contact: Charles C. Self or Barbara Gastel
Phone: (409) 847-9245 or (409) 845-6887
E-mail: c-self@tamu.edu or b-gastel@tamu.edu

University of California-Santa Cruz
Science Communication Program
University of California-Santa Cruz
Santa Cruz, Calif. 95064
Phone: (408) 459-4475
Director/Contact: John Wilkes
Phone: (408) 459-4475
E-mail: scicom@cats.ucsc.edu

University of Maryland
College of Journalism
University of Maryland
College Park, Md. 20742
Phone: (301) 405-2380
Director/Contact: James Grunig
Phone: (301) 405-2416
E-mail: jgrunig@jmail.umd.edu

University of Missouri
Science Journalism Center
School of Journalism
University of Missouri
P.O. Box 838
Columbia, Mo. 65205
Phone: (314) 882-4714/2914
Director/Contact: Robert A. Logan
Phone: (314) 882-4714
E-mail: jourral@muccmail.missouri.edu

University of Tennessee
School of Journalism
330 Communications Building
The University of Tennessee
Knoxville, Tenn. 37996-0330
Phone: (423) 974-5155
Director/Contact: Mark Littmann
Phone: (423) 974-8156
E-mail: littmann@utk.edu

University of Wisconsin-Madison
The university offers formal coursework in both the Department of Agricultural Journalism and the School of Journalism and Mass Communication. The two units offer separate undergraduate and master's degrees and share the Ph.D.

Department of Agricultural Journalism
440 Henry Mall
University of Wisconsin-Madison
Madison, Wisc. 53705
Phone: (608) 262-1464
Fax: (608) 265-3042
Director/Contact: Garrett O'Keefe
Phone: (608) 262-1464
E-mail: okeefe@macc.wisc.edu

School of Journalism and Mass Communication
821 University Avenue
University of Wisconsin-Madison
Madison, Wisc. 53706
Phone: (608) 262-3691
Fax: (608) 262-1361
Director/Contact: Sharon Dunwoody
Phone: (608) 263-3389
E-mail: dunwoody@facstaff.wisc.edu

You may find an internship either through a formal program for interns or informally by contacting a science editor or science writer at a newspaper, magazine, publishing company, radio or television network, or at a government agency or organization. The person you contact may not offer internships. But be aggressive. Suggest an arrangement that would allow you to get some training and some clips, and also be of help.

Seek out an internship that puts you to work as a science writer. Avoid one that turns you into a gopher or desk clerk. In a really good internship program, your supervisors acknowledge that you work as an intern, and agree to pay you something. Sure, an internship should be a great training ground. But if you are writing stories that are published, you should get paid something, at least enough to pay your housing expense.

Science News offers an exemplary internship program. For three months an intern works full time as a science writer under the direction of staff writers and editors, writing one to two published articles a week. Since *Science News* is based in Washington, D.C., it provides interns an excellent variety of news-gathering opportunities, including covering scientific meetings, press conferences, congressional hearings, and other events. Interns also generate their own story ideas. One internship is offered each spring, summer, and fall. *Science News* says the program is intended for people planning careers in science writing, and that preference is given to those who are completing an advanced degree in journalism with an emphasis in science writing. Skilled writers working toward an advanced degree in one of the sciences are also considered. And—*Science News* pays each intern $1,200 per month.

Applicants should indicate what season they are applying for and send a cover letter, résumé, and at least three science writing clips to:
Science News Internship
1719 N Street NW
Washington, D.C. 20036

There's a sea of information on the internet, some of which is useful to science reporters. Because the internet changes every day, it's impossible to keep up with it. What follows is a list, compiled in June 1996,* which suggests a few starting places for science reporters. Because changes are frequent—and because the printed word is not the easiest way to use this information—this list, kept updated, is also available online, at the National Association of Science Writers' web site. So you only have to type in one address: http://www.nasw.org/

SEARCHING THE INTERNET

Often, the best way to begin looking for something on the internet is to launch a search. For example, practically every university and federal government agency has a web site, and more are adding to the web every day. There are many free search "engines" that can help you find an agency, company, organization—in fact, any keyword. Here are a few popular ones.

- MetaSearch (uses several search engines and distills the results)
  http://metacrawler.cs.washington.edu:8080/
- Alta Vista
  http://www.altavista.digital.com/
- Ecola's Simple Search
  http://www.ecola.com/ez/ezsearch.htm
- Lycos
  http://lycos.cs.cmu.edu/
- WWW Virtual Library
  http://www.w3.org/hypertext/DataSources/bySubject/Overview.html
- Yahoo
  http://www.yahoo.com/

This list was compiled by Frank Blanchard, Carol Morton, and Richard Harris, and edited by Richard Harris.

PHONE BOOKS

Need a phone number? Try the internet before you pay for Directory Assistance.

- Switchboard is a national phone directory of individuals and businesses. Certainly not complete, but voluminous.
  http://www.switchboard.com
- ATT 800 Directory
  http://www.tollfree.att.net/dir800/
- University Phone Books (just about all of them)
  gopher://gopher.nd.edu:70/11/Non-Notre Dame Information Sources/ Phone Books—Other Institutions/North America%09+application/gopher+ menu
- American Universities: A listing of every university home page, from which you can find phone numbers, faculty profiles, or whatever information a university has decided to post on the web. Links to international universities, too.
  http://www.clas.ufl.edu/CLAS/american-universities.html
- Public Information Offices at universities, government agencies, museums, and other sites of use to science reporters.
  http://sci.aaas.org/sources/
- National Science Foundation staff phone book
  gopher://stis.nsf.gov/0/NSF/phone/phnalpha
- National Institutes of Health staff phone book
  gopher://gopher.nih.gov:70/77/gopherlib/indices/allphone/index

GENERAL INFORMATION FOR THE SCIENCE MEDIA

These sites have press releases for science journalists, along with other resources for science writers. For example, AAAS's EurekAlert service has embargoed material, a phone directory of public information officers, releases, journal information, and more.

- AAAS' EurekAlert service for science journalists
  http://www.eurekalert.org/
- Sci News/Med News on CompuServe's JFORUM
  Contact: Roger Johnson at rjohnson@access.digex.net or (301) 320-5373
- ProfNet. Send a message to profnet, and hundreds of public information officers around the nation and in other countries get your query and have an opportunity to respond. (800) 776-3638
  http://www.vyne.com/profnet/
- Quadnet—press releases
  http://www.vyne.com/qnetwww/
- Healthlinks
  http://www.hslib.washington.edu/
- The Center for Anthropology Communications
  http://pegasus.acs.ttu.edu/~wurlr/anthro.html

SCIENCE WRITING ORGANIZATIONS

These sites have information about regional meetings and organizations, along with applications for membership. The Northern California Science Writers' home page and the New England Science Writers' home pages have links to other useful science writing resources.

- National Association of Science Writers
  http://www.nasw.org/
- NASW also has a site on Compuserve's Journalism Forum, which is only accessible to Compuserve customers. GO JFORUM and look for the NASW section.
- DC Science Writers Association
  http://www.nasw.org/dcswa/
- New England Science Writers
  http://klaatu.oit.umass.edu/pubaffs/nesw/index.html
- Northern California Science Writers Association
  http://www.lbl.gov/NCSWA/

GENERAL REFERENCE

These sites are useful for looking up specific information on the web, whether it's a patent, details about a company, scientific reference information, or a word on an online dictonary.

- Audio archive of news broadcasts, including ABC News and National Public Radio
  http://www.realaudio.com/
- Biomedical Engineering Network
  http://bme.www.ecn.purdue.edu/bme
- Clinical Trials Listing Service from CenterWatch
  http://www.centerwatch.com/
- Dictionary
  http://c.gp.cs.cmu.edu:5103/prog/webster
- Dictionary of Cell Biology
  http://www.mblab.gla.ac.uk/~julian/Dict.html
- Internet: InterNIC's Directory about everything on the internet, as official as it gets
  http://ds.internic.net/
- Magazines: Electronic Newsstand
  http://www.enews.com/
- Martindale's Reference Desk—everything from the time of day to information about subatomic particles
  http://www-sci.lib.uci.edu:80/~martindale/Ref.html
- Martindale's Science Tables and databases
  http://www-sci.lib.uci.edu:80/~martindale/Ref3.html
- Medical Matrix: guide to clinical medicine resources
  http://www.slackinc.com/matrix/
- Medical Products Guide
  http://www.medicom.com/

- National Center for Biotechnology Information
  http://www.ncbi.nlm.nih.gov/
- Newspapers—general list
  http://www.ecola.com/news/press/
- Thesaurus
  gopher://odie.niaid.nih.gov/77/.thesaurus/index
- West legal publishing—find a lawyer mentioned in the news
  http://www.westpub.com/

SCIENTIFIC JOURNALS

Many journals have home pages on the internet. However, these sites do not usually post information that is embargoed for release. Journals have e-mail distribution lists for this information. Some journals also make embargoed information available.

- *Journal of the American Medical Association*
  http://www.ama-assn.org/register/welcome.htm
- *Journal of Biological Chemistry*
  http://highwire.stanford.edu/jbc/ .
- *Journal of the National Cancer Institute*
  http://wwwicic.nci.nih.gov/jnci/jnci   issues.html
- *Morbidity and Mortality Weekly Report*
  http://www.cdc.gov/epo/mmwr/mmwr   wk.html
- *Nature*
  http://www.nature.com/
- *Proceedings of the National Academy of Sciences*
  http://journals.at-home.com/PNAS/
- *Science*
  http://www.aaas.org/science/twis.htm
- Listing of other journals in the Virtual Library
  http://www.w3.org/hypertext/DataSources/bySubject/Overview.html

LISTSERVS

Listservs are electronic mailing lists that usually cater to a particular group of people with a common interest. These resources can help you find listservs for a particular topic of interest.

- Nova Southeastern University
  http://www.nova.edu/Inter-Links/listserv.html
- Subject index to listservs
  http://www.NeoSoft.com/internet/paml/bysubj.html
- Keyword search of listservs
  http://www.netspace.org/cgi-bin/lwgate

NEWS GROUPS

News groups are freewheeling discussions. Ordinary web denizens contribute to these conversations, so you must always consider the source of the information

contained in these discussions. But sometimes they provide useful news tips. There
are thousands of discussion groups on the web. Here are a few resources to identify
topics of interest.

- Stanford SIFT program. Messages that match the search are returned.
  http://hotpage.stanford.edu/
- Search the list of newsgroups for ones that match your areas of interest.
  http://www.cen.uiuc.edu/cgi-bin/find-news
- Search newsgroup messages by keyword.
  http://www.dejanews.com/forms/dnquery.html
  http://www.excite.com/
  http://www.infoseek.com/

DATABASES

You can find out who has money to study what, if you know how to use these
databases. Some take a bit of work to figure out, but they are valuable resources
for reporters who really want to dig. Follow the money!

- Corporate information (in great detail) from the Security and Exchange Commission
  http://www.sec.gov
- NIH Research Grants and Contracts FY 1992–4 (keyword search)
  gopher://gopher.nih.gov:70/11/res/brownbook
- National Library of Medicine Databases
  http://www.nlm.nih.gov/databases/freemedl.html
- NSF Awards
  http://stis.nsf.gov/wais/awards.htm
- U.S. Patent Citation Database
  http://cos.gdb.org/repos/pat/pat.html
- Patent Abstracts
  http://sunsite.unc.edu/patents/intropat.html
- Patent Search
  http://patents.cnidr.org:4242/access/access.html

Epilogue
VICTOR K. MCELHENY

Victor K. McElheny, Director of the Knight Science Journalism
Fellowships at MIT

In a world where the discoveries and designs and inventions of scientists and engineers and doctors continue to multiply, there's no question that there is now and will continue to be an unimaginable amount of work for science journalists to do. As I have for nearly forty years, I think of it as five lifetimes of work for each science journalist. The growth of stories in science, medicine, technology, and the environment continues to be as luxuriant, to say the least, as it has been for the last several hundred years. And the ways to tell them are as varied as a journalist's character, from one year to the next or between one journalist and another: success, failure, disaster, personality, discovery, disputes, hirings, firings, promotions, in the factory or the school or the office or the home, right in front of your eyes or at the edges of the universe or the bottom of the sea or in the arteries around your heart.

The choices are endless. If one medium of expression fades, as newspapers are said (probably falsely) to be doing, then there are others for people with the skills and commitment to burrow out facts and insights and present them swiftly and simply in everyday terms. And of course you should cultivate those alternate media anyway—including radio and television and public speaking and almanacs on paper and disks—for the lessons they teach about how to tell stories. If it pleases you to regard scientists and engineers and doctors as threatening, or merely politicians in white coats, you can have a career, though in my view a crabbed one. If you are a passionate rationalist, as I suppose I am, there will be decades of happiness for you in working in the gardens of our civilization, where we work, despite inertia and hatred, to solve problems and bring benefit.

We are the ones who tell the world about what is truly new, whether it brings hope or menace. It is work for artists, and the quest for excellence ends only with death.

INDEX

283